50 Years of Cultural Travel

Association for Cultural Exchange | ACE Study Tours

1958
2008

50 Years of Cultural Travel

edited by Paul Brooke Barnes

Association for Cultural Exchange | ACE Study Tours

50 Years of Cultural Travel
Edited by Paul Brooke Barnes

ACE Study Tours
The Association for Cultural Exchange
Babraham, Cambridge CB22 3AP
www.acestudytours.co.uk

Published by the Association for Cultural Exchange, 2008

First published 2008

Printed and bound in the United Kingdom at the
University Press, Cambridge.

*A catalogue record for this publication is available
from the British Library*

Book design Dale Tomlinson
Typefaces FF Clifford · Village National · (FF Signa)
Paper Satimat Club 150 gsm, FSC accredited

ISBN 978-0-9559667-0-5

ILLUSTRATION AND PHOTO CREDITS
Frontispiece: Marble screen from Fatehpur-Sikri/photograph by Philip Barnes
p. 6 Joan Hassall/Leeds Library and Information Service
pp. 16, 18, 19, 20, 21, 22, 23, 25, 26, 27, 28, 180 Philip & Inger Barnes
p. 24 Stephen Briggs
pp. 78, 98, 108, 114, 142, 148, 158 Getty Images
p. 92 Fitzwilliam Museum/The Bridgeman Art Library
p. 104 Alex Koller
p. 118 Chris Gomersall/Nature Picture Library
pp. 124, 126, 127 Philip Allsworth-Jones
p. 128 Peter Exley
p. 132 Warwick Sloss/Nature Picture Library
p. 136 British Library/The Bridgeman Art Library
p. 154 National Painting and Sculpture Gallery, Besiktas
p. 164 Jens Mourits Sørensen/PP Møbler
pp. 168, 170, 173 Mark Powell
pp. 174, 176, 179 Michael Jacobs
pp. 184, 187 Philip Kenrick
pp. 188, 190–194 David Medd
p. 191 Mary Medd

Contents

Foreword

From its original inspiration and foundation by Philip Barnes in 1958, the Association for Cultural Exchange was conceived not as a business in the normal commercial sense, but as an educational charity designed to enable cultural exchanges between people from different parts of the world, and to provide the opportunity for people to travel and learn about the cultural treasures and heritage of other regions, under the guidance of expert leaders. The success of the Association is reflected by the fact that each year ACE now runs educational study tours of various kinds to over 200 locations throughout the world. Whilst the central aim of the Association has remained the provision of such study courses, it has also generated a significant fund to provide support for a wide range of educational and related charitable enterprises both at home and abroad. None of the ten trustees of the Association, needless to say, receives any financial recompense for their services, and they give freely of their time and dedication to the objectives of the Association.

My own association with the Association (to coin a phrase!) reaches back to 1964 when, as a recent graduate in archaeology from Cambridge University, Philip Barnes employed me as a tutor on its then new archaeology programmes for American university students, held in various colleges in Oxford. I subsequently went on to direct these courses for many years, and to organise a major and (with hindsight) highly successful ACE-sponsored archaeological excavation on the island of Oronsay in the Scottish Hebrides (as described later in the present book). I have served for over ten years as one of the trustees of the Association, and for the past four years it has been my pleasure and privilege to act as Chairman of the Trustees.

I personally believe that the greatest strength of the Association has been its status as an essentially old-style "family-run" business – one is almost tempted to say, a cottage (or at least farmhouse) industry. From my own perception, the Association for Cultural Exchange *is* the Barnes family, and it is the combined educational and organisational skills of Philip and Inger Barnes, and their two sons Paul and Hugh (now respectively General Secretary and Operations Director) which have made ACE not only a great success story but also such a personal pleasure to be associated with – now I see (with some amazement) for over 40 years! I know that it is the personal touch which participants in ACE travel programmes especially appreciate, and why so many of them come back for further courses year after year (in one case for a total of over 200 courses!).

Can I simply join in the anniversary celebrations and, on behalf of myself and the other trustees, wish the Association further success for at least another 50 years. For the record, there is no shortage of new members of the Barnes family to keep the operations in safe and secure hands for at least this period!

PROFESSOR PAUL MELLARS, FBA
Chairman of the Trustees

Preface

This book celebrates fifty years of cultural travel and cultural exchange. It is a record of an organisation that has had a unique role in fostering understanding of both historic and contemporary civilisations and of our own cultural heritage. We remain a relatively small family-run organisation, in which I have had an involvement one way or another for most of my life, whether stuffing brochures into envelopes as an eight-year-old, researching destinations as a student, or in my current role as General Secretary. However, it is only in putting together this volume that the true scope of the Association's achievements has been revealed, whether one measures the range of subject matter, encompassing art, architecture, archaeology, history, natural history, literature and music; or the geographical reach, from the UK to Ethiopia and from Mexico to Japan; or the educational aspiration, from student summer schools to life-long learning. The results of education are long lasting but the process, by its nature, is often ephemeral and I hope that this book provides an enduring record of what has been accomplished.

The book is divided into three parts: firstly, a history of the organisation and its role in providing educational course and grants, including an overview of our involvement in archaeological studies and research; secondly, a series of articles, mostly by our course directors, highlighting particular places of interest, which I hope you will find both informative and entertaining, and where perhaps you will even wish to join us on a subsequent tour; thirdly, an objective record in facts and figures.

I would like to thank most sincerely all the ACE course directors who have contributed to this volume; David Medd for his reminiscences of the ACE tour to Sweden in 1967 and for his delightful architectural drawings; Philip Allsworth-Jones for the account of his time as an ACE-sponsored student in Hungary; Paul Mellars for his account of the excavations on Oronsay; Stephen Briggs for researching and writing a history of ACE's involvement in archaeology; Denis Moriarty for writing the introduction; and not least, Philip and Inger Barnes, for providing a history of ACE and advice and assistance in producing this publication.

*None of this would have been possible, or have meaning, without the interest of our partici-
pants, many of whom come on ACE tours year after year. We are extremely grateful for your
support and it is to you that this book is dedicated.*

Dr Paul Brooke Barnes
General Secretary

Introduction

Denis Moriarty

DENIS MORIARTY is both a trustee and one of ACE's most popular course directors. After completing his undergraduate studies at Oxford, Denis spent thirty years at the BBC, where he specialised in producing documentaries on art, architecture and cultural history.

This book is a celebration; a celebration of fifty years of ACE Study Tours. Within these pages emerge the history and testimony of many of those who contribute to a distinguished achievement in a highly competitive business world. We read here, from the founder himself, Philip Barnes, of its origin and development, its ethos and the role of the Trustees. Of the many wide and diverse travel opportunities ACE offers we have the perspective from that fortunate workforce of course directors and tour leaders, and we can celebrate, too, the whole vital infrastructure of tour managers, office staff, fixers and agents around the globe, coach drivers and collaborators who all play a crucial part in this remarkable cavalcade. This is an extra-ordinary travel operator. ACE is something very special.

The Association for Cultural Exchange, to give the organisation its full and perhaps, at first glance, slightly ambitious if not portentous title, was founded in 1958, a hundred years after Darwin's paper on the survival of the fittest and Big Ben struck its first chimes, and in the same year as Explorer 1, America's first earth satellite was launched, J. K. Galbraith published his *Affluent Society*, Parkinson's Law was promulgated, Graham Green wrote *Our Man in Havana*, and Vaughan Williams died.

ACE, always articulated as three separate letters by its founder and all those who closely followed him, but never written with any full stops, is invariably to its loyal and affectionate customers the monosyllabic "ACE" as in the unstoppable winning serve at Wimbledon. The Study Tours hints at its style and ambition; these were, and crucially so to its customers, many regular, devoted and often returning, to be no ordinary tours nor "holidays" but a focus for shared learning in the best traditions of continuing education. Conviviality, companionship, wholly pleasurable, of course, but there was also in accordance with its avowed aims an excitement in discovery, a renewal and reinvigoration from an extended experience, a widening of horizons.

The cultural exchange of the 1950s, primarily summer schools at Oxford for American and Scandinavian students, was to be propitious: in this context Philip Barnes met and married Inger, from Denmark, and during their long partnership she has been at the heart of ACE deliberations, companion and fellow traveller on a number of tours, administrator, discerning and supportive critic, a steady rock and a tower of strength. Their hospitality to course directors, trustees, staff, friends and clients is legendary, and their generosity abundant.

Two sons are now at the centre of operations: Paul, who is General Secretary (and editor of this book) and Hugh, Director of Operations, charged with running the touring activities, the budgeting, setting up, marketing and successful execution of its advertised itineraries. A daughter, Catherine, was also involved in research, and as a tour manager and leader, until marriage and her family determined a move to Norway. The company's activities are run from and around the family home, a handsome, sturdy farmhouse at Babraham near Cambridge. A close family could not be more fully or closely involved; this is the Family Business par excellence and it tells.

Philip Barnes was a pioneer. When, with expanding travel opportunities, the fashion for summer schools had run its course, it was he who saw a need and opportunity for travel with a cultural and educational purpose. Moreover, and characteristically, stemming from his vision, and sensibilities for the wider public benefit, he registered ACE as an educational charity. From well-disciplined business operations and carefully husbanded resources over the years, funds have accumulated, the interest from which enables grants to be made for the advancement of projects, cultural and educational worldwide, in areas where ACE travel programmes have led. Applications are carefully scrutinised and evaluated, and each year the Trustees are able to dispense a sizeable sum to a wide variety of deserving causes. In this way something significant can be put back into situations whence all we travellers have derived so much. This is laudable, comforting even, and a wholly suitable cause for celebration.

These pages celebrate the diversity of ACE. From an early emphasis on archaeology and history, the brochure now reveals an impressive range of tours, expanding into the fields of art, architecture, music, botany and ornithology, and more recently, with an eye on a changing world, nature, climate, energy and the environment. Renewal is of the essence. Expectations too have changed. The tradition of high thinking and plain living, not lightly to be dismissed, has over the years been modified to accommodate more readily available and affordable comforts, sensibly now integrated into our arrangements. We do not need, except in unusual circumstances, to don the hair shirt or take to the metaphorical bed of nails to appreciate the sublime – although sometimes it can help. The pursuit and focus of the serious, and the rewardingly worthwhile, however remains paramount. That must be good for us all.

Course directors – a carefully considered role title reflecting the founding ethos of the early days – write in these pages of ACE's activities. They are representative of a body of talented, knowledgeable and experienced practitioners with personal and pastoral skills, sensitively selected, and responsive to ACE's traditions. They tell their own story, and all of us who have had this privilege of leading tours will immediately acknowledge our gratitude for the extraordinary opportunities extended to us in our association with the organisation. Grateful, too, for that wonderfully spirited and supportive staff in the office, efficient, courteous and helpful to client and course director alike, those friendly, welcoming voices – Marion, Sarah, Michaela, Lotta, Lindsey, Erica, Christine and Edmund. They, too, and David Winter, our man in Paris, are very much part of the ACE family.

Tour managers are now much more a regular part of the ACE travel pattern; arrangements and logistics have become more complicated, and clients understandably have higher aspirations. Tour managers, drawing on many highly developed personal skills, provide support at different levels and enjoy an increasingly conspicuous and appreciated role among participants and course directors. These collaborations work well. Agents and fixers at home and abroad as far flung as Japan and Cambodia, India, Egypt and Malta, Vienna and Oxford, and many points west are indispensable to the smooth and successful running of itineraries and these are crucial links in the chain, as is that stage army of local guides, restaurant managers, hotel staff, transport companies and coach drivers. If it is not invidious to name but one of this last group, it would be Charles Wallace of Richmond Coaches, local to Babraham and loyal to ACE over a decade and more, *primus inter pares*. ACE cherishes its contacts and embraces them all, gently seeking to mould and adapt their many talents to the ACE way of doing things, all part of a valued service to its customers.

In the final analysis, it is the clientèle, and each individual, that counts. Statistics, of course, are always a fascination, manna for some, tedium for others, and the afficionados – and the obsessive – can consult the appendices. Briefly, ACE has conducted around 4,000 courses in its first fifty years, equating to approximately 80,000 participants. Astonishingly, there have been several individuals who have taken a hundred or more courses. We raise a toast to Ron Corbett, well known to many and a specialist in LHR departure lounges, who has honoured us with his company, erudition and kindness on no fewer than two hundred occasions. Scarcely a tour assembles, yellow badged and peeringly seeking each other out, where somewhere between a third and a quarter have not travelled with ACE before and often more. That speaks volumes for its success and reliability. Inevitably, with a complex jigsaw of logistics and unpredictables, snags occasionally arise. All of us will have our Travellers' Tales. Careful and conscientious planning in the office and on location, adaptability, patience, goodwill, a sense of humour and understanding will solve most situations. ACE thrives on its clients and their response.

All they report is analysed and digested, and the intention is that the next tour is always going to be just that touch better than the last. The aims are value for money, a rewarding experience, companionship, pleasure and enjoyment.

To our customers we say: keep coming and ACE can keep going. Fifty years on, from its base in Babraham, this is a family business with a family following, its ethos and purpose firmly established, recognised and admired, by its clients, staff, and throughout the travel business. There is much to celebrate as we look forward to the next fifty years and beyond. Long may such enterprise flourish.

Part 1
The Association

A short history of the
Association for Cultural Exchange

Philip B. Barnes, Founder

In the mid 1950s I was a journalist working as Reuters correspondent in Copenhagen. Whilst I enjoyed living in Denmark, I was also toying with the idea of doing something worthwhile in which I would be my own master. I had grown up in a village in the North Yorkshire Moors as an only child and my father died when I was four. I was an eleven-plus failure and my mother and I left Yorkshire for the Essex coast, near Clacton, but in the autumn of 1939 moved to Chelmsford due to the fear of a German invasion. By sixteen I was a junior clerk in a firm of Chartered Accountants in Chelmsford. However, I wanted to study and found that Birkbeck College, which catered for part-time students, was holding weekend classes. This suited me fine, since I could continue my job Monday to Friday and become a student at the weekend. I enrolled at Birkbeck in September 1943 at the age of seventeen to study for a B.Sc. (Econ.) degree, and stayed there until 1945 when I was called up for military service. London was still being bombed and in 1944 came under attack from the Doodlebug and V2 rockets. Saturday nights were usually spent in the relative safety of a youth hostel in Highgate. After basic military training, I served in the Intelligence Corps for three and a half years, mainly in India and Singapore. During this time I had an opportunity to see many of the historic sights in India and to trek in the Himalayas. India, with all its colour and warmth, poverty and spirituality, was an enormous influence and made me feel I would like to do something creative with my life.

On demobilisation I completed my Economics degree (begun at Birkbeck College) at the London School of Economics, and followed this up with a B.A. degree at Jesus College, Cambridge, in Philosophy, then called Moral Sciences. I had been inspired to do this by hearing Dr Joad on the wireless in the popular wartime *Brains Trust* programme. From Cambridge I got the job at Reuters. I spent two of my university vacations from Cambridge as a waiter in the USA (something very unusual then) and a third summer working for Norsk Hydro in Oslo in Norway. For me, Scandinavia, with its simplicity and clarity in design and architecture, was to become as stimulating an experience as India

Left: Philip Brooke Barnes, founder of the Association for Cultural Exchange, in 1992.

had been, albeit in a quite different way. While in Denmark I came into contact with various Scandinavian adult education organisations and began to think that there was something I, too, could contribute to international understanding. There was already a good interest in the welfare state of modern Scandinavia, but from my first-hand knowledge of the countries and their languages, I knew there was a rich treasury of medieval art surviving in their churches and that their manor houses offered a number of interesting parallels with Britain. Sacheverell Sitwell's book *Denmark* appeared in 1956, while I was working there. In it Sitwell gives a picture of Danish manor house life, which was a revelation to me at a time when Denmark was mainly known for its welfare and modern design. I also soon found that there was a demand in Scandinavia for residential courses in Britain, to study English language, life and institutions, and that this would give me an opening for the organisation I wanted to create.

The next thing was to decide on which form the organisation should take. In 1957, I was commissioned by the Danish Employers' Confederation magazine to write an article about the Scottish Council for Trade and Industry, in the belief that the latter's work in attracting foreign investment to Scotland might have some relevance to Denmark. I visited the Scottish Council's offices in Edinburgh for this purpose and received a copy of the Council's incorporation documents, from which it turned out that the Council was incorporated under the Company Acts as a non-profit company limited by guarantee, each member guaranteeing to subscribe £1 in the event of the Scottish Council going into liquidation. This structure, with a different object, formed an admirable basis for my project: the Association for Cultural Exchange.

Two friends from Cambridge helped me. One, a lawyer, secured the incorporation of ACE as a company limited by guarantee, and the other, an accountant, acted as auditor for many years. As an educational charity we needed a board of unpaid trustees, to advise upon management issues and guarantee the integrity of ACE. I had previously met Tony Crowe, then a lecturer at Farnham School of Art, who soon became an inspiring colleague, trustee and course director. For many years he was my main support. The other trustees of the Association for Cultural Exchange were largely Tony's acquaintances, including the Principal of the Farnham School of Art, James Hockey, although I personally invited Professor John Evans of the Institute of Archaeology at London University, whom I had known as a fellow corporal in the Intelligence Corps in Singapore in 1946.

In the beginning, I had to provide the working capital and to pay all the initial expenses from my own funds. Indeed, I worked for ten years without remuneration whilst ACE became financially sound. To pay the bills I worked as a part-time supply teacher in London schools, and later, between 1962 and 1968, became managing director of a small firm running a local newspaper and printing works in Suffolk.

The maharajah's palace in Datia, described by Lutyens as one of India's finest buildings. The culture and buildings of India made a great impression on ACE's founder, Philip Barnes, who was invited to stay at the palace as a guest of the maharajah whilst serving in the army in India in December 1945, later revisiting during the course of an ACE tour in 1991.

In the autumn of 1957, before the Association for Cultural Exchange was incorporated, I made a publicity trip to northern Europe, visiting student and adult education organisations, which I had got to know through my job as Reuters correspondent in Copenhagen. They included the Scandinavian Student Travel Service, the TBV and FOF adult education organisations in Sweden and Denmark respectively, a similar organisation in Finland, and the Netherlands' Universities Foundation for International Co-operation in Leiden. I sought their support in sending participants on the Summer Schools, which I planned for the following year, in English Language, Literature and British Institutions. The Association for Cultural Exchange was finally incorporated under the Company Acts as a non-political, educational charity limited by guarantee on the 19th of May, 1958.

In that first summer I organised 14 residential courses in Britain covering a period of six weeks, attended by nearly 300 people from Finland, Sweden, Norway, Denmark, Germany, the Netherlands and Portugal. This was a very gratifying response and confirmed that we were offering something worthwhile. One of these courses, for Scandinavian teachers, was held at Exeter College, Oxford. It immediately set a tradition, which held for nineteen successive years, of holding annual summer courses for visitors from abroad at Oxford colleges.

The subject of the first summer school was *Tradition and Experiment in British Society*, but the Scandinavian teachers who took part were probably more impressed by the universality of chamber pots in the college rooms, and the females among them, particularly, by the jugs of "shaving water" brought to their rooms each morning by (male) scouts or college servants. Among the speakers at that summer school was Clement Attlee, who had recently retired as leader of the Labour Party, and had become Earl Attlee K.G. He was somewhat surprised when fifty Scandinavians rose to their feet as one man, when he entered the room, out of respect for him. He gave an excellent, dispassionate speech on British Parliamentary Institutions, in which there was no suggestion that much change or experiment was called for. With Attlee as our guest, we enjoyed a more appetising lunch in College that day. Later, one of the Association's Committee members drove the former Prime Minister back to his modest bungalow in the Chilterns, stopping off en route to help him do some shopping for his wife.

Apart from Oxford and an architectural and art study tour around Britain, the rest of the summer schools were held at Clare in Suffolk. Here the local brewers, Greene King, had made two pubs, *The Half Moon* and *The Bear and Crown*, redundant, selling them to a local businessman who made them available for us to use as a conference centre with accommodation for about thirty people.

Børreby, a 16th century red brick fortified manor on the island of Sjaelland, Denmark. Philip Barnes worked as a journalist in Denmark in the fifties and the country's architecture, in particular the manor houses, and its contemporary society were a revelation and influential in the creation of ACE.

East Anglia, much more than today, was off the beaten track and far more rural in feel. We used Clare, with *The Half Moon* as our headquarters, for three happy years until the problems of running a hotel became too much on top of the administration of the courses.

We also arranged an exhibition of paintings by local artists in Clare, one of whom was Denis Lowson. I still treasure a painting I bought from Denis, whose brother, Ian, got to hear of ACE when visiting Denis after some years of teaching English at Salamanca University in Spain. Thus began a long attachment to ACE by Ian, which took him to the United States, Mexico, Peru, Indonesia and Africa, and many summers teaching on our residential courses in Oxford.

The Bear and Crown, one of two former inns in Clare, Suffolk, that were rented by ACE and used for residential courses between 1958–1960.

During the time we maintained the centre at Clare, our students also benefited from a quite different experience of suburban and metropolitan life, lodging with families in Blackheath in South London. Here the help of the Crowe family was invaluable. We held classes at Charlton House, made available by Greenwich Council, and made excursions to see the Royal Mint, a Fleet Street newspaper office and the Victorian Music Hall.

In 1958 and 1961 I went to the USA to make contacts with a number of American institutions. One of the most successful connections was with Ripon College, a liberal arts college in a small Wisconsin town where the Republican Party was born in 1860, just before the American Civil War. I found it great fun to be entertained to dinner at the Republican Club in Ripon by the President of Ripon College, Fred Pinkham. For nearly twenty years we provided summer courses in European history and art history for students from Ripon College. The courses consisted of a three-week seminar held at an Oxford College, followed by a six-week study tour to Greece, Italy, France and the Netherlands, examining some of the highlights in the development of European art. Philip Conisbee, now a senior curator at the National Gallery in Washington, directed our *European Art and Architecture* course for many years.

Traffic was not all one way. In 1959 and 1960 we selected a number of teachers from Sweden, Denmark, Norway, the Netherlands and the United Kingdom to take part in *American History and Civilisation,* a six-week-long summer school at Ripon College designed primarily to make American teachers more aware of their own heritage. The American Johnson Wax Foundation, which is based in Wisconsin, and the Coe Foundation generously made ten free places available each year. The latter organisation was the prime motive force, having as its objective the furtherance of knowledge of American Heritage. Interestingly enough, this foundation was the brainchild of an English immigrant to America, who thought that the Americans did not appreciate sufficiently their own inheritance.

Participation in the course in Ripon was a most rewarding experience, particularly at a time when American Studies in this country were in their infancy and the volume of travel to the United States was insignificant. Another rewarding contact in the early 1960s was with the Office of Cultural Exchange of the University of Pittsburgh, with whom we co-organised in 1963 an international seminar for educationalists, entitled *Youth and its Search for Identity in Modern Democracies*, held at Helsingør in Denmark. This was followed up the next year by another seminar entitled *Self-realization and Work in a Free Society*, held at St David's College, Lampeter, Wales, which dealt with the problems of leisure and unemployment. Looking back at these seminars, it is illuminating to see how relevant most of the discussions were to problems that became so much more pressing at a later date.

In the early years, ACE was mainly concerned with providing courses and tours for groups coming to Britain from abroad, a large proportion of these from the United States and Scandinavia, but we also offered a number of study tours in Europe, particularly Scandinavia.

For ten years, between 1962 and 1972, we chartered planes to fly participants between Copenhagen and London. This was an era when flights for private individuals were still prohibitively expensive, but we could hire a 100-seater DC-6 for £800 for a return trip. During the course of a day, we could fly Scandinavian course participants to England, and British participants to Copenhagen, while breaking even with 50% occupancy.

Philip Barnes comparing notes with fellow course director Denis Lowson (on the left) in 1961, during an ACE summer school for Scandinavians in Lampeter.

1964 was an important year for ACE. In January, I made another visit to Scandinavia to develop archaeological contacts. I met Professor Mårten Stenberger in Uppsala, Sweden, who agreed to accept an archaeology student on his dig on Øland in the Baltic Sea. Professor Klindt-Jensen in Aarhus in Denmark was very positive and agreed to take British archaeology students on some of his excavations. In exchange, we placed three Danish archaeology students on Martin Biddle's excavation in Winchester. The subsequent year the County Archaeologist for West Suffolk, who was then excavating an Anglo-Saxon site in West Stow, joined a Viking-age excavation in Denmark. The purpose of these exchanges was to give young archaeologists from Britain experience of excavation techniques abroad and provide similar experience for foreign students in Britain. Klindt-Jensen also introduced me to the popular Danish archaeology magazine *SKALK*, for whose readers we arranged a number of archaeological study tours in England, Wales and Scotland. The first of these tours was to southern England and was led by a recent graduate in archaeology from Cambridge, Hugo Blake, who became my first full-time assistant. He played an important role in developing archaeology courses, particularly our programme in Oxford for American students, and exchanges with archaeologists from abroad. These exchanges were particularly important for scholars from Eastern European communist countries, where archaeologists had few opportunities to visit the West. Because of the political difficulties caused by the Cold War, applicants from Eastern Europe were often highly qualified academics who were using our scheme to keep in touch with archaeology in the West. Moreover the communist governments of Poland, Hungary and Czechoslovakia only allowed their nationals to take a pound or two in foreign currency out of the country. This was enough to make a telephone call from London Airport, where we collected them and took them to the excavation. Conversely, the visits to Eastern Europe mainly appealed to young students from Britain.

During the same period we also had an archaeology exchange scheme with the National Museum in Prague. Dr Karel Sklenar, from the National Museum, came to take part in a prehistoric dig at High Lodge in Suffolk, directed by Dr Sieveking of the British Museum. Dr Sklenar spent a couple of days with us at our Suffolk home, where on television he saw the Russian tanks rolling into Prague's Wenceslas Square and taking position outside the National Museum. "I am thirty years old and I have only known freedom for six months of my life. I will never see it again," he said. It was a very emotional moment, but happily Dr Sklenar was eventually proved wrong with the downfall of communism in Eastern Europe in 1989.

In 1967, Tom Burr of the National Trust approached us to make a programme for six conservationists from Moravia in Czechoslovakia. In partnership with the National Trust, we arranged a varied programme of visits in the summer of 1968 to country houses and national parks in England and Wales. Our intention was that a British group should make a return visit in September, but in August came the Russian invasion of Czechoslovakia, putting an end to "communism with a human face". The British group of six, led by myself, postponed our visit to May 1969, when we experienced a belated but interesting insight into Czech architectural heritage.

ACE was a pioneer in providing summer schools at Oxford. The director of this archaeology school for American students at Queen's College in 1968 was Paul Mellars (centre), later to become Professor of Archaeology at Corpus Christi, Cambridge and Chairman of the ACE trustees. He is flanked by lecturers Desmond Collins and David and Ruth Whitehouse.

Throughout the 1960s Scandinavia was an important area of operation, particularly with regard to our courses for professional development. We selected, on behalf of the Danish Ministry of Education, ten British teachers per year to teach English in Danish schools. The idea behind this scheme was to improve the standard of English, at a time when Denmark was going over to a comprehensive system of education. Jørgen Gram, whom I had known in Copenhagen as a journalist, acted as our representative for Scandinavia. He formed a good relationship with Karl Poulsen, gardening correspondent at *Berlingske Tidende*, the largest newspaper in Denmark, who gave us publicity for a number of garden tours in England, Scotland and Wales and Ireland, and this also led us to arrange a number of study tours for FOF, a Danish adult education association, to Britain. In 1961, we ran a three-week-long study tour for Scandinavian teachers,

The first Study Tours were an instant success, proving there was a demand for life-long learning. The photograph captures a moment on an early tour from 1961 entitled *Celts, Saxons and Vikings*. Philip Barnes can be seen in the striped shirt and his wife, Inger, is on the far left.

Rosendal,
Mörarp

Dear Mr Barnes

It was a pleasure to show the members of your party around. Their interest in all they saw and their estimation of "things of beauty" was remarkable and most sympathetic.

The recipe for the cordial is as follows:

25 bunches of elderflowers
50g tartaric acid
2kg sugar
2 lemons
1.5l water

Press the lemons. Cut the peel into small thin slices. Place everything in a large bowl. Pour boiling water over, stir, leave for five days, then strain into containers.

There you are. I hope that the result will be satisfying.

Yours sincerely,
Baron Gerard Bennet.

of England, Scotland and Wales, entitled *Celts, Saxons and Vikings,* which was also very well received. The next year, 1962, I designed and led a comprehensive study tour entitled *Scandinavian Civilisation*. My wife, Inger, who is Danish, played an important role on this tour. Mainly aimed at British teaching professionals, this lasted 23 days and visited all three Scandinavian countries, Denmark, Norway and Sweden, travelling by coach from London and through northern Germany. The tour included visits to Orrefors Glassworks, a textile factory in Gothenburg, a modern Danish furniture factory, and a co-operative dairy in Denmark, as well as more conventional cultural destinations. In Germany we saw the Volkswagen factory in Wolfsburg. Our programme of Comparative Education courses also included one in 1960 giving British teachers the opportunity to study teaching methods in Bremen in Northern Germany and in Copenhagen, Denmark.

In 1966, in co-operation with the National Trust, we planned a tour of Danish manor houses, most of which were not open to the general public (as remains the case today). I arranged the programme together with Harald Langberg of the National Museum in Copenhagen, who was also honorary representative of the National Trust in Denmark. This began a regular series of study tours to Scandinavia, specialising in manor houses and churches as well as contemporary architecture and design. On one of these, to southern Sweden, we were asked to arrive punctually for our visit to the Royal summer palace at Sofiero. The elderly gentleman waiting to greet us turned out to be none other than the King of Sweden, Gustav VI Adolf, who proceeded to show us around personally. The King was already then in his late eighties and his wife Queen Louise, who was sister to Earl Mountbatten, had predeceased him. The King himself died in 1973 and bequeathed Sofiero, which was his personal property, to the Swedish state. It was on another visit, this time to Rosendal Slot, the home of Baron Gerard Bennet, that I tried elderflower cordial for the first time. Baron Gerard Bennet sent me his recipe which is reprinted here (left). Gerard Bennet may seem an unusual name for a Swede, but in fact many Swedish nobles are direct descendants of Scottish mercenaries who emigrated and fought for Sweden in the seventeenth century.

Another innovation of the 1960s in the field of study tours was the result of my personal enthusiasm for German Baroque and Rococo. This introduced the participants to the German concept of the *Gesamtkunstwerk* in which different arts – architecture, painting, stucco, gardens and statuary – all join together in creating an overall effect. The wonderful interiors of churches, palaces, libraries and garden settings were a revelation and have no equivalent in this country.

Meanwhile our summer courses in Oxford for American, and some Scandinavian, college students were going from strength to strength. In the 1960s most were held at Lincoln College and, later, at Merton College during the summer vacation, and we had exclusive use of the college premises. All students from abroad loved the college atmosphere and historic buildings in Oxford. Themes of study included an outline course on *European Art and Architecture*, *English Literature*, with an emphasis on Chaucer and Shakespeare and visits to plays at Stratford-upon-Avon, *18th century Literature*, *Music in England*, *Tudor England* and *History on the Ground* (landscape history). For a three-week course at Oxford, students could earn up to three undergraduate credits; likewise, six-week courses attracted six credits.

Perhaps the most important and rewarding course we offered at this time was a three-week-long archaeology seminar for American students. This was followed by participation in an excavation in one of several different locations. We held this course in Oxford for over ten years and the American students made a valuable contribution to British archaeology at a time when archaeology was underfunded. Cambridge University Press published a small book, written by four of our archaeology tutors, which became the textbook for the course. Amongst the digs to which we regularly sent students was a Mesolithic excavation on Oronsay, in the Hebrides, directed by Paul Mellars, who was also director of our Oxford archaeology seminar. This excavation was featured in an exhibition at the British Museum, in which it was recognised as one of the twenty most important excavations in Britain since World War II.

An attraction of all Study Tours is that they take the learning process out of the lecture room and into the field. Here, course director Stephen Briggs gives an impromptu lecture whilst seated on the walls of a Welsh castle.

The 1960s was a period of rapid change, not the least in the travel world. In 1959, when I first visited the United States to promote our courses, I travelled as a shipboard lecturer on a converted American wartime troopship together with many hundreds of American students. The Atlantic crossing from Rotterdam to New York took ten days. By the early 1960s, student sailings became a thing of the past, and by the end of the 1960s it was almost impossible to cross the Atlantic by sea. Air travel was beginning to open up the whole world to a new audience at modest cost.

We decided at the end of the 1960s that we should plan more study tours for people resident in Britain. An advertisement in 1969 in the National Trust Newsletter resulted in a good response and, remarkably, since then we have done very little advertising, most participants coming as a result of personal recommendation. By 1974 we had 36 programmes, 12 of which were abroad and 24 in the United Kingdom. This compares with the around 200 programmes we conduct today, most of which are abroad.

Many of our family holidays doubled as investigations for new ACE ideas and destinations. Whether *Romanesque Churches* in the Rhineland or *Castles in Castile*, our three children came to accept visits to old castles and churches as part of the natural order of things.

The majority of study tours were built around architectural themes, *French Gothic Cathedrals*, *Chateaux of the Loire*, *Rhineland Romanesque*, *Dutch Manor Houses*, *Plantagenets* to mention but a few. Ideas kept coming, often leading on from one area to the next:

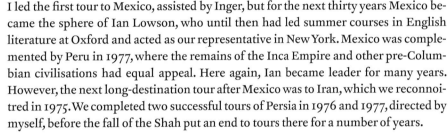

Brittany, *Normandy*, *Aquitaine* and *Provence*. Most tour journeys were by return coach from London. Although travel times were long, there was merit in observing the changing landscape and vernacular architecture as one journeyed through the country.

However, cheaper air travel soon made more distant destinations increasingly viable. While Italy and Greece were always reached by air, it now became possible to envisage travel outside Europe. Mexico became our first long-distance tour and has remained a popular destination for over 30 years. Inger, before we were married, journeyed there in 1958 whilst living in the United States. Looking through her colour slides, I was in no doubt that a January visit to Mexico would make a wonderful study tour of pre-Columbian cultures like the Aztecs, Toltecs and Mayas, of the country's Spanish colonial heritage, and some interesting modern architecture and art. The tour planned for January 1974 sold out very quickly and thus began a whole new chapter in ACE's history.

I led the first tour to Mexico, assisted by Inger, but for the next thirty years Mexico became the sphere of Ian Lowson, who until then had led summer courses in English literature at Oxford and acted as our representative in New York. Mexico was complemented by Peru in 1977, where the remains of the Inca Empire and other pre-Columbian civilisations had equal appeal. Here again, Ian became leader for many years. However, the next long-destination tour after Mexico was to Iran, which we reconnoitred in 1975. We completed two successful tours of Persia in 1976 and 1977, directed by myself, before the fall of the Shah put an end to tours there for a number of years.

In March 1979 we designed a study tour of *Mughal India*, the first of many to the Indian subcontinent. It was very interesting for me to revisit India, more than thirty years after witnessing the last days of the British Raj whilst serving in the Army, not least when we went to Datia, where I had stayed in December 1945 as guest of the Maharajah.

Our first study tour to China followed in 1980, as the country took the first cautious steps towards opening up to the outside world. I was particularly interested in the Chinese Garden and the newly excavated Terracotta Army was being exhibited for the first time. My admiration of Moslem architecture in India and Persia led me to the *Alhambra*, the main Moorish monument in Europe, which I had not visited before. The Andalusian and Moorish monuments impressed me greatly and I immediately planned a tour for the following spring. This was so successful that we have repeated the tour every year since, sometimes twice a year. It remains highly enjoyable, and even though I have done this tour about fifteen times I will never tire of it. Morocco was a natural follow up, tracing back the line of Islamic influence.

Other countries and destinations that followed included: Japan, Burma, Indo-China, Australia, New Zealand, the United States, Argentina, Bolivia, Syria, Egypt, Libya,

Many reconnaissance trips for future ACE tours throughout Europe, from Sweden down to Portugal, were conducted with the help of the trusty family Transit van, here seen on the way to Ireland in March 1969.

Ethiopia and Yemen. On these long-distance destinations it is important to have leaders with broad cultural interests who can make international comparisons with other civilisations.

But Britain was not overlooked. East Anglia, for example, was a great attraction; one weekend programme devoted to *Fenland Abbeys* was so popular that we offered it each year for over 25 years. This was the brainchild of Philip Dickinson, a retired bank manager and talented architectural historian who had written over 80 guidebooks to churches and other historical buildings. Other popular British courses included *Scottish Tower Houses*, *Carr of York* (eighteenth century architecture), *Coventry Miracle Plays*, *Welsh Castles*, *The Cinque Ports*, *Samuel Pepys* and many others.

However, not surprisingly the most popular focus for our cultural tours is Europe. The rich diversity in a relatively small area is appealing and every country has an interesting cultural and artistic heritage. Scandinavia, including Iceland and the Færoe Islands, has a special attraction to me and I have led study tours to all of its major regions. I enjoyed introducing our British audience to the less well-known art treasures of these countries, whether it was pre-historic rock-carvings, medieval churches, manor houses or nineteenth-century paintings.

9 Emmanuel Road, Cambridge was ACE headquarters from 1970–1982.

But for any organisation concerned with art history Italy must be the first priority and we consistently offer more programmes there than anywhere else. In 1970 we had our first study tour of Palladio in Venice and the Veneto, but all aspects of Italian art and history are included in our brochure from time to time.

What then makes a successful study tour? There are three main elements: the academic content and an interesting destination; an inspiring, knowledgeable and caring course leader, who can impart his/her knowledge clearly and simply; and detailed and effective planning of all the practical arrangements. I could ensure the first and the last, but the face of ACE, as far as the participants are concerned, is naturally the course leader or director. I am very grateful for the many people who joined us to take up this exacting but rewarding work.

Part of our philosophy has been to encourage course directors to make their own contribution to a study tour and, in some cases, design a new tour from scratch. We feel it is better for a leader to have a say in the subject and style of a tour than lay everything down for him or her. Joe Acheson, a colleague of Tony Crowe's from Farnham, was both a painter and an art historian, and indeed was our first art historian, leading tours from our first season until his death in 1994. Although the majority of tours have an emphasis on art history, this has never been our exclusive objective. For example, Tony Crowe was a historian and most of his tours had a historical bias. Dedicated course leaders like Tony and Joe, with us for so many years, have given a valuable element of continuity to what we do. But no one, other than myself, has contributed to ACE for as long as Ian Lowson, who was part of our essential team from 1959 to 2006. Many, such as Andrew Wilson, Roger White, Roland Randall, Kevin Hand, Gerald Randall, Denis Moriarty and Malcolm Oxley, have directed study tours for many years, and all contributed to the growth and success of the organisation. Other course leaders such as Frances Vivian, Francis Cheetham, Christie Arno, Roger Jerome, Mark Powell, Colin Bailey, Paddy Baker and Alex Koller have likewise played an important role in the development of ACE. I am grateful to them all and apologise to those not mentioned by name. All have added to ACE through their special knowledge and personal enthusiasm.

The devotion of tour leaders is only one side of the coin – the other is the loyalty of so many of our participants, who have come again and again on tours over many years. We have had at least two customers who have taken part in over 100 tours. The first was an American, Ray Gretencord, who completed 114 programmes with us before he died a few years ago. For years he came over in the summer to join a whole string of ACE courses before returning to the States for the winter. The second is Ron Corbett who has completed over 200 tours and is still adding to the score. Many participants have taken part in more than 50 tours, and at least one has participated in ACE programmes for over forty years – I am thinking of David Medd, whom I first met on a study tour of *Swedish Manor Houses* in 1967.

In 1987 we celebrated the first 25 years of ACE with a party for our participants. So many wanted to take part that for many years we subsequently held an annual reunion for participants, which took place at an interesting venue such as Trinity House and St Paul's in London or Jesus College in Cambridge.

Another gratifying aspect of ACE is the way many participants have formed friendships through taking part in ACE programmes. We hear of many lasting friendships, often across continents, and on every course there is a core of people who know each other from previous programmes. In this respect it has been an asset that we have not specialised in art history only, but have a broader cultural perspective, including: Theatre, Archaeology, Natural History and, not least, Music. Roland Randall and Kevin Hand successfully made Natural History courses part of ACE's repertoire, exemplified by the way they have worked together on spring time visits to Crete.

Our first course in Musical Appreciation was held in 1970 at Merton College, Oxford, for American students, and directed by Professor Denis Stevens. However, it was not until the 1980s that study tours based around festivals such as the *Three Choirs Festival*, the oldest in the country and which rotates between Worcester, Hereford and Gloucester cathedrals, began to attract a wider audience. In 1984 the festival was held in Worcester

We have tried many kinds of transport on our ACE tours, amongst others muleback in Ethiopia.

and this was the base for our first music study tour, led by Brian Richardson. Since 1984 we have expanded to approximately twenty music courses a year. This growth partly reflects a growing interest on the part of the public, but also the talented directors who have led the courses. Brian Richardson, with his experience of higher and extramural education at Chelsea Polytechnic, led the way, and others who have followed in his footsteps include Rupert Scott, Denis Moriarty, John Bryden and Humphrey Burton. Following Brian Richardson's retirement, Rupert Scott, himself a professional violinist, has made a significant contribution to the expansion of our music appreciation courses, while John Bryden, a concert pianist and organist, has often added his own delightful musical performances to the courses he has led. Humphrey Burton is one of Britain's most distinguished television directors and commentators; and Denis Moriarty, with his broad cultural interests, directed the BBC television programme *Face the Music*. Some of the highlights over the years have included *Opera in Vienna*, *Haydn Festival*, *Mozart in Salzburg*, *Melk Baroque Festival*, *Schubert at Schwarzenberg*, *Chopin in Poland*, *Sibelius at the Kuhmo Festival* in Finland, the *Risør Festival* in Southern Norway, the *Tanglewood Festival* in Massachusetts, and the *Thaxted* and *Orkney* festivals.

Since 1982 ACE has been based in part of a late Georgian farmhouse in Babraham, near Cambridge.

After fifty years the trustees have naturally changed. The first trustees took on uncharted waters, but the current trustees all have prior experience of ACE in one way or another. The Chairman, Paul Mellars, Professor of Archaeology at Cambridge University, first joined ACE as a young tutor on the archaeology seminar for American students at Oxford in 1965; Stephen Briggs, also an archaeologist, was likewise a tutor on the archaeology seminars for several years. He has also led ACE tours studying archaeology in Denmark and Ireland. Margaret Braund arranged the teaching on drama and theatre seminars for American students; the architect David Medd has participated on many courses and is our longest serving trustee; Marina, Lady Vaizey, former art critic of the *Sunday Times*, has been both participant and course director; Rupert Scott has led numerous music courses for ACE; Simon Ditchfield, lecturer in History at York University, has directed many tours in Italy; Mike Ferguson, business consultant, has acted as tour manager on tours to Russia; and Denis Moriarty, writer and TV producer, started leading tours for ACE over fifteen years ago and has been active across a broad spectrum of subjects ever since.

I am grateful to all our trustees for devoting their time and knowledge to ACE. The trustees are concerned with the allocation of funds to the educational charities the Association for Cultural Exchange supports. Our work in this area is described in a separate section. We now give away over £100,000 annually, an income derived from our investments, not as a surcharge on the fees paid by participants.

The ACE brochure – together with the course directors the visible face of ACE – is itself witness to the growth of the organisation. The annual brochure, which I wrote myself until a few years ago, has grown from a simple black and white pamphlet in the sixties to a 150-page colour booklet, which is complemented by a newsletter, bulletin and web site. David Winter is now our main writer and he carries on the ACE house style admirably. The technical advances over the years have been immense. We bought our first computer in 1980 – this was in the days before Microsoft and cheap PCs – which ran on an operating system called CP/M and cost £5,000. Of course this was soon outdated, giving way to MS-DOS and IBM PCs. We were early converts to Apple Macs and have used them ever since. In the same period fax machines have come and gone, to be replaced by email; and whilst in the 1970s the GPO charged the equivalent of £1,000 per annum to rent an answer-phone, such devices are now built into other telecommunications equipment. Today it is difficult to imagine travelling without a mobile phone, although in the past there was a certain freedom to being on tour and isolated from distractions. The Internet has made access to information on destinations vastly quicker, but interestingly such advances in technology haven't always resulted in equivalent improvements in productivity. For where a single typed letter was once sufficient to book a visit, a whole flurry of emails, by turns confirming and re-confirming, may now be necessary in order to avoid disappointment on arrival.

Originally we had offices in London and then in Haverhill, Suffolk, where I was managing director of Anglia Echo Newspapers Ltd. In 1968 ACE purchased a property, 9 Emmanuel Road, in central Cambridge, for use as offices. This was subsequently sold, and since 1982 ACE has been based at our home at Church Farm, Babraham, a small village six miles south of Cambridge. In the nineteenth century Jonas Webb, a famous Victorian breeder of Southdown Sheep, farmed Church Farm. Until then I had done the administration myself with the help of my wife and a part-time secretary, but we now had to expand the staff. It was also at this time we decided to call the study tour part of the association *ACE Study Tours*, while the *Association for Cultural Exchange* is the overall company, administering the investments and charity side of ACE, which has been important right from the start.

This has been a very personal account since ACE is very much a personal creation, which has enriched our lives for fifty years. It has been a very busy, exciting and rewarding time. It is hard to overestimate the contribution of my wife, Inger, to the success of ACE. In over forty years her ideas and advice have been of inestimable value and I owe a great debt of gratitude to her. The two of us have reconnoitred, taken part in and led many programmes and got to know many of the participants at first hand, making many good and lasting friendships.

In the autumn of 1992 I handed over administration of ACE's study tours and courses to our son Hugh, whilst remaining as General Secretary and retaining a supervising role. Hugh had already worked for the organisation for eight years and has now worked at ACE for twenty-four out of the company's fifty years in existence. Hugh has reacted to changing demands and phased out college accommodation and continental coach tours in response to customer questionnaires. It has also become clear that there is a demand for shorter tours, so three-weeks-long tours to, say, India and China, are now two-weeks-long, whilst European tours tend to be one-week-long where in the past they would have been two-weeks-long. On the other hand, ACE is now offering many more tours and courses, nearly 200 annually attended by over 4,000 participants, all without losing the personal touch of a small organisation. Many new long haul destinations such as Ethiopia, Libya, South Africa, Japan, Bhutan, Cambodia, Laos, Oman and Bolivia are now reached by ACE. We are also providing tours for other cultural organisations, including the Cambridge University Alumni, Friends of the Fitzwilliam Museum and many NADFAS groups. To further enhance our coverage of natural history, we have recently offered a series of tours in co-operation with the conservation charity Fauna & Flora International. Promoted under the ACE Explorers banner, these tours incorporate more outdoor activities and include an element of adventure. With regard to the office, particular mention should be made of Marion Reeves, who joined ACE in 1984 and is still a tower of strength responsible for preparing documentation for the tours.

I stayed on as the Company Secretary until 2002, a total of 44 years. The workload of the two jobs was now so much greater and more complicated than 50 years ago and our younger son, Paul, succeeded me as Secretary after having served as Assistant Secretary from 1998. I am deeply grateful to my sons, Hugh and Paul, for taking such a deep interest in the organisation I have created, and I am sure ACE is well secured for the future in their hands. Our daughter, Catherine, is still leading tours for ACE though now living in Norway.

During the first fifty years of ACE we have carried out nearly 4000 programmes of which I have personally led more than 200 and I have enjoyed every one of them. I have had very little to do with the active running of ACE for a number of years now, although I remain a trustee, but ACE continues to go from strength to strength, providing stimulating and rewarding programmes, and is no longer a one-man band.

Archaeology and the Association for Cultural Exchange

C. Stephen Briggs

Associated with ACE since 1968, STEPHEN BRIGGS spent most of his working life at the Royal Commission on the Ancient and Historical Monuments of Wales (RCAHMW) where he was sometime Head of Archaeology. His interests include architecture, ceramics and music, and he has written and lectured extensively on prehistoric, industrial and garden archaeology. Stephen established an online database of historic gardens at RCAHMW (Coflein), edits Gerddi, the Journal of the Welsh Historic Gardens Trust, chairs his local branch of the Campaign for the Protection of Rural Wales and his chief recreations are making music and garden-building at home in west Wales.

The Beginnings

The seeds of archaeology at ACE were sown when Philip Barnes met Professor Ole Klindt-Jensen during a visit to Aarhus in January 1964. Denmark by then possessed its own popular bi-monthly archaeology magazine *SKALK*, and with circulation figures around 85,000 in a population area of only 5.5 million most Danes have always had access to it. This magazine has in fact played an exemplary role in raising Denmark's national awareness of archaeology and history. Soon after discovering *SKALK*, Philip set up joint ACE-*SKALK* archaeology tours, first in Britain, then in Ireland and beyond.

In 1964 Hugo Blake was recruited to lead what was probably the first ACE archaeology tour, of Southern England and Wales. A Cambridge archaeology graduate, he was then taken on as administrative assistant for three years with a particular remit to develop the organisation's archaeological agenda. Hugo proved to have a particular flair for making contacts abroad. Today, Reader in Medieval Archaeology at Royal Holloway, University of London, he specialises in Italian historical archaeology and acts as director of Year in Europe degrees and SOCRATES exchanges.

Philip and Hugo were soon working to an unwritten three-part agenda for archaeology at ACE: first, courses would be offered introducing Britain, its archaeology and history to a non-British audience; secondly, archaeology would be brought to the British public through courses at home and abroad; and thirdly, exchanges between archaeologists would be nurtured to foster cultural understanding internationally and, incidentally, to aid career development. Things have naturally moved on in a changing world, so in recent years emphases have shifted so that the most appropriate support is now focused on countries and communities visited by Study Tours. The following narrative otherwise chronicles ACE's archaeological activities as originally conceived 50 years ago.

Courses in Britain for non-British participants

ACE Archaeology Summer Schools

The first British Archaeology Seminar was held in 1965 at Westminster College, Oxford for about fifty students. The Seminar was aimed exclusively at American students and its initial success was owed to a meeting between Philip Barnes and Dr John H. Slocum, a vice-president of the State University of New York, in 1961. Slocum became an ACE trustee and at the outset acted as "Hon. U.S. Representative".

Before the kind of cheap flight nowadays made available through Ryanair, its 1960s and '70s equivalent was the charter flight. Such flights were available to any organised group that registered its members as a club or society. So its student passengers having been made members of ACE for $5, a DC-7C was chartered from New York on July 17th, returning on September 7th at a cost of about $200-275 per head. "Five scholarships of $200 [were] available to outstanding applicants in genuine need of financial assistance" for the course. "Membership of the Association involves no obligations of any kind, though active cooperation in promoting the aims and program of the Association would be welcomed". Six academic credits were recommended for successful completion of the course, and this was to remain until British Archaeology courses eventually ended in 1989.

The first programme consisted of a three-week survey of British Archaeology and a further three weeks working on a dig. It was directed by the Palaeolithic specialist, Desmond Collins, assisted by Paul Mellars (Early Prehistory), Lionel Masters (Later Prehistory) and Tim Potter (Roman). The team was ably assisted by outside lecturers, who included Martin Aitken (dating), Graham Webster (introduction), Tony Crowe (history of Oxford), Grace Simpson (Roman pottery), Philip Dickinson (castles), John Hurst (medieval pottery) and Sir Ian Richmond (Hod Hill excavations). Tough time-schedules were set for attending some practical sessions held at monuments under excavation, like Winchester, Rainsborough in Northamptonshire and Barnsley Park. This course was sold on the basis of the considerable stimulus excavating in Britain would give. Emphasis was placed on the urgency of developmental or "rescue" archaeology, so course promotion also appealed to a sense of global public responsibility. Indeed, promotional hype the following year ran: *A peace corps endeavour in Britain! Urgent need to save archaeology monuments!*

In 1965 participants were sent to seventeen excavations. These included the Iron Age hillforts at Croft Ambrey (Herefordshire), Eggardon (Dorset) and Owlesbury (Hampshire); Palaeolithic sites at High Lodge and Pickens Hole Cave (Somerset); prehistoric sites at Rudston (East Yorkshire) and Weeting (Norfolk); Roman sites at Alcester,

Maryport, Cumbria and Fishbourne; medieval sites at King's Lynn (Norfolk), Lydford (Devon), Southampton, Wallingford (Oxfordshire) and Winchester and multiperiod landscapes in the Welland Valley. Philip Barnes and Hugo Blake visited all the digs the students worked on to see how things were going.

This first programme was repeated at Westminster for the two years following. Both were directed by Bernard Wailes, a British archaeologist with interests in the Dark Ages, teaching at the University of Pennsylvania. In 1966, with sixty students, Wailes was supported by Desmond Collins (early prehistory), Lionel Masters (later prehistory), J. L. Davies (Roman), Eric Talbot (medieval) and Willem Hackmann (conservation). The following year Ruth Whitehouse took over later prehistory, with Tim Potter providing tuition in Roman and David Sturdy in medieval studies. Copies of final written examination papers survive, and the questions were not easy. Indeed, compiling credible answers would still challenge the understanding of many of today's undergraduates.

The course instructions for intending students are of interest for the impression they give of daily life on a college summer school. Details include information on postal rates, and even the whereabouts of the college letterbox. Like the exam papers, getting through the comprehensive booklist would test most of today's students' (and perhaps some teachers') reading skills. Over the next five years, students continued to go to placements on the same or similar excavations, most of which were under serious threat from development.

In 1969, Paul Mellars took over, directing the programmes until 1976 at Merton College, Oxford. Around this time, Philip Barnes commissioned a book to accompany the course. With chapter headings appropriate to ACE's summer course requirements, it was revised and reprinted in 1973 (Collins *et al.* 1970, 1973).

In 1970 Paul opened a series of excavations on a Mesolithic settlement and midden site on Oronsay in the Hebrides. This meant less choice of excavation site or type for course participants, though those ACE American students who provided valuable assistance very much enjoyed the experience of travel to and residence on a Scottish island. Dealt with in greater detail by its excavator elsewhere, this became one of the most important archaeological projects ACE came to be associated with.

In 1973, while still at Merton College, the course was taught once more by Desmond Collins, helped by Andrew Fleming, Dafydd Kidd, John Drinkwater and Clive Bonsall. The course then consisted of 32 hours of lectures covering all aspects of British Archaeology in its European context up to the end of the medieval period. Eight hours each were devoted to archaeological methods, techniques and theory; and to group tutorials in the student's field of special interest.

In 1977 the British Archaeology Seminar moved to King Alfred's College, Winchester, again with Paul Mellars directing. The last programme in this format was held in 1978 at the Theological College, Salisbury under Desmond Collins's direction.

A shorter, revised British Archaeology summer course was later taught at Christ's College, Cambridge from 1984 to 1989, directed by Stephen Briggs. Variety of tuition was provided by visiting lecturers from within and beyond Cambridge and students were taken to institutions or departments of interest within easy reach. These included the University Aerial Photographic Unit, the Archaeology Museum in Downing Street, and the Cambridge County Archaeology Unit at County Hall. A three/four-day field trip examining monuments and excavations in Wessex was also included.

By the mid-1980s rescue archaeology had become a skilled contracting profession and finding student placements was not so easy as it had been twenty years earlier, though some excavators still offered a training component. Accordingly, students were sent to: Cosmeston medieval village, Penarth, Glamorgan; Dryslwyn Castle, Carmarthenshire; Carew Castle, Pembrokeshire; The Raunds and Stanwick in Northamptonshire; and Silchester Roman town.

Courses for British participants

Although some of the courses held in deepest Suffolk from 1958 included strong historical components, archaeological study tours really took off immediately after Philip Barnes returned from Aarhus in 1964, with an *Archaeology Study Tour of England and Wales* led by Hugo Blake. This *SKALK* partnership gathered a particular momentum in 1967 when Hazel Wheeler took an *Archaeological Study Tour of Southern England*, while Elizabeth Shee and Eric Talbot led a similar *Archaeological Study Tour of Ireland*. The format of this Irish tour was adapted and continued by Stephen Briggs 1968–70. These would soon be followed by similar historical and archaeological tour programmes throughout England, Scotland and Wales, the Isle of Man and the Orkney and Shetland Islands. Indeed, the popularity of ACE's tours and courses then grew apace to accommodate a national expansion in the concept of heritage and the historic environment.

Consequently, a strong component of ACE domestic output ever since has included shorter weekend courses as well as extended tours, examining abbeys, churches, castles, country houses and gardens, historic towns, historic villages and the occasional industrial site in the UK. Some of these have been held in conjunction with bodies like the National Trust. All are led by enthusiastic and well-informed specialists. Indeed, since the mid-1970s, archaeology and the historic environment have remained an important and popular component of ACE's tours and courses at home and abroad.

ACE was not only one of the first in its field to undertake specialist archaeology study tours for British audiences: other courses also new in outlook were initiated. For example, during the mid-1960s, organised visits to old gardens were hardly yet a fashionable leisure activity in Britain and Ireland. Interestingly, ACE first ran a course on *The English Country House and its Garden* in 1965. This was followed by *Scottish Castles and Gardens* in 1966, *Welsh Castles and Gardens* in 1967, with Philip Barnes leading a tour of *Swedish Castles and Gardens* that same year. The following April (1968), Dr A.L. (Tony) Crowe (a trustee) led a tour on *Architecture and Gardens in Southern Ireland*. This encompassed the gardens or parklands of Howth Demesne, Powerscourt, Leixlip Castle (Co. Kildare) and Garinish (Co. Kerry), with lectures *inter alia* by Henry Wheeler (Chief Inspector of Monuments, Ireland) and Desmond Guinness (a founder of the Irish Georgian Society). Since bringing together houses, castles and gardens as complete entities of architectural or aesthetic landscapes was not then common among the British scholars then beginning to investigate them, these tours were quite visionary in concept.

Since these early years in which the wider historic environment was first introduced to a broader public by specialists not normally involved in tourism, ACE has pioneered courses involving first-hand examination of archaeology and monuments globally. Paddy Baker, author of *Islam and the religious arts* (New York and London: Continuum, 2004) has set an important example, particularly in the Islamic countries, by forging links with places now difficult of access, some where monuments or museums have been destroyed through insurgency. It is her contacts that have enabled ACE to resource archaeological work on a site destroyed by Genghis Khan in 1215 in the remote Fergana Valley of Uzbekistan.

Grant-aiding archaeology at home and abroad

The First Foreign Exchanges

Soon after Hugo Blake was appointed in 1964, he began making contacts with university departments abroad with a view to effecting scholarly exchanges between archaeology students. This initiative was strongly supported by Prof. John Evans, then Director of the Institute of Archaeology, London and also chairman of ACE's trustees.

Finding sympathetic contacts in the Nordic countries was not difficult and that first year, ACE brought nine Scandinavian students to excavate in Britain: only one English student (Ann Hamlin) went reciprocally to Öland in Sweden. At the time, Britain was in the grip of a growing boom in rescue or salvage archaeology, and central government was making generous funds available to expedite the work. Special arrangements meant that Ministry excavation directors could pay "aliens" or even offer trainee diggers accommodation. Initially, these volunteers were mainly students from home, but some also came from abroad. In 1964, through ACE, two Danes came to a site in Winchester (one of whom, Birthe Kolbye, later married the excavation director, Martin Biddle) and six to other digs in England. In 1966 Anna Bachelier (now Anna Ritchie), a research student at Edinburgh University, visited Eketorp, Sweden, while Richard Manning, a civil servant, went to Drengsted in Denmark.

In 1967, Lisa Jørgensen, a student at Aarhus in Denmark, spent three weeks excavating the chambered tomb at the Ord, Scotland, with Dr John X.W.P. Corcoran, of Glasgow University. The following year Stan West, Howard Thomas and the American, Harriet Stout, separately travelled to Drengsted and excavated with Olfert Voss on a dig organised by Haderslev Museum. Upon West's return he reported that "the evaluation of the West Stow site in Suffolk will depend a great deal upon my understanding of the continental background and to a large extent upon close contacts with excavators of the standing of Mr Voss [who had helped accommodate the Britons at Drengsted]". In fact an immediate result of West's Danish visit was a reciprocal arrangement the following year bringing several Danes to the Suffolk site.

In 1969, Richard Haworth went to dig initially on a Roman fort in South Germany, but feeling standards there were not entirely satisfactory, he left and joined Vladimir Milojčićs multi-period excavation at the Rundemberg, Urach. Hr D. Zylman reciprocally excavated at Meare Lake Village, Somerset with Michael Avery. Everyone felt these arrangements had turned out to mutual satisfaction.

Travel difficulties for Eastern Bloc scholars during the Cold War

Two main factors inhibited young European travellers from studying or working on excavations abroad during the Cold War. The first was an absence of information about the nature or whereabouts of excavations and on what terms they might accept volunteers. This problem was addressed by the Council for British Archaeology, by its issuing a Calendar of Excavations Abroad. The second difficulty concerned only the Iron Curtain countries, for which the British Council offered to facilitate travel arrangements that were hardly sustainable in practice. Basically, the Council was prepared to assist small groups of students or postgraduates to come and go from the Eastern Bloc. But the reality was that it would have been very difficult to find more than a couple of Western European students or postgraduate specialists keen to visit a study project or excavation in East Europe. More importantly, it was virtually impossible for any East European state to reciprocate by sending several students or postgraduates owing to prohibitive currency and visa restrictions. In any case, few of the most senior scholars in the Eastern Bloc then had any access to foreign travel, so it was unlikely that more junior staff or students would have been permitted to travel. Given the freedom of movement in Europe post 1989, these problems are perhaps not readily appreciated today.

The East European connection and ACE

With these difficulties, as Hugo was to discover, initiating archaeological exchanges with some countries would prove impossible. Nonetheless, he doggedly wrote to a number of museums and universities in Eastern Europe with a view to offering exchange scholarships for young archaeologists. In 1965-6 contacts were successfully made with organisations in Poland, Czechoslovakia and Hungary – the countries most enthusiastic to participate. Russia, Romania and East Germany were to prove elusive.

A number of British students or young professionals benefited from exchanges with Czechoslovakia between 1965 and 1970. The first to go were Nicholas Moore (Salisbury Museum) and Joan Taylor (Cambridge University) in 1965. The following year, Vincent Megaw, then a young lecturer at Flinders University in Australia, travelled to Trišov, the important Celtic hillfort in Moravia. He also impressed Czech scholars at a session of the International Congress on Prehistoric and Protohistoric Sciences held in Prague that summer. By way of return, in 1966 Dr Jíri Brěn and Mr Hašek of the National Museum Prague came to Britain.

Then, in 1967 Mrs Hrălowa from the Czech National Museum was placed with Peter Fowler on the prehistoric field system excavation at Fifield Down for three weeks. Mansel Spratling, a research student studying Celtic metalwork at Cardiff, went to Trišov in Czechoslovakia and also visited the Neolithic settlement of Bylany. Hugo Blake dug on the medieval site of Mikulcice that year. In 1968 Dr Sklenar, a Palaeolithic specialist, came to Britain from a museum near Prague and helped on Gale Sieveking's British Museum dig on the Lower Palaeolithic site at High Lodge, Norfolk. He was there when news came that Russian tanks were occupying Prague.

Desmond Collins visited Hungary in 1969 and Dr István Bóna, a Bronze Age specialist and Dr Andreas Mócsy came to Britain that year. ACE sponsored Dr Mócsy to attend the 8th International Congress of Roman Frontier Studies. Although visa restrictions made these arrangements difficulty to expedite, Mrs Bóna also visited Britain in 1971, when she visited mainly Roman sites.

In 1966, the Poles sent Dr Jerzy Gassowski, a scholar of the early medieval period, who was accepted to dig with Martin Biddle at his ongoing Winchester excavations. By way of return Blake had arranged for Mary Jane Mountain (of Edinburgh) to visit Poland to study Mesolithic and Palaeolithic sites. Dr Kempisty was not allowed to travel until

1967, when he requested work on a later prehistoric site, so went to excavate with Don Benson on the long barrow at Ascott-under-Wychwood.

In 1967, another Pole, Dr Boleskawa Chomentowska, owing to ill-health spent limited time with John Collis at Owlesbury. Miss Hollowinska, a Polish national nominated by Prof. Stenberger (Sweden), dug at a number of English ministry sites during June. Irena Gorska, who had medieval interests, also came to Britain that year and excavated at Winchester. Meeting Irena at Sypniewo in 1963 had initially sparked off Blake to think about initiating archaeological exchanges.

A great deal was indubitably achieved through these exchanges, as is illustrated by the following anecdote. On 5th August 1967 Kempisty addressed Blake from Ascott-under-Wychwood in Oxfordshire, where he had been welcomed by the digging team. He described the site as "researched with scrupulosity and knowledge. Mr Don Benson is extremely kind for me and the frequent discussion I could have with him and with Mrs R. Kenward are themselves worth of my visit to Ascott. I profit here immensely and think that I've arrived at the right place".

On 31st July 1968, I myself travelled to Poland and took many colour slides, few of which survived because I posted them home and most were confiscated by the authorities. My modest report explains how I dug with a Polish-American team at Olsanicza, a Danubian Neolithic site and at Iwanovice, where Jan Machnik was directing a Neolithic-Bronze Age settlement site. Don Benson followed a similar path in 1972 and we were both quite taken aback at not being allowed to join in the excavation proper because all digging was undertaken by farm workers. On the other hand we were impressed at the clinical sterility of area excavation, which, as already observed by Mansel Spratling at Bylany, was being undertaken in middle Europe on a scale rarely then seen in Britain. Most western scholars were saddened that because of resourcing problems, little could be done in the way of scientific analysis or radiocarbon dating.

Support for Overseas Archaeologists at British Institutions

From 1968, ACE provided funds for the establishment of a postgraduate fellowship tenable at the Institute of Archaeology, University of London, initially for a candidate from the Mediterranean area. This was the first important area to which ACE gave support in the form of scholarships. The idea was to give young professionals the opportunity to acquire skills enabling them to return to their home countries and set up conservation laboratories or initiate programmes employing laboratory techniques in palaeoecology or other forensic aspects of archaeological investigation. Between 1968 and 1996, eighteen students enjoyed this facility before the arrangement eventually lapsed, happily to be re-established in 2006. The Fellowship eventually attracted applicants from some former Iron Curtain countries.

Although it has not been possible to trace the subsequent careers of all these students, a number have made significant contributions to the life of professional archaeology in Europe. Athanasia Kanta (1968) has for many years been an influential scholar in the Greek government team operating on Crete. Lucia Vagnetti (1970) works at the Istituto di Studi sulle Civiltà dell'Egeo e del Vicino Oriente in Rome and undertakes physical and chemical analyses of artefacts as part of an interest in long-distance trade. Dr Ivan Mirnik (1974) is currently senior research scientist at Zagreb Museum. Renato Nisbet (1978), an archaeobotanist, has, over the last thirty years, conducted research mainly on the history of Holocene forests and early agriculture of Northern Italy, as well as in the near East. He has also directed excavations in the Western Italian Alps.

Rajka Makjanic (1986) is a Roman specialist who has worked in Ghana, and was for some time associated with the publishing venture Archaeopress in Oxford, having been a joint author of the 1994 celebration volume for British Archaeology Reports. Berrin Kusatman (1987) died tragically only six years after finishing the London course. By that time she had established herself as an accomplished zooarchaeologist, working mainly in Turkey. Dr Umberto Albarella (Italy, 1989) is another zooarchaeologist whose career success from the Sheffield archaeology teaching department has involved him in high-profile research and publishing projects throughout Western Europe, the Mediterranean and beyond. Evangelia Kiriatzi (1990) is now Director of the Fitch Laboratory in the British School at Athens, where her scientific work supports a varied research programme. Lydia Zapata-Pena (1991) teaches environmental archaeology at the University of the Basque Country. Lorenc Bejko (1992) has been Director of the Albanian Rescue Archaeology Unit since it was founded in 1999. And Eva Panagiotakoupolu (1996–7) is currently an archaeocoloeopterist working from the University of Sheffield on a variety of high profile investigations into the origins and spread of plagues and other illnesses in antiquity.

The European Association for Archaeology

ACE responded positively to a request for £10,000 from the European Association of Archaeologists, to help support Eastern Bloc participants attend the EAA conference at St Petersburg in 2003. This supportive role is now taken primarily by the Wenner-Gren foundation. Further support (£1,440) was offered towards defraying the translation costs of papers written in East European languages for the *Journal of the European Archaeological Association* also in 2003.

Grant in Aid for Archaeological Projects Worldwide

ACE grant-aided the excavations undertaken by Colin Burgess and colleagues in the Evora Valley, Portugal in 1993, as part of an internationally staffed survey programme which began in 1986. This programme intended to map and undertake selective excavation at a variety of sites ranging from megalithic tombs of Neolithic origin, through Bronze Age settlement sites to large-scale enclosures of Iron Age date.

Since 1998, ACE has supported the excavations of Gennadi Ivanov at Kuva (Kuba), a medieval town in the Fergana Valley in Uzbekistan, destroyed by Genghis Khan in 1215. This site has now been visited by several ACE parties travelling in central Asia with Paddy Baker as guide lecturer.

In 2005, ACE inaugurated a postgraduate Travel Scholarship and Bursary for travel to Syria, Lebanon, Iran or Uzbekistan. In the event, an award was made to Iain Shearer, a postgraduate at the Institute of Archaeology in London. He travelled to Uzbekistan, meeting Gennadi Ivanov, and visiting the Fergana Valley before eventually spending time in Afghanistan examining monuments damaged through recent military incursion.

Conservation Projects

Following the success of the Czechoslovakian archaeological exchanges of the late 1960s, in 1967 ACE was approached by Dr B.I. Písařík (another of Blake's contacts), a conservation architect working for the South Moravian Department of Ancient Monuments (roughly translated), with a view to bringing some colleagues on a study trip to Britain. In the event, two visits were made, the first immediately before the invasion of August 1968, the second in September the following year. In the interim, a team of like-minded British specialists explored Moravia earlier in 1969. The Czechs visited Nigel Nicolson at Sissinghurst. His comment upon the potential of the exchange (*in lit.* 1st December 1967) seems worth repeating: "Of all the iron curtain countries I have visited, Czechoslovakia was miles ahead of the others in their care for historic monuments, and they have a great admiration for the way in which we do the same job in England". Perusal of the contemporary itineraries and contacts made by both sides at this time further underlines the value of the principle then being initiated.

Since 2002, the Trustees have looked sympathetically on a project launched by the Levantine Foundation aimed at addressing the long-term conservation problems of the Coptic Archive in Deir al-Surian Monastery in the Egyptian Western Desert (described in *The Art Newspaper*, no. 129, October 2002, p.22).

Perhaps one of the most pressing conservation problems ACE has responded to arose when the Danube Vltava burst its banks in August 2002 flooding the archives of the Institute of Archaeology in Prague, destroying an important component of the photographic collection, and leaving the remaining material vulnerable to continuing deterioration. In the event ACE assisted funding (of £5,000) towards a programme of digitisation which will at least help save the images of the surviving material.

Since 1998, responding to a request from Professor Sultan Barakat, ACE has supported an annual Masters scholarship at the Post-war Reconstruction and Development Unit (PRDU, est. 1992), at the University of York. This course teaches what might be felt to be the ultimate in conservation studies by linking reconstruction theory to practice, while placing the enablement and development of local communities at the centre.

ACE & the growth of aerial archaeology in Europe
contributed by CHRIS MUSSON, FSA, MBE

ACE made its first foray into the world of aerial archaeology with a grant of £3000 towards an international training school in Hungary in 1996. Since then consistent and invaluable support has been given to a variety of projects and initiatives in this field. The Hungarian school was the first of several promoted by members of the then-British but now pan-European Aerial Archaeology Research Group (AARG). The Hungarian school brought together tutors, pilots and students from countries across Europe for a first experience of active aerial survey, photo-interpretation and mapping. Many of the students have since become leaders in the growing "network" of aerial archaeologists across Europe.

Further schools and workshops followed, frequently supported by grants from ACE, for instance in Poland in 1998 and Italy in 2001 and 2003, first at Siena in Tuscany and then at Foggia, on the "heel" of Italy, over the remarkable cropmark landscapes of the Tavoliere, first brought to light by British army officers at the end of WWII in 1945. For all of these events the ACE grants (amounting to £57,000 in all) worked in tandem with funds from other sources to promote training and discussion of truly "European" scope in the range of tutors and students involved. Students enjoyed both aerial experience and instruction in the ground-based processes which enable aerial exploration to make its special contribution to archaeological research, education and conservation.

The school at Siena in 2001, linked to a Culture 2000 project of the European Union, prompted the writing of the first Italian-language manual on exploratory air survey, a vital step in a country where a change in the law had only recently freed archaeologists to start using this most effective of exploratory techniques in their study of the ancient sites and landscapes of Italy. ACE provided funds towards the preparation and publication of the book, which appeared in 2005 as *In Volo nel Passato: aerofotografia e cartografia archeologica* (Flights into the Past: air photography and mapping for archaeology), by Chris Musson, Rog Palmer and Stefano Campana (Insegna del Giglio, Firenze).

Another initiative, assisted by a "starter" grant of a few hundred pounds in 1997, led over the years to a series of aerial archaeology expeditions to Jordan by Robert Bewley from the UK and David Kennedy from Australia. In 2006 this culminated in the publication of a splendid book on *Ancient Jordan from the Air* (Kennedy and Bewley, British Academy, London). In 2007 this continuing programme saw the first of a series of workshops that in the coming years will foster aerial survey by archaeologists from Jordan and the surrounding countries.

Another initiative lies almost as far afield. With the aid of ACE grants in 2001 and 2005 Rog Palmer, from the UK, has been taking the aerial archaeology idea to Armenia, using a paramotor (a sort of powered hang-glider) in a country that lacks suitable light aircraft or fuel to power them. An Armenian student is at the time of writing (August 2007) attending a workshop on the use of aerial photography at Poznań, in Poland.

The Poznań workshop is one of the final events in a £600,000 programme of aerial survey, research and events made possible by a Culture 2000 project of the European Union under the title of *European Landscapes: Past, Present and Future*. Here again, a generous grant from ACE has given flexibility in mounting exchange visits and events across Europe, particularly in providing financial support for former eastern-bloc students to attend events and to take back the techniques of aerial archaeology to their own countries.

It is timely, at this point in the history of ACE, that there has been a spin-off from this project in Romania, one of the first countries to host ACE tours nearly half a century ago. In this case, a consortium led by the National History Museum in Bucharest has (through AARG) been awarded a grant of £3000 to support the first truly "home-based" aerial survey and presentation of the results in Romania, currently being carried out by research students who were trained in Italy and the UK with the aid of Culture 2000 and ACE.

The contribution of ACE to the growth of aerial archaeology across Europe (and beyond) has been incalculable. Naturally, aerial archaeologists hope that this support will continue in the coming years, whenever innovative and well-directed projects present themselves to the Trustees.

Conclusion

ACE has held a firm commitment to supporting the development of archaeology in its many forms since the mid 1960s. The organisation has progressed its interests from those small beginnings and, by holding numerous archaeology-related courses, now maintains a remarkable position in this area of tourism. More importantly, however, by strategically placed resourcing in vital areas of skills development and on archaeological investigation and conservation at home and abroad, ACE has earned a unique place in the development of archaeology internationally: an enviable reputation.

Bibliography

History of ACE

BARNES, P. B. 1983. *25 Years*, printed by Compton and Sons, Sawston, Cambridge.

BRIGGS, C. S. 2007. *Coming in from the Cold. The Association for Cultural Exchange and Archaeological Travelling Scholars in Europe 1965-70*, lecture delivered to European Association of Archaeologists' Annual Conference, Zadar, Croatia, 22nd September 2007.

COLLINS, D., WHITEHOUSE, R., HENIG, M., and WHITEHOUSE, D. [with foreword by J. D. EVANS] 1970, 1973. *Background to Archaeology: Britain in its European Setting*, Cambridge University Press.

Archaeological Projects

BURGESS, C. B., Gibson, C., and Correia, V. H. 1999. Hill forts, Oppida and Vitrification in the Evora Area, Central Portugal, in P. Frodsham, P. Topping and D. Cowley (eds), *We were always chasing time. Papers presented to Keith Blood*, Northern Archaeology 17/18 (special edition), 129-147.

CORREIA, V. H. and BURGESS, C. B. 2004. Habitats fortificados de tarde Idade do Ferro Romano-republicanos na área de Evora; Quadro geral e problemática, in P. Moret and T. Chapa (eds), *Atalayas y Casa Fortificados: Explotación y control del territorio en Hispania (S.III a de C. - S I d. de C.)* Universidad de Jaén, 55-63.

GIBSON, C., CORREIA, V. H., BURGESS, C. B. and BOARDMAN, S. 1998. *Alto do Castelhino de Serra (Montemoro-o-Novo, Evora, Portugal). A preliminary report on the excavations at the Late Bronze Age to Medieval site, 1990-1993*, Journal Iberian Archaeology, 189-246.

Institute of Archaeology, UCL
ACE Fellowship in Archaeology, 1968–1996

YEAR	NAME	COUNTRY	PRINCIPAL FIELD OF STUDY
1996–7	Eva Panagiotakopulu	Greece	Archaeo-entomology, Textiles
1995–6	Elena Sergusheva	Russia	Archaeo-botany
1994	Mara Migliavacca	Italy	Archaeology of pastoralism
1993	Zana Kamberi	Albania	Museum Studies, computer studies
1993	Joaquin Navarro	Spain	Evolution of urbanism in Ancient Spain
1992	Lorenc Bejko	Albania	Prehistoric Archaeology
1991	Lydia Zapata	Spain	Archaeo-botanical studies
1990	Evangelia Kiriatzi	Greece	Prehistoric Archaeology
1989	Umberto Albarella	Italy	Environmental Archaeology
1988	Nida al-Dindashi	Syria	Western Asiatic Archaeology
1987	Berrin Kusatman	Turkey	Environmental Archaeology
1986	Rejka Makjanic	Yugoslavia	Roman Archaeology
1984	Hassan Ismail	Egypt	Roman Archaeology
1982	Berrin Kusatman	Turkey	Environmental Archaeology
1980	Mervat Ramadan	Egypt	Archaeological Conservation
1978	Renato Nisbet	Italy	Environmental Archaeology
1976	Behin Aksoy	Turkey	Western Asiatic Archaeology
1974	Ivan Mirnik	Yugoslavia	Roman Archaeology
1972	Francoise Hivemal-Guerre	France	Prehistoric Archaeology
1970	Lucia Vagnetti	Italy	Prehistoric Archaeology
1968	Athanasia Kanta	Greece	Prehistoric Archaeology

Review of cultural and educational projects supported by the association

Paul Brooke Barnes, *General Secretary*

Introduction

Since its foundation in 1958, the main activity of the Association for Cultural Exchange has continued to be the planning and running of adult education courses, in which it has been a pioneer from those early days before, for example, the founding of the Open University, through to the development of the current demand for cultural travel. This is true both of the labour expended and the educational achievements, with approximately eighty thousand people having taken part in our programmes. Our founding charter does, however, allow for the making of grants to support other educational and cultural endeavours and this, too, has been a significant part of our activities from our earliest days. From the beginning, Philip Barnes set up the company as a non-profit-making organisation, a Company Limited by Guarantee, so that any surplus from our activities, rather than being distributed to shareholders, is placed in an educational fund, which is either used for developing new courses or distributed in the form of grants. Each year we donate approximately £100,000.

For the first twenty years the grants issued naturally reflected the daily business of the organisation and fell into one of three categories: student scholarships and seminars; teacher training and the theory of education; and archaeological studies. The first two are covered in the founder's history and the third in a separate chapter by the archaeologist and ACE trustee, Stephen Briggs. Towards the end of the seventies, courses for undergraduate students played only a minor part in our activities and they finally died out in the early eighties. It was therefore right that the nature of the grants awarded should change in accordance with our focus on courses for mature adults. Archaeology continued to be a key area of interest and received major funding from the trustees, but three other categories were added: development and education; art and design (both interpreted in their widest sense, to include, for example, music and architecture); and natural history and conservation education.

Development & Education

Prospect Burma

A basic founding principle of ACE is a belief in the value of learning from others and an appreciation of different cultures. In simple terms: not only that dialogue is better than conflict, but that dialogue can prevent conflict. Occasionally this presents problems: for example, when the simple act of visiting a country is perceived by certain pressure groups as an endorsement or support of the country's regime. Such issues are the lot of the international traveller and we leave the decision whether to travel or not to the individual. If we believe that we can devise a study tour in which there can be meaningful dialogue and cultural exchange we will attempt to do so, circumscribed only by practical issues and Foreign Office advice. A good example is Burma. In the summer of 1988, mass demonstrations took place against the one-party system and in support of democracy, but they were put down brutally with the loss of thousands of lives. Many more went into exile, whilst the military government placed the universities, whence many of the demonstrators came, under repressive control. Ever since, a whole generation has been deprived of education, severely damaging the country's future. In 1990 Prospect Burma was founded, with the aim of supporting educational projects for exiled Burmese of all ethnic groups denied learning within Burma because of the country's political and economic crisis. Sadly, the same problems still exist today. Prospect Burma's founding executive director was Evelyn Aris, mother-in-law to Aung San Suu Kyi, the human-rights activist and campaigner for democracy, who since 1989 has been under house arrest by the ruling military junta. One of the first objectives for the trust was to support the education of the thousands of exiled Burmese living in refugee camps on the Thai side of the border. It was soon established, through discussions in the field, that the most effective way to do this was through teacher training courses, enabling the Burmese to better help themselves. The first teacher training camps were established in 1991 and ACE began its support in 1992. Unfortunately, in 1995 the security situation along the border deteriorated to such an extent that work in the region became unduly difficult and dangerous. As a result, Prospect Burma launched a scholarship scheme to enable Burmese students to attend universities in the safety of other countries. One of these was the prestigious Asian Institute of Technology (AIT) in Bangkok and in 2000 ACE funded its first two students, Miss Kyawt Yin Win, to study a Masters degree in engineering, and Mr Myo Min Cho, to study a Masters in waste water management. ACE continues to support Prospect Burma, which now offers scholarships to over 200 students every year, providing hope and much needed skills for the future regeneration of Burma.

Street Symphony, Ethiopia

In 1995 we were approached by filmmaker Andrew Coggins, who requested support for an innovative programme working with street children in Ethiopia. This was at a time when the famine in Ethiopia was still fresh in people's minds, so the proposal to teach children dance and filmmaking skills, when so many other basic human requirements were still so lacking, was at first received with some scepticism. However, we were impressed by his enthusiasm and imagination and the fact that the potential beneficiaries were treated as equals rather than as objects of pity. As a small organisation with broad terms of reference, we are in a position to move quickly to provide seed funding for innovative projects, in the hope that larger organisations will later take over the baton. And so it was that we decided to make an initial grant to Street Symphony. The organisation worked closely with the Ethiopian Gemini trust, originally set up to support families with infant twins or other multiple births. Due to the high levels of poverty and limited healthcare, such children suffer particularly high mortality rates. However, the dance project, known as Adugna, was aimed at the street children of Addis Ababa. The children had never experienced contemporary dance or classical music before and the programme gave them a sense of purpose, away from the dangers of the street, which raised their self-esteem whilst increasing awareness of HIV/AIDS, civil rights and discrimination. Under the guidance of choreographer Royston Maldoom, the children developed rapidly and, as the Adugna Dance Company, gave performances to other children, local communities, NGOs and government officials, and even toured abroad.

The second element of the project was to create a voice for the street children through the medium of film. More ambitious still, the children themselves were to learn the art of filmmaking. The project was called Gem TV and was ultimately to result in two short films. The first, *Stolen Childhood*, recounted the story of Kebebush, one of many child brides in Ethiopia. Married at the age of eight, she fled from the countryside to the city, only to find a life of poverty and prostitution. The film had a significant political impact and was screened to the Ethiopian parliament and received an award from UNICEF. The second film, *Adugna – A Shared Gift*, tells the story of the dance troupe, from first rehearsals through to performances.

Integrated Village Development Trust, India

In February-March 1992 ACE conducted an extensive three and a half week study tour of southern India directed by Philip Barnes. The participants included Margaret and Mike Wright, frequent visitors to India who, in retirement, had been assisting on small-scale development projects. Towards the end of the tour, they gave a presentation on their work to the rest of the group, which resulted in several offers of help in the way of donations. On their return home, the Wrights decided that the work should be put on a more formal footing and so the Integrated Village Development Trust was established as a registered charity later that year. Many of those on the 1992 ACE tour are still supporters and it is very satisfying that ACE can be considered to have been in at the birth of the IVDT. From the outset IVDT has always worked to support local NGOs, with the corollary that its overhead expenses are very low. In IVDT's first year, ACE made a grant to enable a literacy programme in a remote area of Tamil Nadu, followed by a further grant for the building of a small training centre, which has now delivered training to thousands of individuals.

In 1995 Philip Barnes and the trustees of ACE decided to make a grant of £10,000 in honour of the late Tony Crowe, long time ACE course director and trustee, who had provided so much help in the early days of the organisation. Because of Tony's long love of India it was decided that the money should go towards a project in that country and that IVDT would be the best vehicle for doing so. At this time IVDT was working closely with an Indian NGO called Alternative for India Development (AID), which proposed that a training centre be built for women in the very deprived area of Pattireddipatty in western Tamil Nadu. By late 1998 the Tony Crowe Centre was finished and ready for use. Importantly, AID had received a pledge from the Tamil Nadu government to take on the subsequent running costs, ensuring its future success. Margaret and Mike Wright visited the centre in 2001 and were very impressed by what they saw.

Villages in remote rural areas of Tamil Nadu ten years ago lacked, and to a lesser extent still do, the basic facilities we take for granted, such as electricity, telephones, public transport, shops, schools and medical facilities. A number of excellent health and education videos had been produced by government bodies, but there were no means of showing them in the villages. In fact, because there was no lighting and oil lamps were expensive, virtually all activity ceased at nightfall. With funding from ACE, IVDT purchased a jeep, generator, projector and screen, and hired a driver trained in operating the equipment. In the first year, 298 shows were given in Tamil Nadu, attended by over 32,000 people. A tremendous success and a great help in communicating guidance on such issues as malaria, HIV/AIDS and water contamination.

Once the Tony Crowe Centre had been running for a couple of years, it became clear that there were large numbers of women asking for help on simply how to access the resources in the way of grants etc., that were available from local and central government. AID and IVDT, supported by ACE, set up 50 self-help groups, each of about 20 women, and provided training over a period of 12 to 18 months. The result was much improved access to grants and funding that has helped overcome poverty and gender problems.

The southeast region of the state of Bihar (Jharkhand) is home to the Santhal peoples, the original inhabitants of India. Although there are government primary schools in this very poor region, it has always been a custom of the Santhal not to educate girl children. AID discussed with local elders the possibility of setting up some schools for girls on a trial basis. A plan was agreed with IVDT and, with funding contributed by ACE, a total of 20 schools were set up, each providing education to about 30 girls. The girls attended for 4 or 5 hours each afternoon and were taught basic literacy, numeracy and other skills. Another unexpected development was that from the very start the mothers also came to the classes. The trial period was limited to 3 or 4 years, starting from 1998, on the basis that once the tribal leaders had seen the advantages of girls being sent to schools they would start sending them to the local government primary schools.

Travelling in western Bihar in 1996, Mike Wright was struck by the very real problem in remote villages of hundreds of children (mainly boys) aged 14 or 15, who had been "sold" into the carpet industry as bonded labour at 5 or 6 years of age. These children worked in remote villages, often out of reach of the police who were trying to stamp out this system. Few of the villages had electric power, so the children worked on intricate designs in semi-darkness. They were very badly treated, in many cases being chained to the loom and sleeping on a rug under it. They lost contact with their families and received poor food, no education or medical care. After 10 years or so, the loom owners would get rid of the 15 year olds and replace them with new 5 or 6 year old children. The redundant boys faced a very bleak future: a short life, earning what they could by casual labour. IVDT and AID raised the funds to build a residential training centre, where the boys would go for 6 to 9 months to received basic education, vocational training and decent food, medical and pastoral care. The school opened in January 2001 and ACE has subsequently funded the purchase of tools and equipment for some of the vocational courses.

With the economic developments in India, many unskilled workers have travelled from rural areas of Bihar and Jharkhand to seek work in Delhi, often living in shacks in slum areas, their children earning small sums of money by collecting tins, bottles and rags. To address the needs of these children the Kala Kutir project was set up, under the auspices of the Dr Baluga Memorial Trust, to provide a number of centres in the squatter areas at which the children could become involved in music, dance and art, and through these activities eventually become involved in more formal education. ACE helped IVDT fund expansion of the scheme in 2003 and each year Helena Nightingale of IVDT spends time working in the centres and helping the children.

More recently, ACE has supported IVDT's work in the low-lying coastlands of Orissa. The terrible tsunami of December 2005 did not hit the area badly, but a few years earlier another tidal wave killed over 100,000 people in the region. During discussions between local villagers and IVDT it emerged that regeneration of the mangrove forests would be a major factor in saving lives and limiting damage in the future. A key element in the plan was teaching the local community about the value of the mangrove trees, many of which had previously been lost to other development objectives. In December 2005, ACE contributed to the funding of the Chale Chalo project to help protect the area from tidal waves by creating healthy mangrove forests to act as a natural shock-absorber.

St Matthew's Children's Fund, Ethiopia

The St Matthew's Children's Fund was established in 1986 to support the work of local Ethiopian organisation, the Jerusalem Association of Children's Homes, in caring for and educating orphaned children, primarily victims of drought, civil war and the famine disaster of 1984. In the years following the foundation of the trust, homes were established in Addia Alem, Reppi, Debre Birhan, Debre Zeit and Bahir Dar, each home caring for between 100 and 150 children. The children attended local schools and were taught basic farming skills. The trust was named after St Matthew's Church in Addis Ababa, Ethiopia being the second-oldest country to have officially converted to Christianity (during the 4th century). By 1995, the Blue Nile Training School had been established on the shores of Lake Tana in the northwest highlands, providing vocational training for the older children. Philip Barnes visited Ethiopia in 1996 and was able to observe the work funded by the St Matthew's Children's Fund and administered by the local Jerusalem Association of Children's Homes. He was impressed by what he saw, and later that year the ACE trustees issued two grants, one supporting an Agricultural Training Programme in Bahir Dar and the other the Selam Vocational Centre in Addis Ababa. The vocational programmes were designed to provide the skills that would turn the children into self-reliant young adults.

As the immediate effects of war and famine receded, the emphasis of the St Matthew's Children's Fund changed from provision of basic care to education. To meet this need, in 1998 ACE began its support for a Tutorial Scheme for Elementary Students, providing education for both orphans and street children in Bahir Dar. Among the students was Shemelis Mengistu, a blind boy, who had previously demonstrated some musical talent and received training that enabled him to make a good living playing the krar, an Ethiopian lyre, in the hotels and restaurants of the capital. The tutorial schemes received a great deal of interest from local communities and, by 2001, nearly 2,500 students were receiving education, work which ACE participants on study tours to the region were able to witness at first hand. In 2003, we helped fund the extension of the scheme to Debre Birhan, allowing more children in disadvantaged urban areas to benefit from basic education.

Reflecting the increasing focus on education, the Jerusalem Association of Children's Homes changed its name to the Jerusalem Children and Community Development Organisation in 2004. More recently, JeCCDO, as it is known, proposed construction of a community-based children's library in Bahir Dar, next door to the existing adult library, also built and managed by the organisation. ACE is pleased to be supporting this initiative and we look forward to further progress in the future as Ethiopia continues to rebuild from years of war and famine.

Mathieson Music Trust, India

The Mathieson Music School was founded in memory of the late Father Theodore Mathieson, who joined the Anglican Brotherhood of the Epiphany and devoted his entire life to an orphanage run by the Oxford Mission in Calcutta. His enthusiasm for music - he was a keen amateur cellist - resulted in several of the boys developing careers in the musical world, both in India and abroad. One such student was Anup Kumar Biswas, who, after coming to England at the age of 16 to complete his studies, has established himself as an international cellist and composer. Eager to continue the strong musical tradition after his death, Father Mathieson approached Anup and together they planned the founding of the Mathieson Music School to serve the children of Calcutta's poorest families. The school was founded on February 7, 1994, shortly after Father Mathieson's death, and the Mathieson Music Trust, a registered charity to support the school, later the same year.

Anup has a love of both Indian and Western classical music and was determined that both should be a core part of the curriculum. Many of the children come from destitute and emotionally disturbed backgrounds; music is not only a means by which they can express themselves but also a key to opening a world of education. On a vocational level, the flourishing Indian film industry, military establishments, and the hotel and entertainment sectors all have a strong demand for musicians trained in Western music. The school is a Christian institution but is open to children from all religious backgrounds, with general education running alongside the musical tuition. Remarkably, the school also provides accommodation, full board, clothing and medical care for the children. At first the school was situated within the compound of the Oxford Mission, but after a fund-raising tour of the UK, during which thirty of the children played over a hundred concerts, in venues ranging from village halls to Westminster Abbey, three acres of verdant countryside not far from the city was purchased and the first purpose-built accommodation constructed. In 1999, ACE funded the completion of a new dormitory, providing accommodation for forty girls together with a large room doubling as chapel and rehearsal space.

The young performers of the Mathieson Music School returned to the UK in 2000 and their concert tour included a performance at Great St Mary's Church in Cambridge, sponsored by ACE. Anup himself gave a recital at the Royal Overseas League, London, in November of that year, in a concert organised by ACE which raised over £1,000 for the school. A further grant in 2001 enabled the construction of a boys' dormitory. Sadly, on September 11, 2001, the school was invaded by an angry mob which vandalised the buildings. As a result the school was closed for a year. The events demonstrate the difficulties experienced from time to time in development work, particularly when working in as challenging an area as cultural exchange. A rumour had been spread locally that the school was endowed with limitless funds, causing resentment and envy in a deprived area that itself desperately requires more educational resources. The comings and goings of Westerners, mostly voluntary teachers and gap year students, added to the feeling of "them and us", a sentiment that was encouraged by religious fundamentalists who opposed both the tolerance and Christian teaching of the school. Eventually, with the assistance of the Minister for Minority Affairs, Mohammed Salim, the misunderstandings were resolved and the authorities were able to guarantee the safety of the school.

Anup Kumar Biswas has been an inveterate fund-raiser for the school and in 2006 he embarked on another UK fund-raising tour, this time accompanied by friends including Donald Boothman, baritone, and Clifton Noble on the piano. In June, we were delighted to invite the group to a musical garden party at ACE's headquarters in Babraham, during which almost £2,000 was raised for the school.

Feedback Madagascar

Feedback Madagascar was founded in 1991 by Jamie Spencer, an anthropologist who first visited the country aged 22 to write his university dissertation. He was so moved by the poverty yet generosity of the Tanala people, and their kindness when he was taken ill, that he was determined to repay the debt by returning to help the Malagasy. Madagascar is one of the poorest nations on earth, but amongst the richest for endemic wildlife. The majority of people are subsistence farmers and the country has a rapidly growing population. Under current systems of agriculture the land is struggling to support them, resulting in further deforestation and erosion. Integrated development and land management are therefore important priorities.

The aims of Feedback Madagascar are to advance education and provide assistance in the relief of poverty whilst conserving the environment. A founding principle of the organisation is that the projects should be driven by the views, or feedback, of the local people. The first major project was to build irrigation dams for the village of Sandrakely and then to rebuild a local school destroyed by a cyclone. ACE was approached by

Feedback Madagascar's director, William Self, in 1997, with a proposal to fund a secondary school forest reserve. Already a primary school reserve had been created, attracting the support of the World Wide Fund for Nature and Madagascar's Ministry of Education. Impressed by this first step, the village elders in Tsaratanana donated land for the school forest reserve, situated on the eastern border of the Ranomafana National Park, whilst ACE agreed to fund the training of teachers and staff and the provision of educational courses in the environment, sanitation and agriculture. Pupils and their parents were to learn how to manage the reserve and to utilise a variety of forest products, creating a financially self-sustaining project, and exchange visits were arranged with both UK students and a number of other Malagasy tribes. An important element was the creation of a locally staffed and run partnering organisation known as CCD Namana. Unfortunately all this was against the backdrop of a financial crisis in the country which resulted in 4,000 rural primary schools being closed and 12,000 teachers being laid off. Coupled with the Ministry of Education no longer being able to provide support, it sadly became apparent that the scheme could not proceed and that an alternative direction would need to be found.

Feedback Madagascar returned with a proposal to help support an Agricultural Training Centre in Ambalavao, Fianarantsoa province, a project that had previously been visited by an ACE group during a study tour to the country. The centre played a key role in re-establishing the traditional, home silk industry, as well as instruction in improved agricultural methods for other crops, whilst its tree nursery provided 65,000 saplings in 1998. Young women from female-only households particularly benefited from this scheme. Previously, many had been reduced to begging or forced into prostitution at the weekly cattle market and, without access to healthcare, sexually transmitted diseases had become a silent epidemic. Their children were undernourished and did not have access to education, reducing the chance of breaking the cycle of destitution.

The silk industry in Madagascar is founded on two species of sericious insects. Firstly, *Bombyx Mori* or mulberry silk worm, introduced to the island by Europeans in the 19th century and which became the basis of widespread household production, particularly on the high plateau region. Secondly, *Borocera Madagascariensis*, an endemic species whose cocoons are harvested directly from the forest (wild silk). By the late 20th century the tradition had almost died out, undermined by mass production of cheaper fibres and poor marketing. However, Feedback Madagascar reasoned that there would be a demand for individual products made from natural fibres and produced in an ethical manner.

In Ambalavao, the first stage in the re-introduction of the silk-making tradition was the establishment of a mulberry plantation within a 25-hectare site and the training of an initial group of 15 women in all stages of silk production, from mulberry propagation to weaving of cloth on small locally made looms. In September 1999 an ACE party was privileged to visit the new centre and contribute directly to the project by purchasing some of the beautiful silk scarves. ACE provided further support in 2005 to Feedback Madagascar's work in reviving the silk industry. The focus on this occasion was the central high plateau region of Amoron'Mania, with the emphasis on providing the skills necessary for increased production and for selling.

Whilst the revitalised silk industry played a useful part in raising local incomes, Feedback Madagascar was keen to do more to improve local healthcare, and in 2001 requested ACE's support for the Traditional Birth Attendant project, a programme of training and exchange between illiterate traditional birth attendants and doctors and midwives. The provision of modern healthcare is extremely limited in the area, with high rates of infant and maternal mortality. One of the few resources available to expectant mothers are the traditional birth attendants who, whilst respected and trusted by local communities, have very little medical knowledge. The training provided over 120 traditional birth attendants with information about such matters as vaccination, breast-feeding, diet and family planning, and experience of at least two births in a hospital environment. With this knowledge the traditional birth attendants have become a vital conduit between the medical profession and the villagers.

Wilkins Memorial Trust, Nepal

On September 28, 1992, Pakistan International Airlines flight PK268 crashed on approach to Kathmandu airport. There were no survivors. On board were the Wilkins family from Peterborough: Andrew, 38, Helen, 36, Hannah, 10, Naomi, 8, and Simeon, 6. Andrew was an engineer working as a field consultant and adviser for micro-hydro-electric schemes for poor rural communities. Helen was a social worker planning to participate in a children's programme at a local hospital. The whole family loved Nepal and were concerned for its future. Following their tragic deaths, the Wilkins Memorial Trust was inaugurated in the family's memory with the aim of continuing their work, chaired by Cambridge botanist and ACE course director, Dr Roland Randall.

There is no national health service in Nepal and most doctors and hospitals are based in the Kathmandu valley or the larger towns. In many rural areas there are extremely limited facilities and many illnesses, some fatal, are from preventable diseases. In 2001, ACE helped the Wilkins Memorial Trust provide a number of health education camps run by Aparna Bhatta, from the Nepal-based Self Reliant Centre. The aim of the camps was to teach villagers about disease prevention, hygiene, sanitation and nutrition. Local women were instructed in primary gynaecological care and many patients were treated for gastro-intestinal diseases and skin conditions.

ACE also gave its support to a project training the Sarki caste in villages of Sindhupal-chowk to use traditionally tanned leather in new ways for the urban and export market. The Sarki caste have been regarded as untouchables and with very little income have been unable to pay towards education for their children, therefore perpetuating the cycle of economic and social poverty. Nepal is a Hindu kingdom and so the cow is sacred; cattle are not killed nor beef eaten, but using leather is generally accepted. Disposing of dead animals and processing of hides is considered a job for those at the bottom of the caste ladder and has traditionally been carried out by the Sarki. Over time, the demand for locally produced leather has been replaced by that for factory-made and synthetic materials, leaving the Sarki, unable to adapt to a changing market, with less and less income. Organisations working with local communities, such as the Wilkins Memorial Trust, believed that there was a market in developed countries for individually made products fabricated from the delightfully supple, naturally tanned hides. The training therefore included analysis of sales and marketing techniques as well as quality control methods, and was provided by the Village Leather Training Association, a local NGO. The raw hides are soaked in a pit of quicklime for about 3 weeks. Every day they are turned and macerated, by being trodden, for 10 to 15 minutes, removing the hair. The hides are then placed in a tanning pit for 3 weeks in a solution containing locally sourced herbs. Again, they are worked daily, before being stretched out to dry. The next process is skiving, to remove any surplus material, and finally the hides are applied with mustard seed oil.

Another low caste are the Danuwar, an ancient people with a love of nature who traditionally made a living from fishing. In more recent times, the men have tended to work as agricultural labourers for landowners, with the women and children working as house servants. They are a poor and mostly illiterate society, but with a culture, religion and language of their own. In 2001, we were approached by Kishor Rai, a young Danu-war who, against all odds, was the only member of his caste not only to have excelled at school but also to have graduated from university. We put him in touch with the Wilkins Memorial Trust and together we funded him to produce the very first dictionary in Danuwar, a vital step in both improving literacy and enabling the language and related culture to be sustained. We also funded the university studies of Aruna Shrestha, whose family comes from a small town on the main road from Pokhara to the Indian border. Her parents were unusual in that they encouraged the education of their sons and daughters equally. Supported in her education by the Wilkins Memorial Trust, and through her own hard work and dedication, she was able to attain a place on a four-year degree course at Kathmandu Engineering College to study electronics.

The Wilkins family were very concerned with the environment and sustainable development, so it was only natural that one of the first projects supported by the eponymous trust was Environmental Camps for Conservation Awareness, or ECCA. The project is based in the Southern Lalitpur area. The camps bring an environmental message to school children and their families and are designed to bring real improvements to sanitation, local timber use, food and garden production and general health and prosperity. ACE supported the camps in 2005–6, but, sadly, these were carried out against a backdrop of continuing violence, the culmination of a ten-year Maoist insurgency. The future looks very uncertain, with increasing divisions in society looming and the prospect of further confrontation.

Hantam Community Education Trust, South Africa

Those who brave the dust and heat of South Africa's Karoo region often find themselves traversing vast and silent spaces, seemingly devoid of human activity. But anyone who travels along the dirt road running east from the town of Colesberg towards the village of Steynsburg is nowadays met by an extraordinary sight: in the middle of a huge plain, ringed with hills and ridges, lies a modern educational complex, painted a cheerful yellow and flying the new South African flag. The complex has been created by the Hantam Community Education Trust and provides school education for around 200 children, a pre-school centre, evening classes for farmworkers, and vocational training for teenagers.

The project began in 1989 when Lesley Osler and Claire Barnes-Webb, the wives of two local farmers, decided to establish a pre-school for the children of workers on their and a few neighbouring farms. The Karoo is a semi-desert, filled with fossils and relics of Stone Age communities. It is a fascinating but poor region, its dry scrub supporting only sheep farming. Distances between settlements are huge and in the past education for the indigenous communities, composed of people of Khoi descent and later Xhosa settlers, was rudimentary to non-existent. The next step was to establish a community-run primary school, with parents and farmers working together. Parents would have to help with building work and maintenance, contribute to school and transport fees, and help raise additional funds; farmers would have to give workers time off to attend to school affairs, help with transport, and also contribute to school fees. Crucially, the regional education authorities agreed to recognise the school, pay teachers' salaries and provide basic equipment, whilst allowing the project to be privately co-ordinated. The success of the school led to an award from President Nelson Mandela in 1999, and by 2002 a primary health clinic, teacher development centre, and skills training centre had all been added. By this time many of the pupils had outgrown the school and were seeking further education at high school, college or university. To meet this requirement a further education bursary scheme was established, which ACE was pleased to support in 2003, enabling 13 students to benefit from the scheme, studying subjects ranging from electrical engineering to tourism to fine art. Since then we have continued our support, 22 students now benefiting in studies ranging from metalwork to medicine, teaching to agricultural mechanics.

The Post-war Reconstruction and Development Unit (PRDU) provides research, consultancy, and training of professionals, in the planning and management of reconstruction after war and humanitarian intervention in complex emergencies. A one-year MA course provides multi-disciplinary training of professionals from around the world and is a valuable forum for cultural exchange and comparing professional experiences. The inaugural ACE Masters Scholarship was funded in 2000 and awarded to Saman de Silva from Sri Lanka. Saman came to the course with an honours degree in the built environment and a MSc in architecture. He was a member of the UNESCO-Sri Lanka Cultural Triangle project and was one of the architects involved in the recovery activities after the bombing of the Temple of the Sacred Tooth Relics in Kandy. As part of the study programme, Saman visited reconstruction work in Croatia, and he reported that the experience would greatly enhance his own architectural and conservation skills. This was followed by a six-week work placement with the International Centre for the Study of the Preservation and Restoration of Cultural Property (IC-CROM), Italy.

Our second ACE scholar was Raz Mohammad from Afghanistan, who brought to the course his professional experience as UN deputy regional coordinator for humanitarian assistance to Afghanistan. Raz Mohammad visited the ACE trustees in Cambridge to recount at first hand the difficulties faced in rebuilding Afghanistan after the fall of the Taliban and the long war against Russian occupation. After his return to Afghanistan, Raz Mohammad was employed as a special advisor to the Minister for Rural Rehabilitation and Development, Haneef Atmar, himself a graduate of the PRDU.

Other ACE alumni include Anja Simic (Bosnia), Pango Mashimango (Democratic Republic of Congo), Indika Perera (Sri Lanka) and Raba'ah Otoom (Jordan). Anja's secondary school education was conducted against the backdrop of the siege of Mostar and she brought this first-hand experience of conflict to the course. Following her graduation, Anja returned to the Balkans to work for a German-based NGO working with the United Nations High Commission for Refugees in Kosovo and Macedonia. Pango Mashimango went on to work for the UN in Haiti and Indika Perera returned to Sri Lanka to work on human rights training with local government officers. Raba'ah Otoom joined the course with prior professional experience with the International Federation of the Red Cross in Jordan specialising in emergency preparedness. Her field studies included a visit to Northern Ireland to see how a western state deals with post-conflict regeneration, followed by a work attachment in Yemen to compare methods for emergency and disaster relief. ACE can fairly lay claim to having a group of alumni who have benefited from their scholarships in York and who are now making a difference around the world.

ACE Corpus Christi Masters Scholarship, University of Cambridge

Since 1997 ACE has provided a Masters scholarship for an outstanding student to study either Environment & Development (Department of Geography) or Economics at Corpus Christi College, Cambridge. The underlying objective is to support study of the means by which economic development can be achieved in an environmentally sustainable manner. Priority has been given to applicants from the developing world and from eastern Europe. Our first student was Mr Veluswami Saravanan from India, whose particular area of interest was management of water resources. Subsequent scholars have included: Eero Tohver (Estonia), Monica Wihardja (Indonesia), Krisztina Hamara (Romania), Ivailo Vesselinov (Bulgaria), Bakhyt Murzhukbasova (Kazakhstan), Olga Nosova (Ukraine), Sanjeev Sharma (India), Maria Lourdes Montenegro (Philippines), Juhi Sutaria (India) and Anuja Sinha (India).

Art & Design

European Gardens Scholarship Scheme

The European Gardens Scholarship Scheme was inaugurated in 1991 and based at the Institute of Advanced Architectural Studies in the King's Manor at the University of York. The scheme was founded to enable individuals to develop their understanding of the care, conservation and history of gardens (and parks) by visiting a different European country from their own. The study visits included meetings with other professionals to discuss working methods and the opportunity to gain practical experience from fellow gardeners and landscape architects. The scheme was of particular interest to ACE because the fall of the Iron Curtain allowed a valuable new opportunity for exchange visits with central and eastern Europe. The first ACE-funded scholarship enabled Marek Ehrlich from the Czech Republic to travel to the UK; whilst the second was awarded to the National Trust's John Sales, for a study visit to Poland. Marek Ehrlich arrived from the Regional Institute for the Preservation of Historical Monuments in Ceske Budejovice, a specialist in the care of the historic parks and gardens of Southern Bohemia. Following a week-long residential course at the university, he followed a programme of study visits. In the event, John Sales, who as Garden Adviser to the National Trust designed the winter walk at Anglesey Abbey near Cambridge, was unable to travel, but instead arranged a programme of visits for Tim Wilson who went in his place.

In 1999 we welcomed two more ACE scholars to the UK: Grazyna Novotna, a student from the Czech Republic, and Kalina Todorova, a lecturer in the Department of Landscape Architecture at the University of Forestry, Sofia. Kalina Todorova spent two months in the UK, the first based at the King's Manor researching historic landscapes (then an almost unknown subject in Bulgaria), and the second visiting the North York Moors and Yorkshire Dales National Parks. Grazyna Novotna concentrated on the parks and gardens of the country house; she is now a lecturer at the Silva Tarouca Research Institute for Landscape and Ornamental Gardening, near Prague, and at the time of writing is working on the restoration of Decin Castle park and gardens.

Edward Barnsley Educational Trust

The Edward Barnsley Workshop is unparalleled in forming part of a direct, unbroken line with the Arts and Crafts movement of the 19th century. Edward Barnsley (1900-1987) began his career as a pupil in Geoffrey Lupton's workshop in Froxfield in 1919, whilst his father Sidney Barnsley, his uncle Ernest Barnsley, and their friend Ernest Gimson, were key members of the original Arts and Crafts movement. Edward himself was heavily influenced by John Ruskin, William Morris and William Lethaby, and dedicated his life to making furniture that was designed to have "Fitness for purpose and pleasure in use". He took over the workshop of Geoffrey Lupton in the mid 1920s, in which, to this day, Barnsley furniture continues to be designed and made. The Arts and Crafts movement, in general, and William Morris, in particular, have deservedly been the subjects of exhibitions, books and learned articles, but we must not forget that the story is far from over. At the workshop in Froxfield a marriage of art, craft and philosophy can be found that continues to build on a cultural movement of international significance.

In 1980, Edward Barnsley's failing health led to concern for the future of the workshop, for which he had made no arrangements. Edward had been a pupil at Bedales and, later, with Geoffrey Lupton, built the wonderful Arts & Crafts library at the school. It was therefore fitting that one of the founding trustees of the Edward Barnsley Educational Trust was Mary Medd, acclaimed school architect and former Bedales pupil. The trust was registered as a charity in 1980 to ensure continuity by initiating and financing a programme of training of apprentices. The trust continues to run the workshop, which remains one of the leading makers of craftsman-made furniture in the country. The apprentices work alongside, and are taught by, experienced craftsmen making the high quality furniture for which the workshop is renowned.

The trust also maintains the adjacent cottage, where Edward and Tania Barnsley once lived, which houses an important archive containing several thousands of Edward's drawings. The cottage has been renovated and visitors can view a display of Barnsley furniture, including the large oak dresser designed and made by Sidney Barnsley in 1898, that was featured in the V&A International Arts and Crafts Exhibition of 2005.

What is ACE's role in all this? Well, from 1994 we have sponsored the apprentice scheme, not only keeping this wonderful tradition alive but, equally important, developing skills for the future. Two of our apprentices deserve special mention. In 1997, ACE sponsored James Ryan to spend six months at the Carl Malmsten School in Stockholm, one of three furniture schools in Sweden. Whilst the craftsmanship at the Barnsley Workshop is unequalled, we were keen for apprentices to benefit from international experience, particularly in Scandinavia, which has its own highly developed tradition of furniture making and design. James found the experience very beneficial, both personally and professionally, and highlighted the well equipped workshops, the standard of teaching and the quality of work. Impressed by his skill and enthusiasm, the Barnsley Workshop employed James as a master craftsman following the completion of his apprenticeship. He is now Designer and Manager, creating his own body of work whilst maintaining Edward Barnsley's vision:

> "If I can add to the richness of life a few things which give
> real joy in use and to the eyes, then I am happy enough."

ACE continues to support the apprenticeship scheme and recent alumnus Gary Tuddenham has been recognised as one of the finest craftsmen in the world, winning the 2007 final of the WorldSkills tournament in Tokyo.

Catalogue of English Alabasters

Some readers may remember Francis Cheetham OBE, director of many ACE tours during the 1980s and 1990s. Francis came to ACE after a life's work in the museum world, culminating in his creation of the Norfolk Museums Service in 1974. In addition to his professional achievements, Francis developed a keen personal interest in English medieval alabaster sculpture, a field in which he was to become recognised as the world's leading expert. In 2005, ACE republished Francis Cheetham's book *English Medieval Alabasters,* originally published in the 1980s, which explores the history of these fascinating artworks with particular reference to the V&A's outstanding collection. Having catalogued the V&A collection, Francis began tracking down as many of the other surviving sculptures as he could find, scouring churches, museums and private collections to build up an unrivalled and invaluable archive. In 2000, ACE agreed to provide financial support towards the publication of this archive, which was finally published in 2003 as a book entitled *Alabaster Images of Medieval England*, cataloguing and illustrating the majority of known alabasters outside the V&A collection. Together with its companion volume on the V&A collection they provide the definitive guide to the subject.

Alabaster stone of a quality suitable for carving was excavated mainly in south Derbyshire, carvers of tombs being the first exponents of the art. One of the earliest alabaster images, the effigy of Edward II in Gloucester Cathedral, dates back to 1330. By the end of the 14th century, the alabaster carvers had started to produce vertical panels, designed to be arranged as a series in the shape of altarpieces. The most popular themes depicted are the Adoration of the Magi, the Crucifixion and the Resurrection. Records show that although pieces were produced in Burton-on-Trent and York, the main centre was Nottingham. So successful were the English alabaster sculptors that they developed an important export trade. Their work can be found in churches and museums ranging from Iceland to Croatia, although the biggest overseas concentration is in Normandy. Whole altarpieces as well as individual carvings survive, often in the churches that originally commissioned them. Indeed, an altarpiece of the Life of St James, dated 1456, is still to be found in the Cathedral of Santiago de Compostela in northwest Spain.

Although many alabaster carvings have lost much of their colour, traces of the original paint can often be found in the recesses of the figures. Paint was applied without a ground, for the alabaster itself provides a smooth and non-absorbent surface. The lower parts of the panels were usually painted green and decorated with daisies; the upper background was usually gilded, and the images painted in green, red, brown and black. Although painting was an important part of the finished piece, areas of alabaster were usually left untouched to contrast with the painted colours.

Textile Conservation Centre

Of all artworks, textiles present perhaps the most difficult problems of conservation. From costumes to upholstery, carpets to tapestries, textiles form a huge part of our artistic and cultural heritage, and all ACE participants will have enjoyed viewing them on countless visits at home and abroad. When approached by the Textile Conservation Centre in 2003, we were therefore delighted to be able to inaugurate an ACE Masters Scholarship in Textile Conservation. Our first MA student was Claire Johnston from New Zealand, whose interest in textiles developed from a fascination with Indonesian ikats and Maori feather cloaks. In fact, New Zealand has a wealth of both indigenous and imported textiles but a dearth of skilled conservators. She was therefore drawn to the Textile Conservation Centre, which has established an international reputation for conservation education, practice and research. From 1975 to 1998, the centre was an independent charity based in Hampton Court Palace. In 1999, the centre merged with the University of Southampton and moved to new premises on the University's Winchester campus.

Recent work at the centre has included the study of non-destructive strain measurement techniques, which promise to be of great value in, for example, the care of large tapestries. Structural damage is just one of the problems associated with textile conservation; other threats include insects, fungi, atmospheric pollution and exposure to light. Students are trained in colour mixing of dyes and dye analysis. Using spectral analysis and other techniques, it is often possible to establish the origin of a particular historic textile based on the type of, for example, plant matter used in the dye. The centre also has a team of experienced conservators who undertake conservation projects on a contract basis for institutional and private clients.

Claire Johnston proved to be an outstanding student and following her graduation was succeeded as ACE scholar by Lu Zhiyong, an archaeological conservator from the Shaan'xi Institute of Archaeology in Xi'an, China. Lu's interest in textiles developed when he was working on a Sino-German project focusing on Tang Dynasty objects, including textiles, excavated at Famen Temple. China has a huge wealth of historic textiles but no specific training programme for their conservation; Lu will therefore be able to make a major contribution to the development of textile conservation in his home country. Our current scholar is Shobhakar Adhikari, a chemist and conservator with the National Museum of Nepal. The museum contains a large collection of textile artefacts, most of which are currently deteriorating due to lack of expertise. However, Shobhakar looks forward to returning home to apply his newfound knowledge. Sadly, it looks as if he will be the last ACE scholar for the time being, as in an announcement that shocked the conservation world, the Textile Conservation Centre, recognised internationally for its excellence, is facing closure due to funding cuts by the University of Southampton. We very much hope that this will not be the case and that a solution can be found.

Vaganova Ballet Academy

A private visit to the acclaimed Vaganova Ballet Academy, which counts Pavlova, Nijinksi, Balanchine, Nureyev, Baryshnikov and Ulanova amongst an endless line of gifted former pupils, is a highlight of many ACE tours to St Petersburg. In 2005–6 ACE sponsored two students, Zlata Yalynich, an exceptionally gifted 15-year-old ballerina, and Tarakanov Ilia, 13, one of the most talented boys at the school.

The academy is the training school for the Mariinsky (or Kirov) Ballet, whose home is the famous Mariinsky Theatre in St Petersburg. The academy is named after the brilliant teacher Agrippina Vaganova, whose severe and exacting methods stressed the importance of maintaining the link with the classical tradition. The current regime is no less demanding, but perhaps more sensitive, and ACE was privileged to be able to support two such promising young dancers.

The scholarships assisted the students in buying ballet shoes, typically 3-4 pairs per month are required, and other informal dance clothing. Other vital areas of support included physiotherapy, books, recorded music, visits to theatres and additional education during vacations. The scholarships were presented to the students during an ACE study tour led by Colin Bailey. The principal, Dame Vera Dorofeeva, expressed "her gratitude and hope to be able to cooperate with ACE in the future".

The Levantine Foundation

The main aims of The Levantine Foundation are to preserve and conserve Near Eastern artefacts on paper and related material and disseminate information thereon. ACE was approached in 2002 by the Foundation requesting sponsorship for a project involving the conservation, digitizing and binding of the 10th-century Syriac manuscript "The Homilies of Jacob of Sarug".

The Homilies are part of an astounding cache of manuscripts, up to 1,500 years old, recently discovered at the Deir al-Surian Monastery, in the western desert of Egypt. This Coptic Monastery, established in the 6th century and later occupied by monks from Syria and Mesopotamia, is currently home to 200 Egyptian Copts and has one of the richest ancient libraries in Christendom.

The find occurred when reconstruction work was undertaken on the ancient tower where the library had originally been established and comprised one complete manuscript and hundreds of fragments and single pages. It appears the first floor collapsed around 500 years ago and a new wooden floor was simply inserted above. The rubble of the earlier floor has now been removed and the curator, Father Bigoul, found a complete manuscript embedded in a section of disused water pipe. This parchment text has now been identified as a 9th-century "Book of the Holy Hierothos".

When Elizabeth Sobczynski, conservator and director of the Levantine Foundation, visited the site to examine the entire library, she was disturbed at what she found. Exposure to moisture had resulted in corrosion and serious perforations. Insect infestation was also apparent. It was agreed that urgent action was needed to introduce modern conservation techniques and improve environmental conditions. This is currently being undertaken with the aim of developing a suitable thermal and humidity control for the library. The Architectural Association Graduate School in London is helping with technical advice and equipment, and is developing a passive cooling system for climate control.

During the 17th and 20th centuries the great monastic libraries of the Levantine were plundered by the European powers. At Deir al-Surian almost half of the collection was lost. Now, the Homilies of Jacob of Sarug, one of the great poets of the Syrian-Orthodox tradition, are safe in their rightful home. The book, dating from AD 956/7, is written in Syriac, a dialect of the Aramaic language, which dominated throughout the Levant during early Christianity. Once the conservation work is complete the book will, of course, primarily be for the use of the monks themselves. However, the digitized versions will make these rare documents available for scholars all over the world.

Kuhmo Music Festival Scholarships

Many ACE travellers will have particularly fond memories of the small town of Kuhmo, situated a little south of the Arctic Circle, in the region of Finland known as Karelia. For it is here that the world-renowned Kuhmo Chamber Music Festival takes place, combining high standards of performance with an intimate rapport between artists and audience. Every year, first-class musicians, whether experienced old hands or young students, come together to make music from dawn to dusk in the long days of the northern summer. The concerts take place in and around the Kuhmo Arts Centre, a comfortable, newly built concert hall with a magnificent wooden interior and excellent acoustics.

International music courses have been an integral part of the festival from the beginning, allowing exceptionally gifted young performers the opportunity to study with famous masters. Besides first-class instruction, the students have the chance to listen to a vast number of concerts, and in some cases make their own concert debuts. In 2003, ACE introduced a Chamber Music Scholarship allowing talented young musicians the opportunity to attend the festival music courses. The first scholarship was awarded to Finland's Kamus Quartet and the winning musicians met the members of the ACE group and provided an informal private recital. The 2004 winners were the Lawson Trio from the UK, who very kindly played an exclusive concert for the visiting ACE group. Anna Smith, violinist with the Lawson Trio, remembers: "We enjoyed performing for the ACE Study Tours group. They were a wonderfully stimulating and receptive audience, and it was lovely for all of us to have plenty of time to talk to them at the end and answer all of their questions."

The Lawson Trio were able to benefit from the tuition of Konstantin Bogino, the distinguished solo- and chamber-pianist (of the Tchaikovsky Trio). The group found him to be a great inspiration and his insights resulted in an immediate improvement in their ensemble playing and interpretation. Indeed, the Lawson Trio went on to win the festival's Kees Wiebenga Diploma for the best performing student ensemble. In 2005 the award was won by the Tremor Quartet, who impressed the ACE group with their enthusiasm and musicianship. The winners in 2006 were the Hungarian duo Noemi Györi (flute) and Katalin Koltai (guitar), followed in 2007 by the M-Art trio, a union of three young Russian-born musicians: Alexander Kagan (violin), Polina Semenikhina (cello) and Sofya Kagan (piano).

The Catherine the Great Orchestra & the St Petersburg International Early Music Festival

The Catherine the Great Orchestra was created in November 2001 by the Russian Early Music Foundation as Russia's first professional baroque orchestra. The orchestra evolved as an extension of a masterclass series given by Maria Leonhardt, who together with her husband Gustav Leonhardt inspired a return to performance on period instruments in the 1960s. The orchestra's artistic director, Andrey Reshetin, was from 1987 to 1992 violinist with the legendary Russian rock band Akvarium, and from 1990 to 2003 a founding member of Musica Petropolitana.

For much of the 19th and 20th centuries baroque and early music were ignored by the Russian musical establishment. However, in recent years, Andrey Reshetin and others have carried out extensive research in Russian archives with the aim of bringing to light Russian music of the 18th century. As a result of this research, the Catherine the Great Orchestra has presented forgotten musical masterpieces from the Russian Court by such composers as Ivan Khandohshkin, Ivan Jarnovik, Anton Titz, Giovanni Paisiello, Francesco Araja, Baldassare Galuppi, Luigi Madonis and others.

From 2003 to 2006 ACE provided an annual grant to the orchestra. One of the most exciting developments in this period was the permission granted by the Mariinsky Theatre to play a number of 17th- and 18th-century compositions rediscovered in the theatre archives. These pieces fell out of fashion in the 19th century and later were disapproved of by the communists. The new performances were in some cases the first for over 200 years. Throughout 2003 the Orchestra gave a regular series of concerts at the Sheremetev Palace for visiting ACE tours. Thanks in part to ACE's support, the orchestra also played a major role in St Petersburg's 300th anniversary celebrations, the highlight being a joint production of Giovanni Paisiello's *I Filosofi Immaginari* with the Utrecht Muziek Festival. In 2004 we welcomed the orchestra to Cambridge to an event we organised to celebrate the music of St Petersburg. The day's activities were hosted by the international pianist and organist, John Bryden, and culminated in a concert by the orchestra at West Road Concert Hall. Back home, the orchestra opened the 7th St Petersburg International Early Music Festival with a performance of Pergolesi's *Stabat Mater* with Emma Kirkby.

Originally, baroque music was played in a context in which music was just one of many delights for the senses. It was never unaccompanied: food, wine, candlelight, drama and fireworks would all help create a sensual experience. The word "baroque" derives from "a flawed pearl" and baroque music should be played in this spirit: the music should swing. This may be a surprise to those who consider baroque music (or some performances of it) to be mechanical, even formulaic. Improvisation also played an important part in baroque music and it takes a particular quality of ensemble, combining precise technique and a gift for deft timing, to create truly sensual baroque music. Baroque music certainly has a clearly defined structure, but within that structure there is to be found incredible freedom and great beauty.

Attingham Trust

The Attingham Trust Summer School was founded in 1952 to allow people professionally engaged in conservation to learn more about British historic houses and their collections. The first courses were targeted at American curators, at a time when many works of art were being exported. Indeed, throughout the 1950s and 1960s the trust was invaluable in promoting interest and knowledge in country houses, many of which were then in decline and falling into disrepair. Thanks to the Attingham Trust and other organisations such as the National Trust, English Heritage, and, of course, private owners, the country house underwent a revival in the subsequent decades, leading to the opening up to the public of many houses and collections. Today's summer school examines the architectural and social history of historic houses and gardens and the contents of these buildings – paintings, sculpture, furniture, ceramics, silver, textiles and other applied arts. Museum curators, architectural historians, conservationists and teachers come from around the world to participate in the school and share their knowledge and experience of conservation.

In 2005, ACE was pleased to sponsor Dr Terezia Bardi, Vice Director for Research of the National Trust for Hungary, to attend the summer school. Other scholars came from the UK, Australia, USA, Turkey, Holland, Sweden, New Zealand, Czech Republic and Estonia. ACE felt that it was particularly important to support a conservator from eastern Europe, where many historic houses and collections are at risk. Dr Bardi's own research interests lie in theatre and costume design, but she was particularly intrigued to learn how the costs of conservation could be met through commercial means whilst still maintaining historical integrity. The National Trust's shops and Woburn's safari park definitely sparked a few ideas! Dr Bardi said: "I am so grateful to ACE for giving me this opportunity. I have learned so much that will be useful to me in Hungary and it has been wonderful to share experiences with people of so many nationalities."

Our student in 2006 was Ana Sverko, from Croatia, an enthusiast for the work of Robert Adam. A highlight of the summer school was therefore a private visit to Adam's Kedleston Hall in the company of Helene, Viscountess Scarsdale. The Derbyshire house is a fine example of a neo-classical Palladian mansion. Built between 1759 and 1765 for the Curzon family, who have lived in the area since the 12th century, the hall has the most complete and least-altered sequence of Robert Adam interiors in England. In 2007, we continued our support of the Attingham Trust Summer School and welcomed Steffen Løvkjaer, assistant curator of the Royal Danish Collection at Rosenborg Slot, Copenhagen. Steffen reported, "I believe in the importance of going abroad and visiting fellow museums, houses and institutions. The summer school has been inspiring and very rewarding. It was wonderful to meet colleagues and scholars from other related institutions and the summer school is a splendid forum for the exchange of knowledge." Before leaving for England, Steffen welcomed an ACE study tour, led by Marina Vaizey and Paul Brooke Barnes, to Rosenborg, and provided an insightful guide to the Crown jewels. The summer school held many highlights for Steffen, but he found Arundel Castle of particular interest, as it combines a family home of the twenty-first century and an interesting collection open to the public. In Brighton he discovered intriguing parallels between the Prince Regent's Royal Pavilion and King Frederik III's Chinese-style decoration in the 1650s of Rosenborg Slot.

Sir Stanley Spencer, "Shipbuilding on the Clyde"

During the Second World War, Stanley Spencer was commissioned to illustrate the valuable contribution of the British shipbuilding industry and its workers to the war effort. Aiming to capture the positive aspects of the home front amid the ongoing war in Europe, Spencer focused on the working-class community of Port Glasgow and their collective achievements.

The Imperial War Museum acquired the series of eight *Shipbuilding on the Clyde* paintings in 1946. They have proved immensely popular and have thus far featured in 31 exhibitions nationally and internationally. Unfortunately, by 2007 the paintings had deteriorated to a point where they required extensive conservation work. In a fascinating meeting at the Imperial War Museum, ACE's General Secretary heard from Sir Alex Ferguson and Kate Adie, both of whom grew up in the shadow of shipyards, about what the paintings meant to them personally. It was clear that Stanley Spencer had captured the intense heat and physical hardship experienced by the workers, but also the camaraderie and sense of community. What is so impressive, and now invaluable, is that Spencer records accurately details of construction – riveting, welding and so on – but that the paintings remain so vivid and expressive. Sir Alex Ferguson even remembered from his youth the design of the pattern on the sweater of one of the workers, whilst Kate Adie recalled her street getting darker and darker as the then ship under construction grew and grew, casting an ever longer shadow until, finally, one day the ship was launched and all was light again.

Spencer intended his audiences to view and interpret the paintings together as a series. In the past, time, space and budgets prevented the museum from addressing the project as a whole. Previous conservation treatments tended to address single issues as they arose on each painting. This led to an unintentional disparity and inconsistency in appearance between the pieces. Now, partly funded by ACE, the paintings are receiving the conservation work they so richly deserve. The Imperial War Museum, which houses one of the UK's largest collections of 20th-century art, is working closely with the conservator Phil Young. Once the restoration work is complete, it is hoped that the complete *Shipbuilding on the Clyde* series will be exhibited at Glasgow's new Museum of Transport, due to open in December 2008. This presents a wonderful opportunity to exhibit the paintings to large audiences in a powerful and meaningful context, as the new museum is located directly on the Clyde, the site, source and subject of Spencer's inspiration and vision for the paintings.

Natural History & Conservation Education

Introduction

ACE has worked with a number of organisations that are concerned with conservation education, including the Jersey Wildlife Preservation Trust, the Te Rere Reserve (New Zealand), the Tandroy Conservation Trust (Madagascar) and the Integrated Village Development Trust (India). However, in recent years our main partnership has been with Cambridge-based Fauna & Flora International, the world's oldest international conservation charity.

Flower Valley, South Africa

South Africa's Cape Floral Kingdom, an area of 90,000 square km at the southernmost tip of Africa, is one of the earth's richest but most threatened biological regions. It harbours more types of native plant than any comparable area on the planet and is home to 8,500 plant species of which a staggering 5,800 are endemic. Despite its botanical diversity and outstanding beauty, much of the area is now endangered by urban sprawl, exploitation and agricultural conversion to vineyards. An innovative scheme, initiated by Fauna & Flora International (FFI) and supported by ACE, combines conservation, education and sustainable economic development.

The vegetation type that covers the Cape Floral Kingdom is known as fynbos (Afrikaans for "fine bush" and pronounced "fain-boss"), derived from the fine-leafed shrubby species that make up much of the vegetation. There are also a large number of broad-leafed species and the flowering plants such as Protea, Leucospermum and Leucadendron. In fact the fynbos is the original source of many of our hybridised but best-loved garden plants. Another notable feature of the fynbos is the bulbous plants or geophytes, including many exquisite lilies, orchids and irises – a total of 1,400 species!

There are urgent social demands in South Africa for improved housing, employment, education and healthcare. Understandably, there is great pressure on the government to support whatever economic activity can help feed this demand. Much of the Cape Floral Kingdom is being given over to vineyards, which have been a boom industry in recent years. This was also the fate that faced Flower Valley, a 550-hectare haven of near-pristine fynbos in the Agulhas Plain. However, the local rural community, working with FFI's scientific guidance, realised that it is perfectly possible to pick wild fynbos flowers without any impact on long-term sustainability. Contrary to popular wisdom, picking wildflowers is not necessarily wrong.

The farm has become so successful that it is able to purchase wild flowers from neighbouring farms, encouraging them to practise sustainable and ecological methods. The influence of the Flower Valley project has now spread to over 25,000 hectares of fynbos. The local communities benefit from, and thus appreciate the need to conserve, their natural resources. It is this appreciation of the human element that is characteristic of FFI and is why ACE is a keen supporter of their work. The flowers are made up into bouquets on the farm, arranged in a contemporary and exciting way, further adding to the value of the crop. Art paper products have also been added to ensure year-round employment. Income from the project has been used to provide educational facilities for the children, and the success of the project is such that the South African government wants to use Flower Valley as a model for its poverty relief programme.

Veal Veng Conservation Project, Cambodia

As many as one fifth of the entire population of Cambodia was killed during the Pol Pot period, and many more suffered lasting physical and psychological harm. The country is now on the road to recovery and with peace has come the opportunity for travellers to return. For many the highlight is Angkor Wat, the greatest archaeological site in southeast Asia and one of the wonders of the world. Built by King Suryavarman II as his funerary temple and dating largely from the 12th-century, Angkor Wat is said to be the largest religious monument in the world, the jungle setting adding to its mystical grandeur.

Cambodia's natural history is equally rich and since 1997 ACE has been supporting Fauna and Flora International's work in the country. The Veal Veng district, deep in the Cardamom Mountains, is home to the Por people, an almost extinct highland race with animist traditions and a reverence for the spirits of the forests and hills and above all the crocodile. The O'Som commune comprises 200 families in four villages and depends on hunting, fishing, collecting non-timber forest products and shifting cultivation. Archaeological evidence suggests that the community has been living in considerable harmony with their natural environment for a thousand years or more. Sadly, the effects of war left a shattered and broken community, without food or medicine, afraid even to state their race or culture for fear of reprisal from the Khmer Rouge. The beautiful wetlands, on a plateau 600m above sea level, and the surrounding evergreen forests were further threatened by loggers and speculators.

ACE is not a conservation charity but we were attracted by FFI's innovative proposal to integrate educational support with conservation. The programme began with practical training in field techniques of Cambodian scientists and officials from government departments and NGOs. Further training of representatives from the local community took place in the Veal Veng district itself, followed by an extensive biological and social survey of the region. It has been equally important to raise local, national and international awareness of the importance of the area in terms of its biodiversity. This has been helped by the spectacular rediscovery of the Siamese crocodile, a species thought to be extinct in the wild. The marsh and surrounding forests support a wealth of wildlife including many globally threatened trees, tigers, gibbons and hornbills. New species such as the Cardamom Wolf Snake have even been discovered.

In July 2002 the Veal Veng district became part of a new protected area, the Central Cardamom Protected Forest. Traditional and environmentally sustainable trade, such as in cardamom spices, is being re-established to pay for medicines and schools. The local community has set up Cambodia's first crocodile sanctuary, to protect against poachers, and they are once more able to express their unique cultural and religious heritage. The marsh spirit lives on.

Cambodia Masters Conservation Programme

In 2006, ACE helped to establish Cambodia's first MSc degree course in conservation studies. The programme was devised by Fauna & Flora International as a joint venture with the Royal University of Phnom Penh, and is intended to help Cambodians to become less reliant on foreign experts to conserve their natural environment. The project will provide approximately 40 students every year with essential training and experience in a wide range of environmental subjects. The students include young postgraduates as well as teachers and professionals in need of extra vocational training. Besides receiving classroom lectures, students benefit from practical experience of fieldwork and conservation techniques, working closely with organisations such as FFI and the WWF. The scheme's project manager, Dr Jenny Daltrey, reports that there is severe lack of capacity within Cambodia to conserve wildlife and ensure the country's development is environmentally sustainable. This lack of knowledge has resulted in a catalogue of poor decisions that damage the environment and put rural people's livelihoods at risk. Although foreign environmental experts have been hired by the government to provide advice, FFI believes that what is really required are more Cambodians with the necessary knowledge and practical experience.

The Royal University, along with much of the higher education system in Cambodia, was all but destroyed by the Pol Pot regime, and many of the qualified teaching staff and researchers were either killed or fled the country. Most of the university's lecturers are young and only one third have higher degrees. The university is also desperately short of furniture, books and research equipment. The MSc programme will train the next generation of Cambodian conservationists in the principles of wildlife management, sustainable development, use of natural resources, and project management skills. One of the greatest practical challenges facing conservationists and environmental scientists in Cambodia is simply identifying the country's many animals and plants. There is neither a national herbarium or natural history museum. A major part of the project will therefore be assistance in establishing a national reference collection of plants and smaller animals, including butterflies, amphibians, reptiles and fish.

Emergency Schooling in Aceh, Indonesia

The tsunami of December 26, 2004, caused devastation around the Indian Ocean and destroyed communities and their livelihoods throughout areas of Aceh in Indonesia. More than 200,000 people in Aceh are estimated to have died and 700,000 were displaced. FFI has been operating in Aceh since 1998, conducting wildlife surveys and developing environmental education, and itself lost two members of staff in the disaster. Schools were of course not spared in the destruction and among the dead were teachers and members of the government education department. Although not a relief agency, FFI's staff and equipment were immediately available to help reconstruction work and, in collaboration with UNICEF and the local education department in Aceh Jaya district, facilitated the establishment of 16 emergency schools through distribution of tents, books, stationery, recreational kits and blackboards. ACE was honoured to be able to contribute funds towards this vital work.

Educational projects and grants 1958–2008

1958
British student travel bursary
Finnish student travel bursary

1963
University of Pittsburgh and the Association for
  Cultural Exchange, educational travel grants

1965
Archaeology travel grants
Adult Education Seminar, Great Neck, USA

1966
Council for British Archaeology
Archaeology exchange scheme
Course for UK teachers visiting Danish schools
National Trust donation
Scholarships for USA students

1967
Archaeology exchange scheme
Council for British Archaeology
Course for UK teachers visiting Danish Schools
National Trust
Institute of Archaeology fellowship
Scholarships for USA students

1968
Course for UK teachers visiting Danish Schools
Scholarships for USA students
Institute of Archaeology fellowship
Moravia Conservation Study Group visit to Britain

1969
Course for UK teachers visiting Danish schools
Institute of Archaeology fellowship
Scholarships for USA students
Archaeology exchange scheme

1970
Course for UK teachers visiting Danish schools
Institute of Archaeology fellowship
Towards cost of archaeology exchanges
Oronsay excavation
Scholarships for USA students

1971
Donation to German-English archaeology
  dictionary
Archaeology exchange bursaries
Institute of Archaeology fellowship
Oronsay excavation

1972
Exchange bursaries
Archaeology scholarships
Institute of Archaeology fellowship

1973
Archaeology exchange bursaries
Archaeology scholarships and grants
Institute of Archaeology fellowship
Oronsay excavation

1974
Institute of Archaeology fellowship
Eskmeal excavation

1975
Institute of Archaeology fellowship
Oronsay excavation

1976
Institute of Archaeology fellowship

1977
Institute of Archaeology fellowship

1978
Young Peoples Scholarships
Institute of Archaeology fellowship

1979
Institute of Archaeology fellowship

1980
Oxfam helpers India tour
Institute of Archaeology fellowship

1981
Oxfam travel bursaries

1982
Institute of Archaeology fellowship

1983
Design and Industry Exhibition "Young Blood"
International Congress of Prehistoric and
    Protohistoric Sciences

1984
Institute of Archaeology fellowship

1985
Kettles Yard

1986
Rachel King, Peru Expedition
Travel Grant for Stephen Briggs to study Worsaae,
    Denmark
Institute of Archaeology fellowship

1987
National Trust for Scotland
University of Cambridge
Institute of Archaeology fellowship
International Symposium on the origin and
    dispersal of modern humans

1988
Italian Studies Project, Queen Mary's College
    London
Institute of Archaeology fellowship

1989
Institute of Archaeology fellowship

1990
Institute of Archaeology fellowship

1991
Institute of Archaeology fellowship

1992
Paul Rogers, fieldwork in Nepal, International
    Centre for Protected Landscapes
Prospect Burma, teacher for Burmese refugees
Integrated Village Development Trust, India
Zana Kamberi, Albania, museum studies
Institute of Archaeology fellowship
Butser Ancient Farm, international seminar,
    Peter Reynolds

1993
Friends of Cambridge Botanic Garden
Towards Publishing "Herbaceous Flora of
    Upland Kenya"
Institute of Archaeology fellowship
Excavation at Evora, Portugal, Colin Burgess

1994
Prospect Burma
Ladakh Medicinal Plant Archive Project EAVA
Edward Barnsley Educational Trust
Institute of Archaeology fellowship
Integrated Village Development Trust, India

1995
Aerial Archaeology Hungary
Ethiopia reserve
New Ashgate Gallery, memorial exhibition of
    Joseph Acheson's work
Ladakh Medicinal Plant Archive Project EAVA
Edward Barnsley Educational Trust – James Ryan
    attending Malmsten School in Sweden
Edward Barnsley Educational Trust,
    apprenticeship training
Prospect Burma

1996
Fauna & Flora International, Wildlife and Wetlands
Institute of Archaeology fellowship
Aerial Archaeology Training, Hungary
National Trust for Scotland
Street Symphony GEM TV, Ethiopia
St Matthew's Children's Fund, Bahar Dar, Ethiopia
Edward Barnsley Educational Trust,
    apprenticeship training

1997
Madeleine Davis Memorial Fund
Institute of Archaeology fellowship
Jersey Wildlife Preservation Trust
Feedback Madagascar
Te Rere bird reserve
European Gardens Scholarship
Aerial Archaeology Training, Poland
Kuva Excavations, Uzbekistan
Street Symphony GEM TV, Ethiopia
Edward Barnsley Educational Trust,
    apprenticeship training
Fauna & Flora International, large mammal
    conservation in Cambodia
Postgraduate Scholarship at Corpus Christi College,
    Cambridge

1998
European Gardens Scholarship
Princess Margarita of Romania Trust
Jerusalem Association of Children's Homes,
    Ethiopia
Edward Barnsley Educational Trust,
    apprenticeship training
Integrated Village Development Trust, India
Postgraduate Scholarship at Corpus Christi College,
    Cambridge
Matthew Caines, Sculptor

1999
Feedback Madagascar, training centre in
    Ambalavao
European Gardens Scholarship
Postgraduate Scholarship at Corpus Christi College,
    Cambridge
Fauna & Flora International, wildlife conservation
    in Cambodia

2000
Catalogue of English Alabasters
Postgraduate Scholarship at Corpus Christi College,
    Cambridge

Prospect Burma, Asian Institute of
Technology scholarship programme
Edward Barnsley Educational Trust,
apprenticeship training
Aerial Archaeology Training School, Siena
Fauna & Flora International, Cardamom
Mountains, Cambodia
Integrated Village Development Trust, India
Postwar Reconstruction & Development Unit,
University of York
Aerial Archaeology Training, Jordan

2001
European Association of Archaeologists
Kuva Excavations, Uzbekistan
Street Symphony GEM TV, Ethiopia
St Matthew's Children's Fund, Bahar Dar, Ethiopia
Community Training for Aperon Staff in Mostar,
Bosnia
Wilkins Memorial Trust, leatherworkers
Wilkins Memorial Trust, healthcare
St. John de Britto Home for Aged Women,
Chengai, India
Postgraduate Scholarship at Corpus Christi College,
Cambridge
Postwar Reconstruction & Development Unit,
University of York
Edward Barnsley Educational Trust,
apprenticeship training
Aerial Archaeology Training in Armenia
Feedback Madagascar, traditional birth
attendants programme
Conference on the Theatre of Dario Fo and
Franca Rame
Fauna & Flora International, Veal Veng,
Cardamom Mountains, Cambodia
Garhwa Community College, India
Prospect Burma, Asian Institute of Technology
scholarship programme
Mathieson Music School, West Bengal

2002
Friends of the Fitzwilliam Museum
Edward Barnsley Educational Trust,
apprenticeship training
Aerial Archaeology Training in Armenia
Ujyalo Bhabisya (Brighter Future), Nepal
Schumann House
European Association of Archaeologists,
Annual Meeting in St Petersburg, Russia
Kuva Excavations, Uzbekistan

Postwar Reconstruction & Development Unit,
University of York
Tandroy Conservation Trust, Madagascar
Postgraduate Scholarship at Corpus Christi College,
Cambridge
Hantam Community Education Trust, South Africa
Vaganova Ballet Academy, St Petersburg
Oxford University Society
Fauna & Flora International, Veal Veng,
Cardamom Mountains, Cambodia
Bu De Tang Teaching Project
Hantam Community Education Trust, South Africa
Institute of Archaeology, Prague, digital archives
for archaeology
Aerial Archaeology Training School, Foggia, Italy
St Matthew's Children's Fund, tutorial programme,
Debre Berhan, Ethiopia
Conservation and Digitizing Christian Manuscripts
from the Deir al-Surian library, Egypt
Kuhmo Festival scholarships, Finland
University of Cambridge

2003
The Catherine the Great Orchestra and the Early
Music Festival, St Petersburg
The Georgian Group
Association for the History of Glass, 16th Congress,
Imperial College, London
Postgraduate Scholarship at Corpus Christi College,
Cambridge
Kuva Excavations, Uzbekistan
Postwar Reconstruction & Development Unit,
University of York
Edward Barnsley Educational Trust,
apprenticeship training
University of Cambridge
World Voice Education Programme
Textile Conservation Centre Foundation
Friends of the Fitzwilliam Museum
Integrated Village Development Trust, India
Kuhmo Festival scholarships, Finland
Aerial Archaeology Research Group

2004
Catalogue of English Alabasters
Kuva Excavations, Uzbekistan
Fauna & Flora International, Veal Veng,
Cardamom Mountains, Cambodia
Flower Valley conservation and education
programme, South Africa
Vaganova Ballet Academy, St Petersburg
Mozart Archive, Salzburg

Postgraduate Scholarship at Corpus Christi College,
Cambridge
Postwar Reconstruction & Development Unit,
University of York
Edward Barnsley Educational Trust,
apprenticeship training
Hantam Community Education Trust, South Africa
Wilkins Memorial Trust, ECCA Environmental
Training, Nepal
Wilkins Memorial Trust, Danuwar Dictionary, Nepal
Wilkins Memorial Trust, student Scholarships,
Nepal
English Medieval Alabasters – including a catalogue
of the V&A collection
Feedback Madagascar, silk project
Aerial Archaeology Research Group, manual of
aerial survey for Italy

2005
Winton Trust
Vaganova Ballet Academy, St Petersburg
Edward Barnsley Educational Trust,
apprenticeship training
University of Cambridge
Mozart Archive, Salzburg
Aerial Archaeology Research Group,
Wings Over Armenia
Attingham Trust Summer School
Book-Link, Ethiopia
Banda Aceh rebuilding & education, Indonesia
University of Cambridge
Kuhmo Festival scholarships, Finland
The Catherine the Great Orchestra and the Early
Music Festival, St Petersburg
Postgraduate Scholarship at Corpus Christi College,
Cambridge
Kuva Excavations, Uzbekistan
Textile Conservation Centre
Integrated Village Development Trust, mangrove
forest project, Orissa, India
Fauna & Flora International, Cambodia MSc
Programme in Conservation
ACE Travel Scholarship
University of Cambridge
Hantam Community Education Trust, South Africa

2006
Kuva Excavations, Uzbekistan
Postwar Reconstruction & Development Unit,
University of York
Prospect Burma, Asian Institute of Technology
scholarship programme

Textile Conservation Centre
Attingham Trust Summer School
ACE Travel Scholarship
Public Catalogue Foundation
Kuhmo Festival scholarships, Finland
Postgraduate Scholarship at Corpus Christi College,
    Cambridge
Edward Barnsley Educational Trust, apprenticeship
    training
Restoration of Stanley Spencer's Shipbuilding on
    the Clyde series
ACE Masters Scholarship, Institute of Archaeology
Fauna & Flora International, Cambodia MSc
    Programme in Conservation
Conservation and Digitizing Christian Manuscripts
    from the Deir al-Surian library, Egypt
St Magnus Festival, Malawi music fund
Friends of Babraham Church

2007
Reconstruction in Sri Lanka
Hantam Community Education Trust, South Africa
Attingham Trust Summer School
Aerial Archaeology Survey and Training, Romania
Kuhmo Festival scholarships, Finland
Postgraduate Scholarship at Corpus Christi College,
    Cambridge
Kuva Excavations, Uzbekistan
Edward Barnsley Educational Trust, apprenticeship
    training
ACE Masters Scholarship, Institute of Archaeology
Aerial Archaeology Bursaries for Students and
    Young Researchers
Textile Conservation Centre

2008
Textile Conservation Centre
Edward Barnsley Educational Trust, apprenticeship
    training
ACE Masters Scholarship, Institute of Archaeology
Postgraduate Scholarship at Corpus Christi College,
    Cambridge
Fauna & Flora International, carbon conservation
    programme
Attingham Trust Summer School
St Magnus Festival, Malawi music fund
Prospect Burma, student scholarships
St Matthew's Children's Fund, Ethiopia
Fauna & Flora International, conservation
    education in Romania

Part 2
On the Road

Ian Lowson has been a frequent visitor to the Mayan city of Palenque in the state of Chiapas, Mexico. The site features some of the finest carvings and buildings of the Mayan civilisation.

What *is* cultural exchange?

Ian Lowson

IAN LOWSON has worked for
the Association almost from
its inception. In the early days
he devised programmes and
directed summer schools at
Clare and Oxford in between
teaching literature at Columbia
University. Later he led courses
in the Americas, Indonesia,
Africa and western Europe
covering a wide range of
interests: history, archaeology,
comparative religion, pottery
and poetry among them.
He recently retired, and is now
living in New York and Swanage.

ACE stands for "Association for Cultural Exchange" and all course directors remain acutely aware of our cultural label. Our mission was intended to be reciprocal learning – an exchange of cultures - though for many participants our title suggests the sense of "culture" as refinement or cultivation. But no matter, since our members have always been models of intellectual curiosity and refined taste. So the two senses of the word have blended. From the beginning fifty years ago, our goal has been heightened experience, the enjoyment of art and great music, as well as educational visits to historic places and monuments. This kind of travel means the expansion of consciousness, which some see as the process or goal of human life itself. But this very desirable broadening of the mind comes at a price. As soon as you leave home, cross the threshold of the unfamiliar, you encounter culture shock, and the further you travel, the older you are, the greater the shock. Of course it also works the other way round. It takes a long time for an oriental, an Arab, an African tribesman to adjust to English reality and some never do.

Travels variously described as dramatic, colourful, adventurous, challenging, informative and inspiring all partake of culture shock. For some a rude awakening, for others a revelation, study travel remorselessly broadens the mind and shakes our prejudices. The unsettling effects of all travel are proverbial and may underlie the Taoist adage, which most of us would reject: "To be truly happy, never leave your native village." Admittedly, in an increasingly homogeneous world, the surprises of travel grow less year by year, and it is now even possible to cruise complacently through exotic landscapes in pursuit of the merely picturesque or photogenic, regaled with foreign food and folkloric entertainment. But even as the world shrinks and blurs, ACE's unique pattern still makes it possible to recapture the original enchantment of travel abroad, when even crossing the English Channel was a vivid experience of clashing cultures.

In the course of half a century of Cultural Exchange, I have necessarily endured and enjoyed many a cultural revelation, especially as my tours operated in remote parts like Peru, Indonesia, Burma, Guatemala and Kenya. These challenges have been pleasurable for the most part and beneficial always. There is not much need to elaborate upon the pleasant surprises of travel. We can all remember the unique experience, the gorgeous landscapes, the quickening of the senses, the camaraderie, the new awareness of the kindness and goodness of ordinary people everywhere. You only have to go to your photo album to relive the vividness of your travels, to remember the excitement, the occasions when you felt truly alive. Every tour has its particular challenges and it is the lot of the tour director to be the first to respond to eventualities, to be a model of tolerance, multiculturalism and flexibility. However it must be conceded that some experiences overwhelm even the preparedness of an old hand like myself, as some of the following examples may illustrate.

Religion presents the challenge of culture shock in its most extreme form. Every English group becomes suddenly conscious of bare knees on entering an Italian church, and a pious hush can generally be maintained, but when it comes to a pagan church, temple or shrine it is quite different. Blissful ignorance of "pagan" beliefs is considered acceptable. In our tradition, Christians are not expected to know anything about Hinduism, Islam, Taoism, Buddhism or any other mass delusion, least of all to respect them. On an ACE tour, however, the Director usually warns his tour-members against irreverence and intolerance. I have often found myself offering an impromptu lecture on Hindu blood sacrifice, Mormon tithing, Moslem *haj*, Aztec cannabalism, *Boddhisattvas*, and such like, in an attempt to overcome the preconceptions and biases of participants. Religion is so central to a culture that it affects its language, mores, law, art and architecture and often determines its history. In my view, outside of ACE, too much attention is given in touring to the artefacts of cultures and not enough to underlying distinctions between cultures and their determining factors. Tours should not be too narrowly focused.

On ACE tours to the Americas, we often explored civilisations now extinct – such as Inca, Mochica, Maya and Aztec - as well as the contemporary cultures descended from them. Those ancient civilisations, cut off from outside influence for thousands of years until the Spanish Conquest, are particularly rich in cultural surprises and really challenge the imagination. How can a contemporary westerner envisage civilised life without reading or writing, life without a wheel, roads or sails, without metal or lamps, or beasts of burden or private property, let alone take exotic nature religions seriously? For most it is a positive relief to find that the Inca had roads, though largely for military reasons, and metal, though mostly for ornament; or that the Maya elite achieved a glyphic script, though mostly to record their own grandeur. There always seems to be a qualification, a limitation that slowed the evolution of these societies, but the parallels with our own culture are striking and comforting, helping us to overcome our fear of the alien and the primitive. We reflect that great art is not dependent upon technology or religious belief, and are more ready to open our hearts to the marvels of, say, Inca architecture or Mayan weaving or face the realities of life in a two-culture society. Here is one such revelatory glimpse of the alien.

Some of the original Inca dwellings are still inhabited at Ollantaytambo below the great fortress in the Peruvian *altiplano*. The masonry dates from the fifteenth century, but is still intact, forming a network of connecting patios off paved roadways, each patio with a trapezoidal gateway and single-roomed dwelling, originally intended for persons of some status in Inca society. Our guide, Raul, was born in a nearby town and took us one day to see his grandmother's home in this Inca complex. She had lived there all her life. Raul lingered outside the slab doorway to usher in the last members of our group. There was only room for three of us to enter.

In from the brilliant morning light the interior seemed pitch dark at first. A sheet of plywood served as a door. The room was about two metres square. One ray of smoky light filtered through the blackened straw-thatch roof, and we could just make out a tiny withered crone half-lying on a poncho-covered pile of straw by a smoldering fire of three stones. The upper part of the room was full of choking smoke, but the prevailing smell was of mouldy straw and animals. Blackened pots hung from a rafter and sacks leaned against the back *adobe* wall. The floor too was covered with straw and beneath it we heard a constant rustling as guinea pigs scampered along the channels that bisected the dirt floor. I greeted Raul's grandmother formally in my best Spanish. She blinked vacantly. It was clear that she spoke only Quechua. Besides I was too aghast to speak - a casualty of culture shock. There was not a stick of furniture there, or anything else as far as I could see, though it was too soot-covered to see every detail - and why expect furniture in an Inca dwelling? Here was a sad survival indeed, not just of Inca culture, but of colonial oppression and current apartheid. I have never seen anything so squalid, unless it was a dung-plastered hut in Kenya. I asked our guide why he had taken us there!

"I am proud", he said, of the Inca stonework, "and besides I wanted to show you how eucalyptus wood-smoke blackens everything inside a house with soot, whereas the endemic trees used to burn almost smokelessly in Inca times". At present, the eucalyptus, introduced from Australia, is virtually the only tree of the *altiplano*, and sole source of fire for the Peruvian Indians in the bitter cold of the Andean nights.

Cultural travel is generally humbling. We see not only the huge achievements of past empires but also their fleeting nature. It can make you feel glad that your own culture is now largely out of the limelight. You are able to revise your notions of Western superiority. You become more open to values once considered unthinkable, and are readier to suspend judgement. For instance, most of us are no longer so contemptuous of native remedies and practitioners of medicine in other cultures. Perhaps greater awareness of our own unholy tradition of healing, bloodletting, patent medicine quackery and astrology has made us more tolerant of other traditions. I can recall several ACE visits to shamans in Southeast Asia and the Americas that proved humbling or puzzling in this way.

Once, in the jungles of Ecuador we paddled in canoes down a tributary of the Amazon to visit a celebrated tribal shaman, "curandero" in Spanish. We had three people in some need of a cure at that point, a woman with migraine, a man with a sprained wrist and myself, obscurely nauseous. The shaman in his log hut turned off his television to greet us, then disappeared to emerge later in a skirt with complex upper-body painting and orange (achiote-dyed) hair. On a table were several smooth stones and quartz rocks, a coke-bottle full of the local rum and two guinea pigs in a wooden cage. I told him what was wrong with me and he bade me take off my shirt. I removed it gingerly. Whereupon he rubbed my stomach vigorously with the pebbles, took a swig of alcohol and spat, spraying my torso liberally. The people began to laugh, and I smiled wanly gritting my teeth in rage and nausea. Linda was next and he made her chew a leaf and smoothed her hair with quartz as he pronounced spells or prayers, staring deeply into her eyes. Next he took one of the guinea pigs, held it up to heaven while he said a prayer, and then rubbed it along Alan's arm to the wrist, before breaking its neck and pronouncing us healed. It took only five minutes. We were all a little shaken by the death of the guinea pig, so I paid over a few dollars and we got back into the canoes grumbling our disbelief. "But my migraine is gone", said Linda, "it's unbelievable!". "Well", said Alan with some embarrassment, "I just can't understand this but my wrist isn't hurting any more". There was no recurrence of pain. Luckily for science, I remained nauseous for another hour or two before recovering completely, but for days thereafter people were expressing their incredulity or desperately rationalising the cures as "psychosomatic".

Traditional healing round the world invokes the help of spirits, totems, ancestors, culture heroes and the Gods, added to the skill, herbal knowledge, paraphernalia, experience and magic power of the shaman. This is a formidable combination, not to be dismissed too lightly by the scoffing tourist. Some of these elements can still be found persisting in rites of passage, folkloric rites and fiestas. Anyone who has attended a cremation or tooth-filing ceremony in Bali, a *Semana Santa* in Seville, a *Bar Mitzvah* or even a Moslem wedding will remember their initial cultural impact. Nor is it hard to find vestiges of these elements in our own culture and literature. But there is no pleasure greater than stumbling upon one of these vivid cultural events in the course of travel – a dance performance in India, a saint's day procession in Italy or fiesta in Mexico.

I remember one occasion when our route to the airport in Juliaca, was made totally impassible by an endless procession of chanting, whirling, ecstatic Peruvians celebrating their National Day. We got off the coach and fought our way to the front of the immense crowd of spectators in dazzling sunshine. Then, map in hand, I gave the order, and we joined the parade as a fragile foreign contingent. Everyone but ourselves was in native costume – the red-cheeked women in bowler hats, wearing up to twelve skirts below their bulging silk blouses. We had, as it were, our own maraca and trumpet band in front and hefty girls with hula hoops behind. But we, the pallid bourgeois *turistas*, were the sensation of the parade and soon grew tired of smiling, hailing and reacting to the enthusiastic onlookers. Finally I shepherded the group into a cross-street and our moment of glory had passed. It was quite a relief to reach the deserted airport and to escape the multitude. Then we were waiting a drab hour in the shabby airport, praying that our luggage would get through, which it did, probably on the backs of llamas, in time for the flight to Bolivia.

Mutual incomprehension occurs inevitably, if rarely, in the course of cultural exchange. With good will on both sides, such confusions can easily be overcome and contribute to the learning process, which I have called culture shock. More common are culturally enriching encounters with outstanding personalities: artists, guides, museum directors, intellectuals and representatives of government. Most important of all is the encounter of like-minded participants on our tours. Many of these interactions have a permanent effect and lead to long-lasting relationships.

ACE has enabled thousands of friendships and fruitful relationships over the years, and that perhaps is the final meaning and purpose of Cultural Exchange.

Detail of the high altar at the Cathedral of Santiago de Compostela showing an image of St James (Santiago).

With ACE and the Saints

Malcolm Oxley

MALCOLM OXLEY has led many history and art history courses for ACE. Formerly Sub-Warden of St Edward's School, Oxford, he is a talented art historian, a subject to which he brings a historian's wider perspective. Malcolm is a man of catholic tastes, equally at home exploring the art galleries of his native Yorkshire as he is touring the glories of Florence and Venice.

We live in an age of travel. Never has it been easier or more far-reaching. The means of travel are varied and relatively cheap – although we are increasingly conscious of warnings about our "global footprints". There are many reasons for travelling. Commerce, local and worldwide, has always been foremost. We need to take goods and services to market. We also see travel as a means of "getting away from it all", an escape from the everyday, a change from simply being at home. But some travelling has a psychological and even spiritual dimension. Journeys can be part of the spiritual life. They reflect the passage of life itself from birth to death. We travel through our own life cycle as we journey, examining ourselves, seeking self-knowledge and self-improvement. Holiday travel, adventure travel, can be more than just that: it can also take on the functions of a pilgrimage.

Consider the late Elvis Presley and his house in Memphis. Since his early demise "pilgrims" (fans) have flocked to his former home. Being in touch with his surroundings enables them to identify with him. It is the power of place. Neckerchiefs purporting to be his were sold as souvenirs to his "worshippers" even though, had he worn them all, he would have had to change his neckwear every two minutes of his life. But how many of us return to places from childhood or to settings associated with past happiness to re-capture a golden age? How many of us collect and treasure our souvenirs of past holidays and life events?

Recently, on an ACE study tour in Yorkshire devoted to 18th century houses, we were staying in Ripon so I took the group to the cathedral. It was my "first cathedral" when, as a young schoolboy, I was taken there on a school trip. I can easily recall now the climb down into the dark 7th century crypt of St Wilfrid and experiencing my first relic chamber. Conversion to an interest in art and architecture was not instantaneous, but it was an early starting point for a lifelong enthusiasm. When I return to it 60 years later, and buy a glossy guidebook to go alongside the drab one I bought in the 1940s, the journey seems special and significant.

There have been huge strides in medieval studies during my lifetime. From being made up largely of formal legal and constitutional history, we now possess large new areas of knowledge about economic and social life, intellectual and cultural developments, the world of Christianity and the religious life. As today, so in the Middle Ages there was a lot of travel: travel for trade, for diplomacy, for secular and ecclesiastical administration, for war and for crime. But we also know much more about pilgrimages, those overtly spiritual journeys, and about the pilgrims themselves and the saints whose intercessions, mediations, protection and cures they sought. For some the quest was for a garment or a jewel associated with an important figure of the Christian past, like the Virgin Mary's tunic in Chartres Cathedral, or the hay from the manger in Wittenberg. Even better were body parts, inevitably mostly bones, for at the Last Judgement we are re-united with our bodies, and so, likewise, the saints would be back for theirs. Proximity and association through a visit to pray and venerate could only be a good thing. When I used to take ACE groups to Florence and they naturally wanted to see the wonderful Gothic and Renaissance sculptures in the cathedral museum, I always set great store in visiting a small room usually denuded of tourists. It is a room of reliquaries, which formerly graced the cathedral itself. "This," I would say, "is why most people came to Florence in the past, not to admire the art but to venerate the relics." For here, amongst other bones, is the forearm of St. John the Baptist, a relic of the city's patron, the saint who gave status, meaning and communal identity to the Republic.

Visiting the shrines of saints, usually in splendid architectural settings, has underpinned many of my ACE tours of the last 18 years. Our tours have, I hope, been part holidays, part learning experiences, part secular equivalents of the search for meaning and, no doubt for some people, real pilgrimages. Those medieval men and women who saw their lives as a spiritual journey wanted to bridge the gap between the divine and the material. They sought, as many still do today, to identify with significant people and material artefacts in order to aid their understanding of God himself: artefacts and people which seem to mediate between heaven and earth. In spite of the Second Commandment, images, graven or otherwise, have always flourished in the Christian West. Pictures, wood carvings, stone sculptures, glass, precious objects of all sorts might bring us closer to a sense of God, sometimes so powerfully that they brought not just comfort but certainty of belief and even healing. They could also be, as it were, lightning conductors for miracles, for the eruption of the metaphysical into the physical world. This attitude drew on the theology encapsulated in the Incarnation when God himself became, historically, part of his own creation. Christ himself and his increasingly venerated mother, the Virgin Mary, must have left material traces of their earthly lives, just as the holy places, where they lived and breathed like us, could be visited.

The growth of the cult of saints, be they martyrs, confessors, scholars, innocent child victims, princes, bishops, virgins or whatever, constituted a wider application of the incarnation principle. On Judgement Day they would be resurrected in their former bodies, so parts of their bodies might meanwhile provide comfort, protection and healing while they awaited their former owners. To have access to, say, St Thomas Becket's ring was to be welcomed, but to have access to his corpse was even more efficacious. Some saints were venerated spontaneously; others were formally canonised as the result of deliberate policy on the part of the Church, a monastery or a royal family. Some would remain localised, like St Clether (6th century), one of many local Cornish saints. Others, like St Wilfrid (637–709), began with a local reputation and ended up with 4 sites for his relics and 48 churches dedicated to him. Saints with a Christendom-wide popularity, like St John the Baptist, might find their remains housed in churches all over Europe. We encountered his forearm in Florence but met with his finger in Turin Cathedral. No doubt if all the claimed bones of the saint were assembled there would be a full platoon of Baptists. When Louis IX of France (St Louis from 1297) purchased the Crown of Thorns for his new reliquary chapel, the Sainte Chapelle, he may have been aware there were others and that his piece of the True Cross, united with other fragments, would have constituted a small forest. Then there were the 4 foreskins of Christ – but more on the authenticity issue shortly.

Powerful political interests promoted some of the more popular saints. The remains of St Mark were surreptitiously removed in 829 from what was by now Moslem Alexandria and brought to Venice, where, in the doge's grand chapel dedicated to the Evangelist, he became the cornerstone of the Republic. Similarly, St Denis not only boosted the reputation and wealth of the abbey dedicated to him north of Paris and which held his body but, taken up by successive French royal dynasties, became a national saint displacing St Martin who might have sought that role. By contrast, in spite of having, at various times, two shrines, a chapel and a huge window in York Minster, few ever venerated St William there. He failed to challenge the power and tourist attraction of St Cuthbert at Durham or even St John of Beverley. The pulling power and curative successes of St Thomas at Canterbury seem to have taken pilgrims away from other shrines, introducing an element of competition. Some quiet satisfaction was noted in Oxford when several pilgrims to the regional shrine of St Frideswide were thankful for her cures, which had not been forthcoming from St Thomas.

The veneration of saints and their relics was popular with good reason: there were cures; there was peace of mind after performing a penance; and there was the saint's personal protection for the individual pilgrim and for the institution which housed him or her. It was the power of place combined with the powers of the relic which could perform all these functions.

A localised saint could achieve a more Christendom-wide appeal by becoming part of a longer pilgrimage route to a prestigious shrine. Two such pilgrim routes and their feeder roads dominated Western Europe, one to Rome (Saints Peter and Paul) and one to Compostela in North West Spain (St James the Great). One road to Compostela passing through the countryside of the Rouergue in France enabled pilgrims to venerate St Foy at Conques, who thus became part of a wider network of saints on the long pilgrimage to St James. Pilgrims crossing the Mont Cenis pass on their way to Rome could rest at the Benedictine abbey of Novalesa to seek the aid of St Eldrado, the abbey's patron, who thus became associated with the wider pilgrimage to Rome.

The need for saints in any given locality naturally led powerful patrons to secure the most prestigious ones possible. The great abbey of Vezelay, a key visit on the ACE Burgundy tour, secured Mary Magdalene's body by embroidering the legend that she and her family, including the resurrected Lazarus, had travelled to Provence to convert the inhabitants. The Saracen threat led, it was claimed, to the removal of the Magdalene's body to Burgundy where the cult attracted pilgrims and money, which paid for the wonderful church we visit today and put the little town on the route to Compostela. Only when the Pope declared in 1295 that her remains had never left St Maximin's in Provence did the abbey start its slow decline. Similar claims were made and sustained for Lazarus at Autun where pilgrim income created one of the finest of all Romanesque churches.

The demand for relics generated a thriving trade. In early centuries, when northern Europe seemed to be short of saints other than very localised ones, the Frankish lands acquired the remains of many Roman martyr saints, Rome having vast stores of their bodies. Soissons acquired St Sebastian and no fewer than 23 Roman martyrs were brought to Rouen. If the body or part of it could not be secured, then an object connected with the saint would do. So in 527 St Vincent's stole was brought to St Germain des Prés: shades of Elvis's neckerchiefs. This is a point where travel for commerce meets travel for worship.

What trade could not acquire might be possessed by theft. St Foy had been satisfied at Agen, but a monk from Conques infiltrated her church community in the 860s and stole her relics. The offerings realised at her new resting place built the superb Romanesque church we see today at Conques. Monks from Fleury on the Loire stole St Benedict's body in the early 7th century from Monte Cassino, claiming to provide it with safe-keeping from the Lombards. Their monastery was re-named St Benoît sur Loire. The relic need not be of a whole body. St Hugh of Lincoln, venerating the Magdalene, bit off one of her fingers and, concealing it in his mouth, transferred the piece to Lincoln Cathedral's relic collection.

Not all thefts succeeded. Though Turin acquired the Baptist's finger from Maurienne, an earlier attempt by Archdeacon Rufus in the 9th century failed, the cleric being struck down dead. It was clear why: the saint did not wish to be moved! Conversely, a successful "theft" clearly indicated that the saint in question was willing to be moved elsewhere. Legal procedures were developed to sanction such thefts, allowing saints, dismembered and re-distributed, to spread their power. St Nicholas of Tolentino (1245–1305) was clearly reluctant, for when a young German Augustinian, on pilgrimage to Tolentino, sawed off the Saint's arms to make off with them, he was apprehended. Thereafter the canons displayed the arms in special reliquaries for pilgrims, while the rest of Nicholas's body was buried for safe-keeping and its whereabouts subsequently forgotten. Rediscovery of the body in 1926 enabled Tolentino to take off again as a pilgrimage site.

If I have stressed the modernity of the parallels between medieval spiritual journeys and contemporary ones for cultural refurbishment, then scepticism and disapproval can also be paralleled. The authorities always saw dangers in the pilgrimage. Peasants and townsmen leaving their lands and work could be disruptive of order and social discipline. Were pilgrims simply avoiding trouble, creditors or law suits back at home? Travelling cut across established social boundaries and structures. Thomas à Kempis in his famous "Imitation of Christ" was at the end of a long line of doubters. He saw pilgrimages as distracting, too much about satisfying curiosity, too much about sight-seeing in fact. Attention to one's personal relationship with Christ and regular attendance at the Eucharist were more important then the novelty of dubious travel. Anyway, as was frequently pointed out, pilgrims were often cheated or attacked. The stench of profiteering which so often paid for the great buildings and works of art we see today was constantly condemned, as was the traffic in souvenirs. The "tatty" gift shop is not a recent invention.

Then there was the question of authenticity. From earliest times critics condemned the gullibility of many of the pious and challenged the authenticity of relics and the miracles associated with them. We recall the "pigges bones" of Chaucer's Pardoner. Contemporaries were well aware of the problem, which explains why we have such detailed writings about saints and relics, the burials and translations. There was felt to be a need for scholarly investigation and documentation where possible. This was another reason for making official canonisation a more formal process and looking with disfavour on old and fleetingly popular cults. Yet one Eucharist, according to à Kempis, was still worth a thousand pilgrimages. Of course there was much gullibility, superstition and exploitation, and we can sympathise with the authorities' concerns about it, but did church leaders and intellectuals believe all relics to be genuine or did they just ignore pilgrimages because it suited them? I doubt, but cannot prove, whether the intelligentsia believed in the authenticity of many relics, but they no doubt believed that, in spite of the dangers, religious observances, which encourage the faithful to be in touch with the divine, were to be encouraged. Maybe they thought that the comfort and peace of mind achieved by many justified looking the other way when it came to authenticity.

For several years I was privileged to lead the annual ACE tour to Compostela, covering many of the Aragonese, Navarrese and Castilian routes on the way to Galicia. As we travel from the Somport Pass via Jaca, or the Roncesvalles Pass via Pamplona, we encounter Santo Domingo della Calzada, the treasures of Burgos and Leon, all these and more, before climbing the Cebriero Pass, where we look down from the mountains dividing Castile from Galicia, towards the final goal of Santiago and the relics of St James the Great. Ours was not a religious pilgrimage but a cultural one. Nevertheless, as we enter the city of the Saint there is expectancy not just of viewing the glorious church and its sculpture but also of experiencing that final focus of the journey, the shrine of St James. Above the crypt, which holds the shrine, is a clothed wooden image of the Saint, jewel-encrusted. Pilgrims and tourists alike are invited to approach it by steps and to hug the image. I have done so on many occasions, not always sure whether this is a religious act or cultural homage, or simply gratitude at having got there at all! Pilgrimages are still worth the journey, whether for the believer or the unbeliever, if only because we can - through the journey - enter into something of the experience of our medieval forebears.

As we join ACE on its next 50 years of travel I carry on my key ring the scallop shell of St James and his image within it. *Bon Voyage!*

Martin van heemskee
A° Ætatis 〈?〉XLI
1553

From the Grand Tour to the Study Tour

Simon Ditchfield

SIMON DITCHFIELD led over twenty tours for ACE between 1989 and 1994, principally to the Italian peninsula but also to his home city of Liverpool. Since 1998 he has been a trustee of ACE and occasional tour leader and manager. He teaches at the University of York where he is currently reader in history.

Samuel Johnson's chippiness at never having undergone the experience of the Grand Tour to Italy is well known. Pat Rogers wittily described the good doctor's peregrinations to the Scottish Highlands and Western Isles in the company of the irrepressible James Boswell as "the Grand Detour". Dr Johnson's prickly behaviour can only be understood if one appreciates just how central knowledge of classical Latin language and culture was to the identity and self-image of educated people in *Ancien Régime* Europe. (Greek only became as important in the nineteenth century, as exemplified, for example, in the Homeric scholarship of Gladstone.) Equally important, however, was the degree to which the Grand Tour had become *the* acknowledged rite of passage for scions of those families who considered themselves members of the British political elite.

This cultural pilgrimage to what was regarded as the home of classical civilisation in the Italian peninsula, via France, Switzerland and Germany, only really got under way during the reign of Charles I (1625–49), by which time the confessional struggle between Protestant and Catholics had become muted by a mixture of pragmatism and diplomacy. Charles's own queen, Henrietta Maria, was daughter of the Most Christian (Catholic) King of France and James I had originally hoped his son would marry the daughter of the Most Catholic King of Spain. The number of travellers accelerated during the Commonwealth (1649–60), when a number of Royalists chose exile on the continent rather than residence under the protectorate of the Puritan Oliver Cromwell. By the early eighteenth century, the round trip to Italy, together with the purchase of what antiquities (both genuine and fake) they could lay their hands on (and to a lesser degree old master paintings, the heyday for whose purchase arrived in the nineteenth century as a direct consequence of Napoleon's wholesale artistic looting of Italy), had become almost *de rigueur* for those who aspired to political leadership of the country. The contents and decoration of country houses the length and breadth of Great Britain and Ireland, many of the finest of which have themselves been subjects for ACE study tours, still bear elegant and eloquent witness to this fact; while the tradition of classical Ciceronian rhetoric

Self Portrait of the Painter with the Colosseum in the Background, 1553 (oil on canvas), Maerten van Heemskerck (1498–1574)

was mined deeply and creatively by such parliamentary orators as John Wilkes and Charles James Fox.

By the nineteenth century, the Grand Tour was giving way to the Romantic Tour, in which scenic travel, hills and mountains joined with health spas and sea-bathing to extend the choice of destinations. Significantly, such an expansion of what was considered worthy of visiting by those with the money and leisure – who now comprised not only the aristocracy but also increasingly the commercial, professional and industrial middle classes – not only included such continental sights as the Swiss Alps (the Alpine Club was founded in London in 1857) or the French Riviera, but also such domestic areas of outstanding natural beauty as the Lake and Peak districts, Brighton and Torquay.

During this century, continental travel first became open to the middle classes of Britain; a process that was encouraged by the activities of such travel popularisers as Thomas Cook and John Murray III. The latter's famous Murray guidebooks were almost contemporaneous with the equally popular Baedeker handbooks, both of which shaped the traveller's expectations as well as determining his itinerary. As the journalist Charles Lever put it satirically in his picaresque tale, *Arthur O'Leary: his wanderings and ponderings in many lands* (1844):

> And now, in sober seriousness, what literary fame equals John Murray's?
> What portmanteau, with two shirts and a nightcap, hasn't got one Handbook?
> What Englishman issues forth at morn without one beneath his arm?…Does he not
> carry it with him to church, where, if the sermon be slow, he can read a description
> of the building? Is it not his guide at the *table d'hôte*, teaching him when to eat, and
> where to abstain? Does he look upon a building, a statue, a picture, an old cabinet,
> or a manuscript, with whose eyes does he see it? With John Murray's, to be sure!

One consequence of this phenomenon was the emergence of a powerful distinction between the "true traveller" and the "mere tourist". The dictum: "Tell me where and how you travel and I'll tell you who you are" is by no means a recent topic for dinner party one-upmanship.

By the time one reaches the inter-war years of the twentieth century, this reaction to the commercialisation of tourism had developed into a full-blown nostalgia for the lost art of travel. Writers as diverse as D. H. Lawrence, Graham Greene, Norman Douglas, Evelyn Waugh and Robert Byron memorialised these years as the twilight of an age of travel, now swept aside by the new dawn of vulgar tourism. It was somehow appropriate that by the close of the 1930s the Baedeker printing plant in Leipzig was itself controlled by totalitarians for whom leisurely travel through territory bristling with monuments and places "worth the detour" was replaced by the abhorrent notion of ethnically cleansed *lebensraum* and the guidebooks themselves came to be used to select five suitable targets, all of which had been awarded three stars by Baedeker, amongst the cathedral cities of England for the Luftwaffe in its bombing raids of spring 1942 in retaliation for the wholesale destruction of the medieval, Hanseatic port of Lübeck by Bomber Command.

When the Association for Cultural Exchange was founded half a century ago, Great Britain was barely recovering from the years of post-war austerity (meat rationing only ended in 1954) and currency controls still made overseas travel for leisure a decidedly elite privilege. Given such restrictions, lovers of "abroad" were forced to nourish themselves vicariously by reading such books as Elizabeth David's *A Book of Mediterranean Food* (1950) or her own acknowledged favourite, *Italian Food* (1954). The difficulty of sourcing many of the ingredients for her uncompromising and frequently complex recipes (which still had not been fully resolved when I sought to vary my gastronomically impoverished student diet using David's *Italian Food* at the University of York in the late 1970s) meant that many readers were able to feast just on her powerful evocations of exotic tastes and textures and to enjoy only the spice of her irreverent wit.

All this was to change from the 1960s onwards. The sometimes prurient attention devoted by social commentators to the emergence of a moneyed youth culture, particularly as expressed in the so-called "permissive society", has perhaps obscured a cultural change no less colourful and culturally significant in its own way: the establishment of the cultural tourism of Western Europe as a more broadly middle-class pleasure. Without at least some direct familiarity with or knowledge of the canon of West European artistic, architectural and (more recently) culinary treasures, it is difficult to imagine the present-day ubiquity of "lifestyle" sections in today's media (or indeed the cultural references of so much TV advertising). For they are predicated on their readers' nostalgia for that unforgettable day spent on holiday and the corresponding desire to evoke it by various means: from décor to dining.

ACE's place in this seismic shift in Cultural literacy (and I am unashamedly using "Culture" here with an upper case "C" in the German sense of the word: *Kultur*) has been, and remains, a distinguished one. Since its foundation as an educational charity with the specific mission to promote cultural exchange by, for example, running summer schools for students from North America and mainland Europe (initially Denmark), ACE was for many years almost alone in offering participants at a reasonable cost the possibility of retracing the footsteps of their aristocratic forbears who made the Grand Tour. But with ACE one was in the company of like-minded, enthusiastic participants who counted the highlights from the churches and museums they had visited each day rather than the stars of their accommodation. Furthermore, one was led by knowledgeable and resourceful course directors. (There were no tour managers for course directors to delegate the humdrum business of ascertaining the opening times of local sites or counting the group on and off the coach to until very recently.) By contrast, their eighteenth-century counterparts were led by put-upon tutor-cum-servants who not infrequently expended more energy trying to distract their wayward young charges from catching venereal disease than they did to sketching the Venus de Milo.

The other operators in the field of cultural tourism at the time of ACE's founding included Cox & Kings, at 200 years old the longest established travel company in the world, and Swan Hellenic. Perhaps fittingly for a company founded by Richard Cox in 1758 to act as a regimental agent for the Grenadier Guards whilst on campaign in Flanders during the War of Austrian Succession, for much of its history Cox & Co's core activity was the facilitation of the travel requirements and financial needs of colonial administrators and army officers throughout the British Empire and even today its tour destinations noticeably reflect (and celebrate) this rich colonial heritage. Swan Hellenic, on the other hand, established its reputation in the post-war years as a purveyor of luxury (and correspondingly expensive) cruises to the Mediterranean heartlands of Western Civilisation, during which passengers enjoyed the evening lectures of big name speakers and the daytime services of rather less grand local guides when on dry land.

ACE has gone from strength to strength and now offers an unprecedented range of tours to embrace music as well as art; nature as well as architecture. In the 1980s ACE was joined by a number of competitors in the niche market of affordable cultural tourism. ACE, however, remains unique not only in the geographical and thematic range and number of its courses and the extent of its commitment to those within the UK, but also in the charitable support it makes to projects that further the vision of cultural exchange and understanding which first inspired that remarkable Anglo-Danish couple Philip and Inger Barnes to found the company in May 1958.

Palladio's Villa Rotonda, Vicenza, Italy.

Andrea Palladio – *architect of perfection*

Charles Hind

CHARLES HIND is associate director of special collections and H. J. Heinz curator of drawings at the Royal Institute of British Architects, which owns the majority of Palladio's drawings. He has led ACE architectural tours for many years and is also a member of the executive committee of the Georgian Group.

It is nearly twenty years since I first saw a villa by Andrea Palladio. The Villa Rotonda is a square, domed building that sits comfortably on a low hill overlooking the road leading southwards from Vicenza to Noventa Vicentina. It was both familiar and strange, known to me from a hundred photographs in the architecture books on my shelves at home, yet the reality was unsettling. The building is full of subtleties that the photographs struggle to convey. On that first visit, the interior was closed but the custodian allowed us to wander round the outside. It was nearly an hour before we left, remarkable when you consider that the house is not large and is precisely symmetrical on every front.

Many people before me have been mystified and entranced by the building. Goethe called on 22 September 1786. "Today I went to see a magnificent house called the Rotonda. … It is a square block, enclosing a round hall lit from above. On each of the four sides a broad flight of steps leads up to a portico of Corinthian columns. Architecture has never, perhaps, achieved a greater degree of luxury. Far more space has been lavished on the stairs and porticos than on the house itself, in order to give each side the impressive appearance of a temple. The house itself is a habitation rather than a home."

Goethe's last comment is interesting. Though the villa is still privately owned and occupied and its furnishings are simple and appropriate, somehow the overall impression is not home-like, unlike many other villas by Palladio. Was that indeed Palladio's intention? I think not. Immensely knowledgeable about Roman buildings as he was, almost certainly Palladio saw it as his most direct tribute to the architecture of antiquity, with its quotations, as we shall see, from Classical buildings, sacred and secular. The name Rotonda is a reference to the popular name for the Pantheon. Even Palladio's description of the Villa's splendid setting was in terms that contemporaries would have recognised as deriving from Pliny's account of his own villa on the slopes of the

Apennines. But first we must look at Palladio's background and why he came to base this villa so firmly on antique precedents.

2008 is the 500th anniversary of Palladio's birth and it will be the excuse for looking at his own work as well as his posthumous influence on Western architecture through exhibitions, conferences, books and articles. Even more important than his buildings was the book he published in 1570, *I Quattro Libri Dell'Architettura*, which achieved an international audience that his buildings, apart from his Venetian churches, initially lacked. In later life, Palladio's opinion was sought from Constantinople to Madrid. Buildings reflecting his thoughts on architecture could be seen all over Europe in the 17th century and his influence had reached north America and India by the 18th century. By the 19th century, he was a worldwide phenomenon.

Andrea Palladio's background was relatively humble – his father was a millstone dresser. Although associated particularly with Vicenza, he was actually born in Padua. There are indications that his parents had good connections, for young Andrea's godfather was Vincenzo de'Grandi, a well-known sculptor. In 1524 (aged 16), Andrea was apprenticed to one of the leading stonemasons and carvers in Vicenza, in due course becoming a partner. In the mid-1530s, the firm was employed to work on remodelling the villa of Giangiorgio Trissino, a gentleman scholar and amateur architect. Trissino changed Andrea's life. He gave him the name Palladio (a nickname with a suitably antique sound), let him loose on his library and took him to Rome in 1541 to see the monuments of antiquity.

Rome inspired him and he came to know its ancient and modern buildings well, but in designing buildings for the Veneto he fused contemporary needs with local and antique traditions. Palladio picked up his first villa commission in 1540 but the work that really launched his career, consolidated his reputation inside Vicenza and established his fame beyond it was the design of the new Classical arcades around the Basilica, the largest public building in the city. This irregular, 15th century structure in the main square was the meeting place for the Vicentine nobles, under the watchful eye of Venice, which had ended the city's independence in 1404. The Gothic loggias that surrounded the building had partially collapsed soon after their completion in 1496 and after long delays caused by war and the ensuing economic recession, the Vicentines wanted something special and modern. Fitting a regular Classical design onto the irregular existing Gothic building had defeated a number of eminent architects such as Sebastiano Serlio of Bologna, Giulio Romano from Mantua, Jacopo Sansovino from Venice and Michele Sanmichele from Padua. None of them could provide the city with an elegant and affordable solution and the general view was that the only answer was to reconstruct the old Gothic loggias on better foundations.

Lurking in the wings was Andrea Palladio, who was quietly being promoted by a number of influential local friends, including present and future patrons. Palladio's first villa had been built in 1540–42 for the wealthy Girolamo Godi, who happened to be a member of the committee charged with rebuilding the loggias. A colleague was Count Alvise Valmarana, who later commissioned a palace, while a third supporter was Bonifacio Poiana. Palladio's wife Allegradonna had been a favourite maid of Poiana's wife Angela, who had given her a generous wedding present. In due course, Palladio built a villa for the Poianas.

Palladio's ingenious proposal for the Basilica, begun in 1546, was not completed until 1616, 36 years after his death. His solution demonstrated a practical attention to detail (derived from his experience as a mason) combined with a flair for adapting the rules of Classical architecture to suit particular circumstances. These two skills were key to Palladio's success. He made himself a master of Roman architectural theory, particularly the work of Marcus Vitruvius Pollio, the first-century AD author of the only treatise on Roman architecture to survive from antiquity. Palladio clambered over Roman ruins, making measured drawings and speculative reconstructions of them as far afield as Provence and Istria (now part of Croatia) as well as and most importantly in Rome itself. Many of Palladio's buildings contain quotes from Roman structures – for example he used the cornice from the Pantheon on a number of villas and many of his porticos (including those of the Villa Rotonda) are loosely based on the Portico of Octavia, a first-century AD building also in Rome.

The source for the general appearance of Palladio's four identical façades at the Villa Rotonda was not, however, from any surviving building that he had seen. Goethe had commented that Palladio had wanted to give the house the appearance of a temple, but porticos on antique temples are always at the narrow end of rectangular structures. At the Villa Rotonda, Palladio applied a portico to the middle of a long façade, with windows to either side and high walls flanking the steps to the main door. In his *Quattro Libri dell'Architettura*, Palladio's illustration shows the staircase walls with statues at the ends, and a trio of statues on the pediments. The only possible source for the façade, now a commonplace in thousands of buildings worldwide, was a Roman coin, a *sestertius*, first minted by the Emperor Tiberius in the 30s AD. Tiberius had recently restored the Temple of Concord in the Roman Forum. Fragments of its foundations were discovered in the twentieth century but nothing was visible in Palladio's day. Unusually, the Temple had a portico in the middle of its long side, approached by a staircase adorned with statues like the Villa Rotonda's and flanked by windows.

Like the Greeks, the Romans took a strong line on which buildings could appropriately have porticos. In their view, porticos should only be applied to sacred buildings. This key fact was unknown to Renaissance theorists, who argued that Roman domestic buildings had also included porticos. Knowledge of Roman domestic architecture was extremely limited before the excavations of Pompeii and Herculaneum. Until then, it was necessary to rely on written descriptions surviving from antiquity and almost everything assumed from these sources was wrong. Unhelpfully, Vitruvius's surviving text had barely mentioned Roman houses at all, concentrating on temples and public buildings. Palladio championed pedimented porticos "to give emphasis to the entrance and render the building grand and magnificent". Practical as ever, he also pointed out that pediments were useful places to display the arms of the owner.

The arms in the pediments at the Villa Rotonda are those of a later owner. Palladio's client was Paolo Almerico, a wealthy, retired priest. After a dodgy start (despite being in holy orders, as a youth Almerico spent two years in prison for killing a man in a brawl), he had made a successful career in Rome working in the Vatican civil service. On retirement, he commissioned this house, inspired by the Pantheon, on the outskirts of his native city, halfway between a town house and a country villa. Work began about 1566 and continued till Almerico's death in 1589. His illegitimate son subsequently sold it to the Capra family, who commissioned Vincenzo Scamozzi to finish the building. Despite suggestions that the present dome, significantly different from the one published by Palladio in his *Quattro Libri*, is Scamozzi's, it is more likely that he was only responsible for some of the more elaborate interior decoration and additional farm buildings that flank the approach to the house from the road. It is unlikely that Almerico would have lived in his little house for 20 years with the central room unroofed. Palladio's dome as built resembles that of the Pantheon whereas the one he published is more like those of his two Venetian churches, S. Giorgio Maggiore and the Redentore. These were in turn based on the traditional Venetian church dome, a hemispherical, light timber structure quite different from the massive domes of Florence Cathedral and St Peter's Rome. Probably Palladio felt that it was not entirely appropriate to use a traditional ecclesiastical feature on a private house, an inhibition not felt by his North European imitators who preferred the fancier published version. It may be that he also thought such a high dome would dominate the building too much, a charge that can certainly be levelled at its nearest imitator, Mereworth Castle, Kent, begun about 1720 by Colen Campbell, which externally is otherwise very close to the Renaissance original.

Internally, the Villa has changed much since Almerico's day. I have mentioned the elaborate plaster decoration added by Scamozzi. The central circular hall has rather gross mural paintings applied by Louis Dorigny in the late seventeenth century and the opening in the roof like that of the Pantheon, which allowed air and rain in, has been glazed. Inigo Jones in 1614 noted that it was closed with a net to exclude birds and flies. The top floor, designed as a granary in common with almost all of Palladio's villas, became bedrooms in the eighteenth century. But the exterior remains magical and even modern development has failed to spoil the extraordinary setting. Palladio described it thus in 1570:

> The site is as pleasant and delightful as can be found, because it is upon a small hill, of very easy access, and is watered on one side by the Bacchiglione, a navigable river, and on the other it is encompassed with most pleasant risings, which look like a very great theatre, and are all cultivated, and abound with most excellent fruits, and most exquisite vines: and ... it enjoys from every part most beautiful views, some of which are limited, some more extended, and others that terminate with the horizon.

Approaching the Villa after all these years still gives me a shock of surprise and pleasure at its perfection, probably just the reaction that Palladio hoped for.

Discovering Japan

Alex Koller

Born in Vienna, ALEX KOLLER has lived and studied in Salzburg, Oxford and Cambridge and has travelled extensively. He gained his PhD in the History of Art from Magdalene College, Cambridge, and has lectured and supervised at the University. Alex has directed many tours for ACE and, in addition to his interest in art history, he is also a linguist: he numbers German, French, Italian and Russian amongst his languages. He counts his work for ACE in Japan as amongst the most exciting and stimulating experiences of his working life.

Until recently, Japan did not advertise itself as a destination for anything other than business travel. News of Japan in the West is mostly dedicated to the economy or technological innovation and sometimes to the country's arcane and bewildering social mores. The image of a land of bullet trains, multi-storey expressways and high-rise buildings is often conjured up. Of course, one has heard of the tea ceremony, geisha girls and, perhaps, kabuki theatre. Typically, as an art-historian I had come across Edo-period woodblock prints because they influenced French artists in the late nineteenth century. Yet nothing had prepared me, for example, for the architectural and sculptural treasures of Nara, the first permanent capital (eighth century), and the first site I ever visited in Japan. Many of the monumental Buddhist images survive in their original surroundings, in temples that have kept alive the scholarly traditions of early Japanese Buddhism for the last 1,300 years. Horyu-ji Temple, just outside Nara, has the world's oldest surviving wooden buildings (seventh century) and a collection of religious art which some might argue is unrivalled in Asia. It is virtually unknown outside Japan.

Japan's treasures are hidden. It is impossible to cross Rome, Florence or Paris without at least catching a glimpse of some monumental, world-famous sight. Kyoto has close to 2,000 religious sites, many of them of outstanding historical and artistic value, yet one can travel through the city from end to end without noticing any of them or seeing even anything remotely attractive. At this stage, the words "country of contrasts" and "Japanese aesthetic" are often mentioned, the former supposedly explaining the difference between the traditional and the modern, the latter referring to the simple, understated nature of a great deal of Japanese design. Yet as soon as we look beyond these stereotypes, we realise the complete lack of universally applicable aesthetic principles. For instance, the garishness of the Toshogu Shrine at Nikko, the much more muted sumptuousness of the Shogun's Castle in Kyoto and the mannered simplicity of Katsura Villa all go back to the same period (seventeenth century), yet display largely differing, even contradictory, aesthetics. The list could go on. There is no single Japanese aesthetic, just as there is no Italian or British aesthetic.

Detail of shrine gate at Inuyama Castle with cherry blossom.

The variety of Japan's cultural, and also natural, features may indeed appear infinite and confusing. Similar to Britain, it is an island nation, off a culturally extremely fertile continent. From that continent came the stimuli for the great innovations in Japanese history, the introduction of the Bronze Age, of Buddhism (sixth century) and of the political and cultural institutions of Classical China (seventh to eigth centuries). In several phases of its history, the country opened itself to these outside influences, adapted them at great speed (as occurred with Western influences after 1868), made these new elements its own and then entered a phase of isolation, such as the "Closed Country Policy" from c.1640 to 1868. At the same time, the nation always held on to some of its most ancient traditions. One example is the survival of the native, animist Shinto religion next to culturally dominant Buddhism. In the same vein, a single Imperial Family has ruled over the country, albeit mostly nominally (another characteristic of Japanese history), since the mythological age; some of the religious accessories of this monarchy go back to the Bronze Age. Things never seem to be replaced in Japan, they are merely added to.

The assimilation of foreign influences can easily be misunderstood. In Japan this does not represent a tendency to dilute one's identity but it stands for an extraordinary ability to give a home to essentially alien ideas in a thoroughly Japanese environment. Historically and culturally speaking, the most important such act of assimilation was the adoption of Buddhism from Korea, and subsequently China, from the middle of the 6th century. It brought with it learning, writing and art, as well as a highly complex religious and philosophical system, including access to the cultural achievements of Classical China. T'ang-period sculpture survives better in Japan (Nara) than in the country of its origin; the same could be said of the Classical Chinese Court music.

There is an ancient belief that the Japanese islands are sacred and form the abode of myriad *kami* (Shinto deities). In fact, the love of the natural environment is a logical and easily understandable element of the Japanese mind. There are no wild beasts, the scenery is, by all standards, beautiful, mostly mountainous and heavily wooded, the climate temperate, and the seasons afford plenty of variety. If one were trying to find a common denominator in Japanese culture, it would probably have to be this highly developed and sophisticated interest in the beauties of nature, the changes of the seasons and the character of particular places. To return to the same examples, the Toshogu Shrine at Nikko is notable as much for its spectacular location, surrounded by the giant cedar trees typical of Northern Honshu, as for its buildings, and Katsura celebrates the beauty of natural purity in a paradoxically artificial way while the screen paintings at the Shogun's Castle in Kyoto show almost exclusively trees, plants and birds.

This love of the natural environment may be difficult to believe for the casual or first-time visitor to the great population centres of the Pacific seaboard, where the majority of Japan's 128 million inhabitants live. Open countryside is nowhere to be found between Kyoto, Osaka and Kobe for tens of miles, just a steady rhythm of industrial, suburban and downtown areas. Nevertheless, most of the surface area of the country is covered in forest, hills and high mountains, from the majestic cedar forests of Tohoku to the subtropical jungles of Kyushu and Shikoku, most of them pristine and empty. Similarly, there is more unspoilt coastline to be found in Japan than in the Mediterranean, including stretches as spectacular as the Amalfi Coast, for example, in Chugoku and Shikoku, yet without any overcrowding or tourist industry. However, particular spots are sought out at certain times of the year by millions of people, Yoshino in the Kii Peninsula for the Cherry Blossom, Takao near Kyoto for the autumn leaves, the temple of Daigo-ji near Kyoto for the Cherry Blossom, and so on: large sections of a nation on a kind of aesthetic pilgrimage to the – often highly stylised – natural beauties of their country.

In fact, an extraordinary pursuit of beauty of form can be discerned in much of Japanese life, in the domestic arrangement of houses, presentation of food, bodily posture etc., often against the laws of practicality or comfort. It is obvious that this beauty takes many forms, from the abstract, "dry" compositions of Zen gardens, to the lavish feudal parks of the Edo period to the appreciation of extraordinary natural phenomena (Mt Fuji being the most famous example) or particular landscapes of outstanding appeal. An even older tradition, however, is the veneration of nature and natural deities in Mountain Buddhism and Shugendo, the physically challenging ascent to the top of a holy mountain to "meet" the deity (often with a later Buddhist interpretation), as at the Upper Daigo-ji near Kyoto. Here aesthetic appreciation and ascetic practice appear very close to each other, including a kind of spiritual intensity that is rarely associated with the country and even less often admitted by its inhabitants.

The most impressive example of this "hidden" side of Japan is probably the pilgrimage of 88 temples of Shikoku, the smallest of Japan's main islands, and maybe the safest haven of traditional life and culture. The pilgrim covers a route of about 1,400 km around the island and visits each temple, following a tradition of more than 1,000 years of ascetic practices in this island. The scenery is stunning around the mountain temples and along the Pacific Coast, yet one also dives in and out of industrial and suburban areas on the one hand and thick, forbidding jungle on the other. There is no goal or single highlight to this circular progress through Shikoku, it is like a symbol of the cyclical nature of all existence and the emptiness at its core that Mahayana Buddhist philosophy teaches. Most of the temples would be rather unexceptional without their natural surroundings, yet the latter make them the most memorable encounters with the country. This is a long way from the refined aesthetic of Kyoto Court culture, its tea ceremonies, manicured gardens and finely painted screens, but it recalls the words of Motoori Norinaga, eighteenth-century Shinto revivalist, who says

"Should some ask about the Japanese spirit,
  it is the wild cherry blossom, glowing in the morning sun."
This could be the cherry tree that overlooks Yokomine-ji, the sixtieth temple of the Shikoku Pilgrimage, high up in the mountains of Shikoku.

China guides and places

Gregor Benton

GREGOR BENTON, a fluent Chinese
speaker, graduated in Oriental
Studies from Cambridge University.
After holding professorial posts
at the University of Amsterdam
and the University of Leeds, he was
appointed Professor of Chinese
History at Cardiff University.
He has published books on Marxism,
political humour, the history of
the Chinese Communist Party and
dissent in China and Hong Kong.

Most China tours are clinically sealed against contact with Chinese – not that there is much time for it anyway in the short time most tours have available. However, there is an exception to this cocooning, the guides. They are probably the nearest you will get to a real Chinese and potentially as interesting as any stone monument. The *quanpei*, or national guide, stays with the tour for the whole trip: we can get to know him or her well. Our encounter with the *dipei*, or local guide, is shorter but more intensive, for while the *quanpei* may sit snoozing on the back seat, the *dipei*'s job is to explain the sites and count us on and off. However well or poorly they guide us, they are our window onto Chinese character. Also, they have more power than most tourists think: alienate them, and you risk ruining the visit; show them warmth and respect, and you will receive their co-operation.

I took my first group to China in 1980, four years after Mao's death. Our *quanpei* was Comrade Zhao, a woman of 22, with pigtails, a blue Sun Yat-sen jacket, baggy pants … and patent-leather shoes. After the post-Mao switch from spartan egalitarianism to bureaucratic pragmatism, Deng Xiaoping said bare-foot doctors (his metaphor for ordinary Chinese of Mao's day) would one day graduate to leather, a prediction Zhao bore out. She worked tirelessly and selflessly in the manner of the hero Lei Feng, a martyr of the 1960s held up posthumously as a model of altruism and the object of a communist cult. Today, the idea of a "living Lei Feng" (with its connotations of a living Buddha) is a joke in China, but in the years before capitalism worked its magic Zhao took Comrade Lei as her lodestar. On the bus to the airport, she sang a romantic song about her love for China followed by Jingle Bells (although it was September). Most were too embarrassed to join in, but Geoff and a couple of others happily belted it out. Geoff, a young man, liked Comrade Zhao a lot. At the airport, he tried to give her a fancy pen she had admired. She blushed and politely turned down the gift. Geoff secretly left it behind on the bus, but she came running back to return it. I met Comrade Zhao a second time in 1991. More of that later.

The Great Wall of China.

In Xi'an, Zhao took us to the terracotta warriors, which had just opened to tourists. The site, under a metal hangar, rose incongruously from among the maize fields. My first glimpse of Qin Shihuang's soldiers was literally staggering – I had to grip the railing above the pit to keep my balance. At the back of the hangar, behind the restored front lines of generals, infantrymen and archers, hundreds more warriors seemed locked for perpetuity in a struggle to free themselves from the clay, like Michelangelo's Awakening Slave. Severed heads and mangled limbs lay scattered across the surface, tragic and unsettling, poking out at unlikely angles.

Until the mid 1980s, Chinese graduates were assigned to their jobs, often arbitrarily, and many ended up in unsuitable or uncongenial occupations. One unhappy conscript to the tourist industry was Polly Pang, our *dipei* in Shanghai. She wore fashionable sunglasses, a pretty frock, a floppy Japanese-style hat to frame her nice curled hair, and Western-style trainers. She was angry and desperately unhappy about being a guide, and made no secret of it. Unkind spirits in the group teased her with questions she could not or would not answer:

"Polly, what's that building?"

"I don't know."

"What's the population of Shanghai, Polly?"

"Please ask Mr Greg."

The *quanpei*, a stern-faced young man, leaned over the back of Polly's seat for a quiet word. Polly screamed back in Shanghai dialect and flounced off the bus at the first opportunity, without a backward look.

The next day a new *dipei*, Sally, turned up in Polly's place. I asked her what was going on. At first, she was reluctant to say. Eventually, she opened up.

"Miss Pang is the daughter of a senior Party cadre," she whispered. Clearly, Polly had set her sights higher than China tours.

Four years later, Sally was again our *dipei*. She told me Polly had gone to America on a scholarship to study English. At university, she had an unhappy unfair with a fellow student and withdrew from the course after a nervous breakdown. She then obtained a green card and became ... a tour manager in San Francisco.

While Miss Pang sulked, we visited the Jade Buddha Temple. After a quick look at the 3-ton Sitting Buddha, a representation in sparkling white that some visitors find vulgar, I took the group to my favourite, the tiny Recumbent Buddha, showing Sakyamuni at the point of death, hidden from view in a backstairs chamber. For me, the image forms a trinity with Cuba's Lady of Charity, in her remote shrine above the high altar in the Cobre Basilica, and the Black Madonna of Montserrat – an exquisite, doll-like Mary hidden away at the end of a corridor where devotees queue to file through in a state of wonderment. Today, Shanghai's Jade Buddhas are the focus of a Southeast Asian-style cultic enterprise that attracts ever greater pilgrim throngs. Its prosperous trustees park their luxury cars round the back.

*

In the early 1990s in China, parts of the tour industry became a shark-pond. Guides worked the tourists hard for "sponsorship" to go abroad, for themselves or their "relatives", and shook them down in every way possible. The shop-stop, and the chance of commission, became their prime focus. If they were lucky, someone bought a Tianjin silk carpet or an expensive jade. That was when I met Mr Chong in Chongqing, on a Yangtze River tour.

Mr Chong immediately saw I hated the shop-stop, so he did his best to elbow me aside and take control of the group, for example by putting me in a room in a different part of the hotel from the group and forgetting to let me know when he changed the time for dinner. Mr Chong and I waged our leadership battle in murmurs, but everyone could see what was going on. The group discussed tactics. At a certain point, the tour bus parked in a back street outside an abandoned building done up as an "art gallery", where Mr Chong's cronies were selling tour groups trashy paintings and calligraphy at sky-high prices. The group got out, trooped mechanically round the shop, and trooped straight back onto the bus, without buying a thing. The same evening, behind my back, Mr Chong went round the guests' rooms hawking a video his mates had secretly filmed of our local visits, with us as the unwitting stars. Again, no one bought. Mr Chong was furious, and set out to make my time in Chongqing hell.

By then, tipping had taken off in a big way and the *hongbao* or red envelope, a feudal tradition said to date back to the Song Dynasty, was back in fashion. There was no way I was going to tip Chong, but we had a whole day on the bus before boarding the evening boat to Wuhan and I didn't want him plotting against me or sitting around with a long face. So I got out two of the red envelopes I had started using for gratuities (my own prankish comment on refeudalisation and money-grubbing) and inscribed one with the character Chong and the other with the driver's name. I propped the envelopes conspicuously on the seat beside me. Chong noticed and kept quiet for the rest of the visit, which ended at the quayside. I hope the driver was happy with his fifty yuan, and Chong with his flyer for the art shop.

Chongqing, perched on fog-bound hills above the Yangtze, has few cultural attractions and serves principally as a point of embarkation for river tours. In 1991, the cliffside rock carvings and Buddhist statues in Dazu County were not yet within easy reach by bus, and there was little else to see. Today, Chongqing seeks international notice in an unconventional and even desperate way by promoting a weird "toilet culture", with exotic urinals in the shape of open crocodile jaws, environmentally friendly toilets made of withered grass and charcoal, a toilet culture street, and a four-story public convenience occupying more than 30,000 square feet. Chongqing's leaders have submitted the toilet to the *Guinness World Book of Records*, as "the world's largest restroom". It has an "Egyptian-style" façade behind which soothing music is piped to the more than 1,000 cubicles.

*

In 1991, to my amazement and delight, who should be at the airport to meet us but Comrade Zhao, now called Lulu, aged 33. At first, I didn't recognise her. She wore acid-wash jeans, a lumpy sweater, short-cut hair … and Chinese granny slippers. My students in East Asian Studies at Leeds used to return from their year abroad in Beijing or Tianjin with all sorts of Chinese affectations, of which granny slippers (also known in the West as kung-fu shoes) were one. Made of cloth uppers and rubber soles, together with Mao caps they were by then the height of naffness for urban Chinese youth, who used to laugh at the foreigners for wearing them. By this time, Lulu had been transformed by years of hanging out with tourists and language students into a "fake foreign devil", although the students she aped were themselves "fake Chinese". This produced a double take, or what the postmodernists would call "self-orientalisation". Lulu had chilled out since 1980, but her basic goodness and altruism continued to shine through, despite the collapse of the Lei Feng cult and her own "modernisation". This time, however, she accepted the gifts pressed on her.

*

Xi'an was again on the itinerary. By then, far fewer terracotta warriors lay trapped in the earth, and more than 6,000 soldiers and horses stood in battle formation in Pit No. 1. Today, the hangar remains, but the peasant vendors have been kicked out and replaced by an ugly mall of shops and "galleries". In 1980, while we were in Xi'an, two half life-size scale-model chariots, built in bronze and cast bullion, were unearthed in a heap of thousands of broken strips representing the reins and harnesses. By the late 1980s, each had been reconstructed and unveiled in a new chamber. Where the soldiers are master-pieces on a human scale, the chariots are an exercise in stunning realism and technical virtuosity, adorned with gold and silver gears, sliding windows, and a back door, and engraved with geometric and cloud patterns. According to Sima Qian (ca. 145–90 BC), the ceiling of Qin Shihuang's nearby tomb has a map of the stars depicted by pearls, above a map of the world's seas and rivers formed from mercury (high concentrations of which have been revealed by magnetic scans). However, the Chinese will probably not excavate it in my lifetime, for they are determined to wait for their own scientists to develop the technological means to do so rather than rely on foreign expertise.

*

My most recent trip to China was in 2007. Our guide's English name was Greg, like mine. He was a likeable, easygoing fellow, familiar with foreigners' ways and immensely tolerant. He was more a Confucian than a Maoist – he carried himself gracefully and with dignity, acted kindly, and spoke slowly and correctly, three cardinal virtues of the Confucian *junzi* or gentleman. However, he was also a child of Mao's Cultural Revolution and therefore more or less my age, so we sang Mao songs together over a beer or two and moaned about modern change. He was a real professional. He told good stories, knew his sites, and had time for everyone.

*

In 2007, Beijing was gearing up for the Olympics. Giant canvases masked scaffolding over the gates and halls of the Gugong (known to foreigners as the Forbidden City), where thousands of decorators were freshening up the colours. The canvases, flapping and billowing like backdrops in a draughty theatre, were painted with rough approximations to the buildings they screened. Luckily, the restoration of the Tiantan (or Temple of Heaven) to the south of the Gugong was already complete. I first visited the Tiantan in 1980, just after an earlier facelift. It was the most wonderful building I had ever seen. Below the steps, a quartet of young foreigners were playing Mozart for an American travel advert. In the Cultural Revolution of 1966–76, Western music was banned as "bourgeois", so the scene was symbolic of China's reopening. Elderly Chinese bystanders wept. Physically, the Tiantan in 2007 sparkled and glistened even more luxuriously than in 1980, and I wish the sports fans a happy visit. For me, however, nothing could ever match my memory of 1980, when Comrade Zhao proudly introduced us to a building that she, too, was viewing for the first time.

Classical Archaeology

Andrew Wilson

ANDREW WILSON, born and educated in Edinburgh, studied archaeology then theology before working overseas as an archaeologist, specialising in Roman frontier systems and Byzantine mosaics. He has led many tours for ACE in the Graeco-Roman world, and also several in Britain, with a particular emphasis on the archaeology of his native Scotland. Andrew is a Fellow of the Society for Libyan Studies and belongs to the Society of Antiquaries of Scotland and the Classical Association of Scotland.

Classical archaeology is a lifelong pursuit and a continual source of delight. My own journey began when captivated by stories about Troy as a boy, after which the stepping stones led across the Mediterranean via Bronze Age Mycenae to fifth-century Greece in all its glory and then the majesty of Imperial Rome. Sailing to Byzantium, as Yeats puts it, was the next port of call, and the journey continues, courtesy of ACE Study Tours. Touring, travelling and classical archaeology are comfortable cabin companions, so aptly and eloquently summarised by Samuel Johnson in one of my favourite quotes, when he said:

"…the grand object of travelling is to see the shores of the Mediterranean. On those shores were the four great Empires of the world; the Assyrian, the Persian, the Grecian, and the Roman. All our religion, almost all our law, almost all our arts, almost all that sets us above savages, has come to us from the shores of the Mediterranean."

My travels round the Mediterranean have taken in the great classical sites, places that require little introduction and that will evoke happy memories for all present-day devotees of the Grand Tour. We can wander over the sites and admire the surviving buildings, but classical archaeology is more than studying *metopes* and *triglyphs*, more than counting the *cunei* in the *cavea* of theatres and more than distinguishing the *tepidaria* and the *caldarium* in Roman baths, pleasurable and satisfying as those pastimes are for participants on ACE tours. No, for me classical archaeology is standing in the agora in Athens, near where Demosthenes the great orator warned against the danger of Philip the Great, and picturing him utter the words *"neither the Greek not the barbarian world is big enough for the fellow's ambitions"*. I can hear him spitting out the word "fellow" contemptuously. It is strolling through the forum in Rome and imaging Octavian "conveniently" removing Anthony's will from the custody of the Vestal Virgins, and then claiming Anthony under Cleopatra's influence planned to move the capital to Alexandria. I can see the outcome, Octavian being given a personal oath of allegiance

Delphi, Greece.

from *senatus populusque romanus*, his first steps on the campaign trail to becoming Emperor. It is walking though the streets of Pompeii, and seeing the political slogans and graffiti engraved for ever by the eruption in 79 AD, names that will never grace the classical archaeology textbooks. I can imagine a political activist scrawling *C. Cuspium Pansam aedilem aurifices universi rogant* (all the goldsmiths ask [you to vote for] Gaius Cuspius Pansa [as] aedile). It is sitting in the Hippodrome in Constantinople, and considering the Nike riots of 532 AD, when Justinian was preparing to abandon everything, before being admonished by Theodora who suggested that *"for one who has been an emperor it is unendurable to be a fugitive and may I never be separated from this purple"*. I can visualise Justinian ordering in his tough general Belisarius to secure his throne, culminating in a great renaissance of learning, culture and architectural enhancement across the Byzantine empire. This for me is the challenge and fulfilment from a life experiencing classical archaeology; that is what makes it all come alive.

But travelling round the shores of the Mediterranean with ACE is not just about the big classical sites. For every Palmyra, where some of the group arose before dawn to watch the rising sun emerge behind the splendid Temple of Bel, there is the hardy company who braved the cold plateau to admire Trajan's triumphal arch at Mactaris in Tunisia, or who endured the long coach journey between Fez and Marrakech to walk through Caracalla's arch in Volubilis. For every adventurer who scrambled up to the High Place of Sacrifice in Petra, to be rewarded with molten chocolate at the actual spot where previously blood flowed, there are the even more resolute who clambered down into the Oracle of the Dead at Necromanteion in Epirus, where the "treat" this time was to hear Homer's chilling words describe how Odysseus encounters the soul of Achilles, who longs to be back in the land of the living. And for every crowded Ephesus when the cruise liners are berthed nearby, there is the pleasure of enjoying the companionship of a traditional Turkish gulet cruising along the Lycian shore, anchoring in small picturesque bays. Was it here that Caesar was captured by pirates in 78 BC, promising after his ransom that he would return to crucify them? Did Pompey anchor here while clearing the Mediterranean of pirates in 67 BC, allegedly in some forty days? Was Cassius here in 42 BC, frantically trying to pressgang men into his fleet before the approaching defeat at Philippi? And did St Paul land here on one of his missionary journeys, always unsure what reception awaited him?

Sailing in a small boat gives us a taste of how challenging journeys were in the classical world: although we are in considerably more comfort, we have the opportunity to arrive in small places like Xanthos as the ancients did – from the sea. Here is a small, dusty site, overgrown in places, that has everything for the classical enthusiast, with lots of interpretation required. The lower acropolis, with its difficult to detect temple podia, reminds us of two occasions when the inhabitants chose suicide rather than capture: the first when Cyrus' general Harpagus came rampaging through Asia Minor in 546 BC; and the second, when Brutus, supporting Cassius on land after Caesar's assassination two years earlier, actually tried to restrain the Xanthians when he was horrified by what he saw during his siege of their city. The theatre recalls numerous performances over the years by ACE players who recited adapted versions of *Antigone*, *Agamemnon* and the *Bacchae* in various theatres in beautifully located towns such as Priene, Pinara and Kas in Turkey, or memorably in Greece in a Venetian/Turkish fortress in Nauplion, beneath the Temple of Apollo in Naxos or, best of all, in the sacred precinct of Athena Pronoia in Delphi. The large basilica church in Xanthos, with sand now covering its mosaics, conjures up glorious other mosaics from the more famous classical sites, starting in Pella, birthplace of Alexander, with the simple but effective pebble mosaics and reaching their peak in the magnificent pavements in Justinian's royal palace in Constantinople 900 years later. Finally, as we stand near the gate at Xanthos before the scanty remains of the so-called Nereid Monument, its full splendour now residing in the British museum thanks to Charles Fellows and the British Navy in the 1840s, we reflect on all the great archaeologists and travellers of the past who discovered and explored these classical sites, often at considerable risk to their health, safety and wealth.

Johnson also said that *"the use of travelling is to regulate imagination by reality, and, instead of thinking how things may be, to see them as they are"*. But Classical archaeology is more than seeing sites and buildings as they are today: it opens up the possibility of adding the imagination to the reality in front of us, and of picturing how things might have been. So when we stand before the great temples at Paestum, for example, yes it is important to know archaeologically their construction dates and whether they are *tetrastyle* or *hexastyle* and *Doric* or *Ionic*, but how much better to engage in some debate and conjecture? What prompted the Greek colonists to arrive on those shores: war, famine, land shortage or over-population? What was their religious understanding of how best to placate their deities and secure their benevolence? Why did they feel the need to build three temples in the space of 100 years? And best of all perhaps, reflect on the description in Homer when Odysseus encounters Nausicaa, in a land where her ancestor had *"laid out the walls of a new city, built them houses, put up temples to the gods, and allotted the land for cultivation"*. The privilege of visiting the shores of the Mediterranean to explore classical archaeology with ACE is to arrive at places where people stood centuries before and use the surviving evidence to consider the challenges of founding a new colony, or consulting an oracle at Dodona or Delphi, or whether it was indeed Mausolus himself who was buried in the eponymous tomb in Halicarnassus. Such musings add to the enduring pleasure of classical archaeology, and, after 50 years, long may ACE continue to provide those opportunities, for *ars longa vita brevis* and there is so much more to see and enjoy.

The Oronsay excavations

Paul Mellars

PAUL MELLARS is Professor of Prehistory and Human Evolution at Cambridge University, where his research interests include the archaeology, evolution and behaviour of early human populations, especially Neanderthal and early 'modern' populations. His first involvement with ACE was directing archaeological courses for the organisation in the 1960s and he is currently chairman of the trustees.

The archaeological excavations sponsored by the Association for Cultural Exchange on the island of Oronsay spanned a period of ten years, from 1970 to 1979. For the preceding four years I had been directing a series of summer-school courses in archaeology for American students, and in all these courses we had followed up a three-week series of lectures and seminars in Oxford with a further period of three weeks in which the students took part in archaeological excavations in various parts of Britain. In the summer of 1970, in discussion with Philip Barnes, we developed the idea of organising our own ACE excavation, as an integral part of the annual Archaeology programme. We chose to do this on a small, windswept island in the Inner Hebrides, just off the west coast of Scotland, involving a two-hour (sometimes bumpy) voyage by McBrayne's ferries from the Scottish mainland (initially from West Loch Tarbert and later from Oban). Perhaps owing to the romance of these Celtic fringes of Britain in the minds of our American students, this proved an extremely popular choice among the students taking the course, and for a period of ten years we took up groups of around 10–15 students to take part in the Oronsay excavations. As a base-camp we lived in a succession of farmhouses on the adjacent, much larger, island of Colonsay. From there we travelled either by boat or (at periods of very low tide) by Land-Rover, across the narrow "strand" which lies between the southern tip of Colonsay and the tiny island of Oronsay, one mile to the south. Since Oronsay was permanently occupied by just a single farmer and his wife (with occasional visitors), our transatlantic crew vastly increased the population density of the island during our annual invasion!

So, why did we choose Oronsay for this pioneering excursion by the Association into the archaeological field? This was closely tied in with my own special research interests at the time (while I was a Lecturer in Archaeology at the University of Sheffield) which were centred on the so-called "Mesolithic" (or "Middle Stone Age") period, which intervened between the end of the last ice age in Britain around 10,000 years ago and the arrival of the first farming populations from the European mainland around 4,000 BC.

The beautiful and remote Scottish island of Oronsay was the setting for an ACE-sponsored archaeological excavation in the 1970s, leading to important discoveries in our understanding of the hunting and gathering communities who occupied Britain 6,000 years ago.

The island of Oronsay had been well known to archaeologists since the nineteenth century for its extraordinary series of so-called "shell-midden" sites, dating from the very end of the Mesolithic period, only shortly before the arrival of the earliest farming (i.e. "Neolithic" or "New Stone Age") communities in the region. Although the existence of these sites had been known since the 1880s, the last excavations on the sites had been carried out in 1913, using methods of excavation and material analysis which, by late twentieth-century standards, were woefully inadequate. There was clearly an exciting opportunity here for ACE to make a major contribution to British archaeology, as the results of the ten years of work on Oronsay (eventually published as a book by Edinburgh University Press) were to reveal.

The challenge of the Oronsay work was to explain why the final, late Mesolithic "hunter-gatherer" populations in northern Britain had chosen to occupy this tiny, gale-swept island, and to establish five separate occupation sites dotted at various points around the coastline of the island. At present, Oronsay has a total land area of only around one-and-a-half square miles, and at the time of the Mesolithic occupation this would have been reduced to only half this size, by the effects of the slightly higher sea levels (relative to the land) that prevailed at that time. The sites themselves were only around 20–30 metres in diameter, and can only have been occupied by very small groups of people, perhaps amounting to just four or five families. The occupants seem to have sheltered in small, rather flimsy huts, of which some faint traces could still be detected in the deposits of dune sand which immediately underlay the middens.

When we embarked on the excavations, the sites were believed to consist almost entirely of mounds of shells (mostly limpets, periwinkles and dogwhelks), with a few scattered remains of sea birds (including the now extinct Great Auk) and a few remains of larger animals such as the grey seal, wild boar and red deer. Remains of otters were also fairly frequent in the middens, perhaps because of the utility of their skins. Interspersed with the shells were large numbers of shaped bone and red-deer antler tools, most of which appeared to have been used as "scoops" to remove the flesh of the limpets from their shells. In addition, there were a few sharply barbed antler spear- or harpoon-heads, probably used for hunting seals and red deer, and many bone points or awls, probably used for working skins. The shell middens also contained thousands of small flint flakes, struck from small flint pebbles collected from the adjacent beaches. Pottery and metal tools of course were totally lacking from the sites, since these were only introduced into Britain during the ensuing Neolithic and Bronze Age periods. Perhaps the most intriguing finds were hundreds of small cowrie shells, carefully perforated for suspension, and presumably employed either as beads or as decorations for skin clothing. In archaeological terms, in other words, these were decidedly "impoverished" sites, which may perhaps explain why they had been effectively ignored by archaeologists throughout the fifty-year period before we commenced our new excavations in the 1970s.

In reality (as of course we were hoping) the new excavations on Oronsay proved to be far more interesting and rewarding than most of our archaeological colleagues had anticipated. From the start we had a strong hunch that no one could possibly have survived mainly on limpets, at best a rather tough and tasteless morsel (although interestingly these were still occasionally eaten by the modern inhabitants of the Hebrides down to the present day). We guessed that the prehistoric occupants must have practised some fishing, and to investigate this we employed very fine-scale "water-sieving" of the shell-midden deposits (down to a one-millimetre mesh size) to recover even the smallest fish bones, which had been totally overlooked in the earlier "pick-and-shovel" excavations by the previous excavators. Following hundreds of hours of meticulous "sorting" of these sieved residues (much of this undertaken by my long-suffering wife Anny!) we were rewarded by the recovery of thousands of small fish bones, most of which were identified as belonging to very young "saithe", or coalfish. These fish are still extraordinarily abundant in the immediately inshore waters of the Hebrides during the summer and autumn months, and are known to have formed a staple element in the diet of human populations in the Hebrides down to the present century. How the fish were caught by the Mesolithic groups still remains something of a mystery. There were no traces of fish hooks in the middens, and we assume the fish must have been caught either by nets (of which of course all traces would have long ago decayed in the archaeological sites) or perhaps by tidally operated fish traps or "fish-weirs", set within the intertidal zone of the adjacent beaches. In any event, it soon became clear that fishing for saithe (and a few other species) probably provided more food to the Oronsay groups than the collection of shellfish. The fish would no doubt have been cooked on some of the numerous fire-places that we encountered throughout the midden deposits, and some may well have been dried or smoked for use during the winter months, when the young saithe retreat into deeper, offshore waters and are very difficult to catch. Some of the older modern inhabitants of Colonsay still dry and preserve saithe in this way. Combined with occasional seal meat, venison, birds and crabs, this would have amounted to quite a palatable diet, reasonably appropriate to any modern sea-food restaurant!

But the most remarkable – and ultimately exciting – discovery was the recovery of thousands of tiny "otoliths" (i.e. "ear-stones") of the saithe, scattered throughout the midden deposits. Although only between 5 and 10 millimetres in size, these otoliths have highly distinctive shapes and surface markings, which allow the species to be identified with complete certainty. A detailed study of these otoliths provided even more fascinating information. We could easily estimate the total numbers of fish represented in the sites (by counting the numbers of otoliths and dividing by two!) and we could estimate the size and age of the fish caught by comparisons between the lengths of the otoliths and those recovered from present-day saithe caught off Oronsay at different times of the year – a topic taken up as a PhD project by a student of mine at Sheffield University. The final, extraordinary discovery was that the exact size distribution of the saithe otoliths varied systematically between the five different shell-midden sites, which could only be explained on the assumption that the fishing for saithe had been carried out at different seasons of the year at the different sites, extending from the early summer months (June–July) through to at least the late autumn or early winter (November–December). In other words, it became clear that the small human groups on Oronsay had moved systematically between the five shell-midden sites at different times of the year, both to catch the saithe and to "harvest" the limitless supplies of limpets and other shellfish on the adjacent, rocky beaches. This was the first time that this kind of seasonally rotating settlement pattern had been documented from Mesolithic settlements in Europe, and the methods of demonstrating this from a study of the fish otoliths was a fairly radical contribution to the methodology of archaeological "science", subsequently applied in many other archaeological contexts. Oronsay in fact became something of a classic case-study in British archaeology – and for the study of archaeological coastal sites in general – as several generations of archaeology undergraduates facing exam questions have come to discover!

There are, admittedly, many other questions about the Mesolithic occupation of Oronsay which remain to be resolved. How did the groups survive over the mid-winter months, when the saithe could not be caught without deep-water fishing expeditions? Did the human groups live predominantly off shellfish during this period, or did they supplement this with supplies of dried fish (and perhaps seal meat) as discussed above? More fundamentally perhaps, why did the late Mesolithic groups choose to occupy this tiny island in the first place, and what kinds of contacts did they maintain with other human groups on the Scottish mainland, or the other, larger Hebridean islands, such as Islay, Jura or Mull? Clearly, the Mesolithic groups must have had efficient boats to get to Oronsay in the first place. In fact, we can now show that they must have made regular visits to the Scottish mainland or larger islands to obtain supplies of red-deer meat and antler, since it is highly unlikely that red deer herds would have been present on the island itself. And one or two of the rare, scattered human bones recovered from the middens (perhaps disturbed burials?) would appear on the basis of analyses of the carbon and nitrogen isotopes in the bones, to have come from individuals who must have spent part of their lives on the Scottish mainland. (Clearly, the Oronsay groups had to get their wives or husbands from somewhere …)

With hindsight, all of these results of the Oronsay research have proved to be crucially important new contributions to understanding the ways of life of the final hunting and gathering (and fishing) communities who occupied the northern fringes of Britain shortly before the arrival of the earliest farmers from the European mainland, around 6,000 years ago. The Association for Cultural Exchange can I think be justly proud of its pioneering role in initiating and supporting this important contribution to British and European prehistory.

Footnote: It should perhaps be added that the main archaeological finds from the Oronsay excavations are now housed in the new Museum of Scotland, in Edinburgh. The full monograph on the excavations (*Excavations on Oronsay: Prehistoric Human Ecology on a Small Island*) was published by Edinburgh University Press in 1987. Readers may also be intrigued to know that the Oronsay excavations were visited by Her Majesty the Queen during an unscheduled and totally unexpected stop-over on the island during a summer cruise on the Royal Yacht Britannia in 1971. Formal recognition of this Royal service to Her Majesty is still awaited…

Hungary 1971

Philip Allsworth-Jones

PHILIP ALLSWORTH-JONES
is a former lecturer in the
Department of History &
Archaeology at the University
of the West Indies at Mona,
Jamaica. An expert in
Palaeolithic archaeology,
his research interests cover
the archaeology of Jamaica,
West Africa, and Central and
Eastern Europe. In 1971 he
received an ACE Archaeology
Scholarship and here
recounts his experiences.

I spent six weeks in Hungary in August and September 1971 thanks to a scholarship which I obtained from the Association for Cultural Exchange. At the time I was a post-graduate student of Emmanuel College, Cambridge, working on my doctorate under the supervision of the late Professor Charles McBurney. My subject was the transition from the Middle to the Upper Palaeolithic in Central Europe. I say Central Europe because the peoples living in this part of the world regard it as that (and why not? When they were governed by the Habsburg emperors nobody would have considered it to be otherwise). At the time, however, Hungary and the other "People's Democracies" were definitely regarded as part of "Eastern" Europe, a remote sphere under Soviet rule. The particular concern of my dissertation was the Szeletian, a Palaeolithic "culture" named after a cave in the Bukk Mountains in northeast Hungary, which was supposed to have played a vital role in this transition. Clearly therefore a visit to Hungary had to be included in my work.

I had just completed ten months in Czechoslovakia, based in Brno, thanks to the support of the British Council. I bought an old Volkswagen in Germany, which cost me all of £100 (there being 10 Marks to the pound at that time) and hence arrived in Budapest by road. The person in charge of the exchange programme was Dr Istvan Bona, who was not concerned with the Palaeolithic at all, but who had excellent connections and was very helpful. I was given accommodation in a student hostel right in the middle of *Buda* on Menesi Street, very near to Moricz Szigmond Square. From there it was a convenient tram ride to the centre of *Pest*, where the Hungarian National Museum was situated. I parked my car in a designated area opposite the hostel, empty apart from a couple of Trabants. The hostel itself was a rather decayed building, probably an old private house, but with a delightful garden in which at the weekends I studied the learned journals that came into my possession. Since it was the middle of the vacation, the hostel was practically deserted, but the ladies running the place were very pleased to see me, and I was given a palatial room, as well as a giant bathroom, where the taps certainly looked as though they were made of gold. Every morning on Moricz Szigmond Square I was able to partake of a small cup of espresso coffee of maximum strength, the type

Szeleta cave, Hungary, photographed by
Philip Allsworth-Jones in 1971.

for which the Hungarians are justly famous. I usually had lunch in a workers' café behind the Museum, cheap but good. This was the time of "goulash" Communism, as it was known. In other words, the deal was that the Kadar regime would ensure that nobody went short, but in return you were expected to keep quiet about political questions. In private, my impression was that people could pretty much say what they liked.

As I discovered, it was a strange time to arrive in Hungary to study the Palaeolithic, but on the whole this strangeness worked to my advantage. It was a period of hiatus: Hungarian Palaeolithic studies had been dominated by Laszlo Vertes, but he had died suddenly in 1968, and effectively no one had taken his place at the Hungarian National Museum. Officially, Viola Dobosi had succeeded to his position, but she was on maternity leave, so I did no more than visit her in her flat on the outskirts of Pest. The person in charge therefore was Dr Ilona Kovrig, the head of the prehistoric section, and she handed over the day-to-day care of my affairs to Dr Amalia Mozsolics, a formidable lady and a specialist in the Hungarian Bronze Age. Both these persons did their best to ensure that I had access to all the material that I wished to study. For the most part, this material had been excavated before and during World War I, by the then leading exponents of the Hungarian Palaeolithic, Ottokar Kadic, who dug at Szeleta, and Jeno Hillebrand, who dug at Jankovich, in the Gerecse Mountains west of the Danube. It is both the triumph and the tragedy of Hungarian Palaeolithic archaeology that these sites were dug (and dug out completely) so soon. By the standards of the day, Kadic was an excellent excavator, but in the nature of things he could not tackle the problems nor use the methods of today.

Apart from the material at the Hungarian National Museum, I wished to examine the collection at the museum in Miskolc, Hungary's second largest city, in the immediate vicinity of the Bukk Mountains. Here again, I was fortunate. Athough no Palaeolithic specialist was working in the museum at that time, one of Vertes's close collaborators, Lajos Toth, was in attendance. He was tremendously helpful. His position was that of senior research engineer at the Lenin Metallurgical Works in Diosgyor in the western part of the city. He arranged for me to stay in the guest room of the factory at no charge. In the evenings and at the weekend I had the place to myself, and I used to have dinner at a local restaurant in Diosgyor. It had an authentic gypsy orchestra, the hottest goulash, and the strongest Tokai it has ever been my pleasure to consume. Toth himself had a villa on Avas hill, within the city boundary (an area which I understand has now been totally built over), and I visited him there. I also went with him to the Tatar-Arok valley, which he had ascertained was the place of origin of the predominant raw material used in the Szeleta cave, which he described as "glasiger Quarzporphyr". Having a car, I was able to explore the Bukk Mountains and likewise the mountains west of Budapest on my return to the capital. Coming back from Jankovich along the coast road one weekend, I gave a lift to two Hungarian girls. These were the days of hot pants, so who wouldn't? When they discovered that despite the "D" on my car I was in fact English they became most friendly.

Split-based bone point found in 1928, during a joint excavation by Louis Clarke from Cambridge University and the Miskolc Museum, Hungary. The finds suggest the contemporaneity of the Aurignacian and the Szeletian, split-based bone points being characteristic of the former and leaf points of the latter.

Leaf point of glasiger Quarzporphyr (90 × 32 × 13 mm) also found in the Szeleta cave in 1928.

By Jankovich, however, hangs another tale. Dr Kovrig explained that I could not study material from this site, since she had received a specific request to that effect from Dr Miklos Gabori and his wife Dr Veronika Gabori-Csank. These Palaeolithic specialists, both very well known, worked at the Budapest city museum, not at the Hungarian National Museum (and, as I understood from Toth, there had been no love lost between them and Vertes). I decided that I would have to meet them and ask them about this ban; after all, the material had been excavated many years before. It became apparent that the reason for the ban was that Veronika Gabori-Csank had recently excavated another site west of the Danube (the cave of Mariaremete) and was engaged in a reassessment of the entire "Jankovichian". Miklos Gabori was adamant and gave a flat refusal, saying finally, since the conversation was in French, "nous sommes les maîtres dans notre maison". This evidently embarrassed his wife, and it was finally agreed that if I came back the following year I could study the material. I don't suppose they expected me to come back, but I did (this time without the assistance of ACE, though I stayed at the same hostel, being greeted as their "dear Englishman"). Dr Kovrig, also embarrassed by the lack of cooperation, was pleased to give me full access, although it so happened that the Gaboris were away in Moscow at this later date, which may have helped. I learned not to speak of this story, since when I told my Polish colleagues, they did not believe me, and I was regarded as a liar. But Toth was not surprised, and in his opinion, if Vertes had been alive, I would not have obtained access to any of the material at the Hungarian National Museum.

Even this episode has a positive conclusion. Gabori-Csank published her account of Mariaremete in 1983, and the results were included in my book, *The Szeletian,* which was published by Oxford University Press in 1986. It is ironic that of all the reviews the book received, hers was by far the most favourable (Germania, vol. 66, 1988, pages 531-535). Among other things, my book was said to be thorough and fair-minded and actually benefited from being a "look from outside". I am grateful to her for this. In subsequent years, of course, access to the former "Ostblock" has become much easier, and there have been a number of new developments and new standpoints concerning the transition from Middle to Upper Palaeolithic in Europe in general. Nonetheless, in my opinion, the viewpoint which I expressed in 1986 is still basically correct and I have recently restated it (The Szeletian Revisited, Anthropologie, vol. 42/3, 2004, pages 181-196).

What about ACE in all of this? As I told Mr Barnes at the time, and again when my book was published, I think that the Association did a great job in keeping open links to "Eastern" Europe at a difficult time, and they certainly helped me greatly. Such understanding between East and West is still needed today, when old suspicions of Russia have resurfaced and (as Anatole Kaletsky recently remarked in The Times) the legitimate security concerns of that country are ignored or misunderstood.

In search of the wild ... *from violas to oysters*

Roland Randall

ROLAND RANDALL is a Fellow of Girton College, Cambridge, where he specialises in coastal botany. He acts as an ecological consultant for the National Trust, Natural England and Scottish Natural Heritage. Roland has been instrumental in developing natural history courses for ACE, including Madeira, Crete, Mallorca, the Scilly Isles, Barbados, the Algarve and numerous islands off the coast of Scotland.

Most of the ACE wildlife courses are "general interest" and emphasise birds, flowers and wildlife, but we also include aspects of the local geography, geology and archaeology as these subjects fit together well. Consistently we find that the most interesting archaeological sites have exciting birds and special flowers. Tours to the Mediterranean take place mainly in spring to see the best of the flowers and the northward bird migration. In summer, tours to Scotland and more northerly locations catch the breeding moorland and sea birds and the later flowering season. Autumn tours provide an opportunity to see the southward bird migrations and the beautiful fruits and seeds present at that time.

ACE wildlife tour groups may join survey teams as part of their study. On whale watching trips to La Gomera in the Canary Islands, for example, the study tours work with MEER, the island's whale and dolphin study group. All cetaceans seen during the group's boat trips are recorded, and the findings help MEER to form a detailed picture of distribution and abundance in the area. The records are also being used to make the case for the creation of a protected marine reserve to the south of La Gomera. ACE clients have been able to write letters of support to local government regarding the proposed reserve, and to ferry companies questioning their safety measures with regard to cetaceans.

During many of the ACE wildlife tours records of species seen are kept. These records are shared with national recorders when needed. Although these records are only a snapshot of what is seen during a week or so, they can be most important in areas that are rarely visited by naturalists. In Crete, for example, lists of all birds seen during the annual or twice-yearly visits have been kept since 1992. Sea birds seen during the La Gomera boat trips are counted and details passed on to MEER and the Canary Islands bird recorders. During this year's tour to Shetland we were able to see first hand how declining stocks of sand eels were impacting on the success of many breeding seabird

Oysterplant (Mertensia maritima) with Sea Mayweed (Tripleurospermum maritimum) and Silverweed (Potentilla anserina) on Urafirth Ayre, Northmavine, Shetland.

species. We also saw how a minor change in land-use impacted upon water-levels in a lochan on Fetlar and thereby changed the feeding distribution of red-necked phalarope.

Some of the records collected by ACE groups have fed directly into research. Studies of the changing flora of olive groves in Crete over the years we have been visiting the island, led in part to a publication in the journal Land Degradation and Development (vol. 17, pages 249-273, 2006 – *The impact of changing olive cultivation practices on the ground flora of olive groves*). In this paper we showed how many of the more remote olive groves were being less well managed and were changing from grasses and herbs to scrub, whereas others were being more intensively managed and ploughed (encouraged by subsidies from the EU) so that orchids and aromatic herbs were disappearing. This was also having a knock-on effect on the birdlife. Other implications are the potential for increased risk of soil erosion in the bare areas and fire-risk as a result of increased fuel loading as flammable shrubs invade abandoned terraces.

During the time the ACE group spent on Tory Island, Donegal in 2003, a complete survey of the island's plant species was undertaken. This was published as: *An annotated flora of Tory Island, Donegal*, in the Irish Naturalists Journal, 27, 373-381, 2004. The survey found 199 plant species including a few not seen before. It was enlightening to compare our results with previous plant records for the island since it showed a marked decline in arable weeds (34 now extinct) as the cultivated area has decreased over the years with declining population. On this tour we also witnessed a shipwreck and rescue!

Some of our greatest fun has been the annual search for dwarf pansy *Viola kitaibeliana* in the Isles of Scilly. ACE groups have been visiting these islands for over 15 years and each year we have recorded the success of one of Britain's smallest and rarest plants. It has meant a dedicated crawl over the dune pastures of Bryher with a lunchtime reward for the first person to locate this tiny flower! Some years we have found only tens, other years thousands, depending on weather conditions and human activity over the previous year. With the help of ACE records, the species was written up in the Biological Flora of the British Isles: *Viola kitaibeliana* Schult(es), *Journal of Ecology*, 92, 361-369, 2004. Also the story was developed as *Viola kitaibeliana* Schult (Dwarf Pansy) in the Isles of Scilly in: S. J. Leach, *et al.* (eds.) *Botanical Links in the Atlantic Arc*, BSBI, London, UK, 277-280, 2006. In Extremadura, a few ACE aficionados who had been with me in Bryher were able to see the more robust variety: *Viola kitaibeliana machadiana* (Coutinho) Coutinho, which grows along the riverbanks north of Trujillo.

Another plant we have studied in detail is the oyster plant *Mertensia maritima* which grows on shingle beaches in Scotland and Ireland. This plant is dynamic in distribution but also has been declining rapidly over the last 25 years partly as a result of global warming. Low winter temperatures are necessary as a prerequisite to germination but enough water is required in summer to stimulate growth. Hence it has tended to retreat northwards. More frequent winter storms and increased coastal trampling and grazing have also impacted on its biogeography. This species has been looked for and its population vigour recorded on ACE tours in Arran, Islay, Jura, Shetland and Donegal. By visiting a large number of sites around Britain we have been able to build up a composite picture of the changes that are happening to our coastal habitats. Coastal defence, agriculture, public access and control of alien species are all important and intriguing factors in habitat management. This story was written up as *Management of coastal vegetated shingle* in the Journal of Coastal Conservation, 10, 159-168, 2004.

For many of the locations that ACE visits natural history tourism is a significant and growing aspect of the local economy. In the Isles of Scilly it has replaced fishing and agriculture as the main source of income and it has been amusing to notice that where ACE goes, BBC Springwatch seems to follow: Scilly, Shetland, Islay! The popularity of ecotourism represents a change in tourist perceptions, increased environmental awareness, and a desire to explore natural environments. Within this area, islands have proved extremely popular destinations whether around Britain, in the Mediterranean (Balearics, Sardinia, Aegean) and Atlantic (Canaries, Madeira, Azores, Faroes) or even further afield (Madagascar, Barbados). Some ecotourism has a poor name because much of the income generated goes into the coffers of international hotel chains or cruise liners. However, ACE has attempted to use locally owned hotels, restaurants and coach companies and thereby to feed money directly into the local economy.

If I were to be asked to provide a highlight day on a natural history ACE tour it would be a beautiful day on Islay when we walked along a beach in the morning and saw oyster plant and grass of Parnassus in flower and seals basking in the water with choughs overhead. On our return in the late afternoon we took a remote moorland road and stopped to watch golden eagle overhead being mobbed by raven and curlew. In the evening we ate locally caught fish for dinner and sampled Islay malt whisky!

My thanks to Kevin Hand, Peter Exley and Diana Ward for joining me as co-leaders on the tours mentioned.

Island Life

Kevin Hand

KEVIN HAND is a conservationist and ornithologist and has developed and led an impressive array of natural history tours for ACE, from Norfolk to Madagascar. His work as a conservation consultant has included extensive field work – including animal surveys – for the Cambridge Wildlife Trust.

I hope you will indulge me, as I should like to recount a few traveller's tales, which summarise for me what is so special about taking part in an ACE tour. Firstly, picture yourself on Tory Island, a Gaelic-speaking community of 100 souls, some miles off the Donegal shore, and known for its treacherous rocks and history of wrecking. Our ACE group had just arrived on a wave-tossed ferry, chased by seabirds, and were resting in the hotel bar. We were delighted to observe a large wooden-masted schooner sail by on the horizon. It was Friday 13th June, 2003.

A few moments later, as we began our tour of the island, we could not help noticing a bustle of activity. In a place where there was rarely any need to hurry, people were actually running. I asked what was happening and found that the beautiful ship had run aground. We quickly changed our plans and went to help, but the islanders had everything under control and soon got all the crew ashore. Righting the ship proved more difficult and, despite everyone's best efforts, we had to watch as she was reduced to matchwood within hours. As we returned to the hotel we found out more about the disaster, which turned out to be a very twenty-first century variant of an oft-repeated chapter in the history of Tory.

The ship, *Carrie of Camaret*, was host to a reality TV show called Cabin Fever, which was topping the ratings on Irish TV. No one was quite sure what had happened, but her amateur crew were now holed up in a farmhouse, recovering and trying to evade the media and fans who filled the daily ferry and whirled overhead in helicopters. I spoke to the producer and suggested she bring them down to the hotel for a meal; our ACE group was unlikely to mob them, and reporters were unable to stay here as we had booked all the bedrooms. We enjoyed a memorable evening talking with these young "stars" and helping them to come to terms with the strange events that had happened to them.

Madagascan wetlands with Baobab tree.

It is tempting to tell you more about Tory, of our welcoming audiences with the King of the island, or of the wake we attended as honoured guests, having purchased an unprecedented three paintings from the island's gallery of local "primitive" artists the day before. But I must move on, to the larger island of Madagascar, and to recount a tale that does not involve bars (although we could tell of the local band who, spotting we were British, regaled us with a Malagasy version of "Roll Out the Barrel" in a dingy wooden bar as we supped vanilla-flavoured rum...). No, of many unforgettable experiences on this incredible island, I should like to recall our ACE tour which included the total eclipse of the sun. We had altered the programme and dates to include this event, and found ourselves at a beautiful campsite on the edge of a sandstone plateau, amongst savanna trees. Skipping over the party the night before (more rum, with different flavourings), we began by discussing as a group how we all wanted to experience this unique moment. We decided to take some chairs out of the camp, and to walk up the hillside to some flat rocks well away from any other people. We all had our special glasses, and I set up my telescope to project the sun's image onto the ground beside us. We read out loud some descriptions of what happens during eclipses, both about the science and astronomy and about that other-worldly feeling which occurs as we are made aware of our tiny place in the universe. Some people chose to sit together, to enjoy the experience as friends, while others climbed further into the rocks to be alone. There were clouds over much of the area, but for us the sun appeared on cue. For three and a half minutes the world changed from light to dark and back again, birds stopped singing and then restarted. We walked back down to the camp together, an unspoken bond between us.

I am lucky enough to have been leading tours to Crete for over 15 years, and it is more than 20 years since I first visited the island, but I never expected to be doing anything as exciting as this when I first went there on a package holiday. I have many happy memories from my long association with this magical island. One story is particularly relevant to what it means to be part of the ACE family. On one of my earliest visits I was sitting in a taverna called Aouas in Aghios Nikolaus, one I still visit with ACE groups. It was a warm evening so we sat outside, amongst the bougainvillea and ficus bushes. Suddenly, through the greenery, a dark, moustached Cretan appeared, with a memorable face and a twinkle in his eye. He was a friend of one of my colleagues from the travel firm I was working for. We did not have much common language, but we got on well. He arrived on a scooter, but I learnt he had a taxi too, a wonderful old Mercedes, and he became my driver of choice whenever I needed transport around the town or to and from the airport. Over the years Yiorgios, or George as he preferred to be known (he was a bit of an anglophile), became a great friend, and he acquired a bus. When I began to lead ACE tours to Crete, I suggested we use his bus. He is a very safe driver, which is most important on the winding Cretan mountain roads, even though he does have a penchant for using his phone while driving, sometimes seemingly using two phones at once (hands-free of course). I watched as his bus fleet grew. He married, I watched his children grow up and his bus fleet decline as he went into semi-retirement. Enjoying George's company, his quick wit and ready smile, and his constant kindness, is, I think, one of the highlights for everyone who takes part in the ACE trips to Crete. We only meet once or twice a year, but somehow it is special, in that way ACE have of getting the best from everyone they work with. It is like a family, and even agents and drivers become part of it. Everyone we work with seems to welcome us back year after year.

Finally here is a tale from one of the latest ACE Explorers tours, back on Crete again in 2007. Our group spent a morning on the beaches near Rethimnon with the Greek sea turtle conservation society Archelon, helping them to search in the sand for the nesting sites of the rare and endangered loggerhead turtles. As the Archelon researchers dug down into a recently emerged nest site we did not expect to see more than just hatched shell fragments, as the little turtles dig their way out of the ground at night, when the risk of predation is lowest. However one of our group, Roy, was relaxing a little way apart when he saw a movement. It was a baby turtle, a hatchling that had just emerged into the sunshine. We all watched it slowly orientate itself and head roughly towards the sea. There were false turns, long trails up sand ridges in the wrong direction, and agonising pauses as its strength seemed to fail. Our instinct was to help but we could not, as the young turtles need to walk unaided to strengthen their flippers, and to learn to recognise the feel of their natal beach. If they are females somehow they will return here from across the oceans to breed, although not for another 30 years, when they reach maturity (males may never return to land). All we could do was hold up a tattered beach mat to protect the little chap from the sun ... it may well have been a lady, but we had christened it Little Roy after its discoverer. Many hatchlings never make it to the sea, particularly if they emerge after dawn like this one. After an extremely long 20 minutes, Little Roy finally approached the sea. He paused as a wave washed over him. I know we should be objective about wild creatures, but I am proud to say we all cheered as "our" turtle finally dipped into the sea and swam away. Most of the researchers had never seen live hatchlings on their first journey, so this was a very special experience that we would never forget.

I should like to thank all the wonderful people who have travelled with me over the years and made each tour so special. In particular I should like to thank those who have shared touring duties with me, including Roland Randall, Edmund Lowson, Mark Northfield and Jon Stokes.

ACE Music Tours: A Minor Triumph!

RUPERT SCOTT studied violin, piano, composition and conducting at the Royal Academy of Music, and took his Bachelor of Music degree at King's College London under Professor Thurston Dart. For some 25 years he was a professional orchestral violinist, firstly in London playing in all the major concert halls and opera houses, and later joining the orchestra of Opera North as a founder member. In 1992 he left orchestral playing and joined the music staff at Leeds University, where he remained for 8 years. He led his first ACE tour in 1998 and has since directed over 80 tours, specialising in the orchestral, operatic and chamber music repertoire.

In the early summer of 1997 I first talked to ACE about leading music tours in succession to my long-standing predecessor, Brian Richardson, who had decided to retire. Leipzig was a possible destination and as it happened Hugh Barnes already had the performance schedule for the coming season. It must have been the quickest and easiest decision I have ever been called upon to make: the St Matthew Passion was to be performed on Good Friday, 1998, in St Thomas Church, the very church where Bach had worked and performed for his last 27 years. It was the perfect match of time, place and music. Purists may argue about details of the performance, but in my opinion there is nothing to equal the musical and spiritual impact of hearing Bach's masterpiece, one of the towering glories of Western music, on the day and in the church for which he wrote it. Ten years later this annual pilgrimage remains the quickest selling ACE music tour of all.

Leipzig is a fascinating city. And what changes it has seen, not least in our lifetime. I was sad that they were unsuccessful in their Olympic bid for 2012 (they made the final 12 but not the final 5). From their plans it seemed to me that the games could be of so much more benefit there than in London.

As a violinist I had played in Leipzig in 1985 during the Bach tercentenary celebrations and during my stay had gone to a service in St Thomas Church. It was a Sunday in Lent and the church was packed to hear, *inter alia*, a highly political sermon. Little did anyone suspect that some 4½ years later the Berlin Wall would be torn down and the whole Soviet and Eastern European systems collapse. When I returned with the ACE group at Easter in 1998 renovations were taking place on the distinctive massively angled roof and in the interior: renovations which continued until just a few days before the next big Bach anniversary in 2000 – 250 years since his death on 28th July 1750.

Leopold Mozart and his two children, Wolfgang Amadeus and Maria-Anna, by Louis Carrogis Carmontelle (1717–1806).

The church has never been seriously damaged by wars or conflict since Bach's time and contemporary engravings show the exterior almost exactly as we see it today. At the end of the nineteenth-century some of the Baroque interior was restored to its Gothic original. But the large organ loft at the west end remains essentially as it was (although the organ itself has of course been replaced). It is there that the performance takes place as it did in Bach's time, and it takes but slight imagination to see him there where a colleague observed him in the 1730s "playing the organ with both hands and feet most virtuosically, while controlling his vocal and instrumental forces, giving instantly the pitch and rhythm to any who erred".

We are the Association for Cultural Exchange. The exchange in almost every case involves an exchange of place and time. We travel to a different place and we imagine ourselves in a different age. A change of country means generally a different language, in both the literal and the wider metaphorical meaning of the word. Leipzig is German speaking, but Bach is quintessentially German in his musical language as well as in his mother tongue: in his restless desire to probe the very fundamentals of music and explore the potential of his often fragmentary musical material. C.P.E. Bach identified this last as his father's greatest musical gift. For Italian composers melody is paramount; for Bach and his German successors it is harmony and form. Neither is intrinsically better or worse but they represent different aspirations. To travel to different countries and to hear music in its original setting, which opportunity the tours offer, brings one closer, in my opinion, to the essential qualities of the composer and his work and enables a deeper appreciation – a cultural exchange.

One of the responsibilities I most enjoy in my work leading ACE tours is the freedom to plan the tours in every detail. ACE does not impose a "house style", and every tour leader will find his own way. It is (almost!) always a delight when I find past participants returning for another course. If they like me and what I have done it is likely the feeling will be mutual. Planning the tours starts at the stage of suggesting which festivals or performances to offer, and this presents various challenges. Festivals where the performances take place only at weekends, of which there are several in France, are fine for locals but no good for those who have paid to travel and want a week immersed in events. Russia is always problematic in that they do not announce their music programmes until a few weeks before the event; no time even to get visas, let alone make the hotel and flight reservations which often have to be done up to a year in advance. The cliché of Globalisation has affected music: the same performers, and sometimes the same programmes, which might be on offer in Vienna or Chicago can nowadays often be heard in London – so why travel? In proposing tours my "bottom line" is that the standard of music-making must be of the highest order: worth travelling for, worth spending precious money on. Some places are inextricably bound up with a particular composer and make for a special bond: Bach in Leipzig, Mozart in Salzburg (despite the irony of Mozart's personal detestation of Salzburg!), Sibelius in Finland, Haydn in Eisenstadt – every year one of the most joyous of festivals, the result I am sure of Haydn's joyous spirit. Both players and audience (including the ACE group) are happy to be immersed in Haydn's wonderful work in the place which he knew so well for his whole working life. The Baroque Music festival in Melk does not concentrate on any one composer, but is again the perfect match of place and period – Baroque music in one of the most spectacular Baroque complexes in Europe, and often with a surprising and richly rewarding off-the-beaten-track repertoire. Two festivals of chamber music – Kuhmo in Northern Finland, and Risør in Southern Norway – have been special for the very reason of their remoteness from any urban centres – ideal for chamber music. In Risør the unnumbered seating can involve a queue of 45 minutes or more before each concert. But far from being a chore, this has been stimulating in enabling us to get to know the local people queuing with us, asking questions, sharing knowledge and enthusiasms. And what delightful people the Norwegians are!

Highlights? Too many to mention, but most recently a Meistersinger to die for at the Met in New York, with the great James Morris as Hans Sachs. Five years ago Leif Ove Andsnes and Emmanuel Ax played fourhanded Mozart piano sonatas in a lunchtime recital of pure magic in Risør church. They dressed informally, played as friends, and communicated the sheer joy of making music. With 350 people the church was crammed full, and the tickets cost about £10 – they must be the only things in Norway that are cheap!

Sometimes, mercifully rarely, the eagerly awaited event does not live up to expectation. More often the opposite is true. Who would have thought that a lunchtime recital of trio sonatas by a young hitherto unknown Japanese group, a programme which promised a pleasant concert but no more, would be the highlight of last year's Melk festival, sending us all out in a state of euphoria. Ten years ago the young and then little known Berlin-based Artemis Quartet, in my opinion the finest string quartet in the world, played the Beethoven op. 132 quartet only, in an unforgettable concert (also in Risør church) which started at midnight and ended just before 1.00 a.m. Then there was the enormous joy and privilege of hearing the only just 18-year-old Yundi Li win the Chopin competition in Warsaw in 2000. At that competition one takes a formidable technique, which Yundi Li has in abundance, for granted, but he also has those qualities that elude so many: wonderful pedal control (not too much), a natural sounding rubato (so elusive in Chopin) and innate musicality. How strange, our ACE group reflected, that it takes an 18 year old from China to teach us how to play Chopin.

Although many festivals include daytime performances, it is still true that most performances take place in the evenings. This leaves the days free for more cultural exploration apart from music. In planning this aspect I try to give, over the week as a whole, an overview of the essential cultural life of the city or area – in modern jargon "where it comes from" or "what makes it tick". In a big city like St Petersburg, Vienna or New York (to name my three favourite cities) this is relatively easy. St Petersburg, despite being, at just over 300 years old, younger than several American cities, is more steeped in history – political, literary, musical, and architectural – than almost any other city I know. St Magnus festival in Orkney is at the furthest remove from a big city, but with its mix of music – from the most high-brow, old and new, to folk and local fiddlers – almost unbelievable archaeological treasures, some predating the pyramids, and wild, undisturbed and magical landscapes it has quickly become a favourite.

Planning these extra-musical aspects of the tours I have found immensely enjoyable and rewarding. In anticipation of a visit to Herman Melville's house "Arrowhead", near the Tanglewood site, I embarked, with considerable trepidation at its length, on my first reading of *Moby-Dick*. It is an obsessive book: written by an obsessive writer about obsession for obsessive readers. As anyone who has travelled with me during the last few years must know, it quickly obsessed me and became my favourite book of all time. It has also cost me a fortune in whale-watching journeys around the world! In those cultural areas the group and I learn together, but the exchange also takes place within the ACE groups. I have learned so much more from group members than they can ever have learned from me. Over the years there have been experts in geology, architecture, medieval manuscripts, international law, many aspects of medicine and countless other specialities. At dinnertime or in informal meetings conversation may take any turn, and it is by no means only the experts who provide food for thought as we tuck into our borsch or schnitzel.

The tours have many moments of deep seriousness, such as the Bach Passions with which I started this article, but they also turn on the other cultural aspects of the places we visit, on the various expertises and interests of the participants, and, oh yes, on fun! I do like to hear laughter. When all these work together then we really live up to our name in both long and short form: the Association for Cultural Exchange – ACE.

Oh, Vienna!

Humphrey Burton

HUMPHREY BURTON CBE was BBC Television's first Head of Music and Arts and a founder-member of London Weekend Television. He has worked alongside such illustrious names as Menuhin, Walton, Bernstein and Rattle and his biographies of Bernstein and Menuhin have become standard works. Humphrey has won four Emmies and two British Academy awards for his work as a film director.

Just down from Cambridge and on my first visit to Vienna, what impressed me most was that my taxi driver had a score of Beethoven's *Fidelio* in his jacket pocket. And when I dropped in for a beer in one of the historic Judenplatz's cellar bars, the resident trio were playing Schubert's *Unfinished Symphony* on violin, cello and … accordion (!) with all the colour and intensity of the Vienna Philharmonic. The year was 1957 and I was representing Britain's fledgling Youth and Music organisation at the World Congress of the Jeunesses Musicales. I was a rather impressionable young man which may explain why I fell in love with Christa Ludwig as she sang a radiant Cherubino in *The Marriage of Figaro*; this was a magically intimate production given in the Redoutensaal of the Imperial Palace. We were also taken to hear *Otello* at the State Opera; Karajan was conducting and the baritone singing Iago was Paul Schoeffler, a local favourite. The audience broke into the music to give him a huge ovation after his spine-chilling *Credo* but in the pit the maestro refused to stop, rightly so, since Verdi made no provision for any hold-up: for the next five minutes pandemonium reigned. Karajan won the battle of wills that night but he didn't last long as *Generalmusikdirektor*! It was my first experience of an opera house *skandal*!

Our musical congress of Vienna held a few earnest meetings at the Konzerthaus, the delightfully airy *Jugendstil* building that is Vienna's second concert hall. But the gathering was essentially about young people making music and having fun. To my bedazzled eyes the Austrian girls all seemed witty and beautiful, the men intelligent and progressive. Everybody was out to entertain the foreign visitors, an Austrian characteristic that still prevails. The top attractions for us were visits to the magnificent Benedictine abbey at Melk, dominating a bend in the Danube, and the ruined castle of Duernstein, where Richard Coeur de Lion was imprisoned on his way home from the Third Crusade. The excursion included a lazy trip on a Danube pleasure boat through the Wachau, marvelling at the neat vineyards that slope down from the hills to the river's edge. The discovery of Austrian wine gave almost as much pleasure as such culinary

Georges Prêtre conducts the Vienna Philharmonic Orchestra in Vienna's 'Goldener Musikvereinsaal.'

delicacies as the *wiener schnitzel* and the slabs of boiled beef the Viennese call *tafels-pitz*. (Emperor Franz Josef had it every day for lunch.) And once tasted who could forget the coffee with *schlagobers* (whipped cream)? I was hooked by Vienna's geography, too. The four-nation military occupation so vividly evoked by Carol Reed in *The Third Man* had ended only three years previously. In the Schwarzenbergplatz a road sign pointed to Budapest. Yes, the Iron Curtain was only a few miles down the road, indeed the Hungarians had had their traumatic run-in with the Soviets just one year prior to my visit. The city was shabby and still bore many scars from the Allied bombing but spirits were high and the sun shone every day.

My work for BBC TV (and later with Leonard Bernstein) has taken me back to Vienna almost every year since that idyllic first encounter. It was in Vienna that the BBC forged its first musical co-production with another country: a studio opera taped in two different languages with the same performers on successive days (*Susanna's Secret*) and then a documentary, *The Golden Ring*, still available on DVD, about the gramophone recording of Wagner's monumental epic, *The Ring*. The sessions were held in the complex of seedy ballrooms in the third district known as the Sofia Halls, the Sofiensaale (since destroyed by fire). To capture the performances of an international cast and the Philharmonic at full stretch we used Austrian TV's crack outside broadcast unit and imported a British film crew. The police were very co-operative and shut off whole streets when total silence was required. Georg Solti, the musical genius behind the operation, became a close friend and so did Decca's John Culshaw, who was my successor at the BBC. His team loved practical jokes. At the end of *Twilight of the Gods*, when Brunnhilde summons her horse and rides into the funeral pyre, they arranged for a real horse to be led on to the platform, much to the mirth of the entire orchestra and superstar soprano Birgit Nilsson. Luckily the steed, a thoroughbred racehorse, behaved itself. It was from the Decca "boys" that I learnt a bit of Viennese slang and also the best cafés and restaurants. There weren't too many attractive eating places in those days: the Dubrovnik hinted at the oriental spices originally imported by the Turks centuries previously, and the White Chimney Sweep (*Weissesrauchfangkehrer*), close to the house where Mozart died, had many cosy nooks where one could flirt in safety while enjoying the herrings *hausfrau-art* and the blueberry pancakes. The building with Mozart associations has, alas, been replaced by an ugly department store, but in compensation the recently restored Figarohaus, not far from the St Stephen's Cathedral, shows us how Mozart lived in the year he composed *Figaro*; it boasts a magnificent display of Mozartiana and you get an audio guide in the price of the ticket.

In 1970 the Viennese rolled out the red carpet for another in their massive portfolio of great composers, Ludwig van Beethoven – it was the bicentenary of his birth. I had the good fortune to be hired by CBS as producer/director of a two-hour "Special" called *Beethoven's Birthday* in which Leonard Bernstein narrated a biography, conducted

Fidelio and the Ninth Symphony and played solo in the first piano concerto in the Golden Hall of the Musikverein. So now I got to know another landmark in Viennese musical history, the Theater an der Wien, built just outside the old city walls by Mozart's librettist Emanuel Schikaneder (using the profits from *The Magic Flute*; Schikaneder was the first Papageno). Beethoven lodged there while composing his only opera. I filmed the new *Fidelio* production, which starred Gwyneth Jones and James King, and during the rehearsals managed to distinguish myself by setting fire to the brand new stage curtain with a rogue television light. That was a *skandal* I prefer to forget! Heaps of CBS dollars had to be deployed to buy our way back into the production, which I'm proud to say won an Emmy. We filmed many of the houses where Beethoven had lodged in his stormy life and my editor Mike Bradsell later assembled a brilliant montage in which he cut to a different flag-bedecked façade on every beat of the bar, using a chunk of the Scherzo from the Ninth. Breathtaking stuff! The best preserved of the *Beethovenwohnungen* is in Heiligenstadt, then a village and now a suburb in Vienna's 19th district. Here Beethoven, aged 31, wrote his famous testament, facing up to the fact that he was going deaf. He told his brothers that he had contemplated suicide, but love of life and the creative force he felt within him drove him onwards. (These days I'm allowed to play the piano in the museum (the first movement of the Moonlight sonata goes well) and then from a balcony in the courtyard I declaim the Testament to my ACE group.)

In 1971 Bernstein launched a new era in his illustrious career by signing with the Unitel film company to conduct a complete cycle of Mahler symphonies. I seemed to be playing Boswell to his Dr Johnson: my life, like his, took on a regular Viennese tinge with filming assignments twice a year for the next couple of decades. "Gloomy Gustav", as my family nicknamed him, was followed by symphonic cycles of Beethoven, Schumann, Brahms, Haydn, Sibelius and Mozart, not to mention liberal helpings of Bernstein's own compositions, which of course he adored hearing played by the world's top orchestra. Top orchestra? Well, he once confessed that despite his close orchestral links with New York and Israel and London (to name but three) when push came to shove Vienna took the crown because of their total commitment and love of the music. "I operate on love", he explained to me, and he responded with music-making of a rare order. So I got to love the Golden Hall, with its gorgeous acoustic, its sinuous and sexy caryatids who hold up the balcony and its bars where both coffee and open sandwiches are as tasty during rehearsals as they are during concert intervals. And to continue in this epicurean vein, it was in the seventies that I learnt to love the Hotel Sacher, just across the road from the opera house. Okay, the staff could be obsequious. But they know the meaning of service and their restaurants are, well, classy.

The summit of my Musikverein experience was in 1987, when I was first invited by ORF to direct the worldwide telecast of the annual New Year's Day concert of waltzes and polkas. The Philharmonic professors bestowed the ultimate honour of presiding over this colourful event upon their ailing ex-chief conductor, Herbert von Karajan. (Since Bernstein and Karajan were allegedly great rivals, it was quite a coup for me to get the job: I was rather outrageously likened to the Viennese courtesan who was said to have slept with both Kennedy and Khruschev at their 1961 summit meeting.) Karajan was close on 80 and could hardly walk because of horrendous back pain but he propped himself up at the rostrum with a polo stick topped by a bicycle saddle and a very good time was had by one and all. One of his programmatic innovations was to invite a singer to perform along with the orchestra and Karajan caused a furore in conservative circles by selecting the black American soprano Kathleen Battle, who dashed off *Voices of Spring* with exquisite verve. But I almost preferred the Anna Polka, because at the maestro's suggestion I was allowed to film the horses being exercised at the famous Spanish Riding School as a visual accompaniment to the orchestra. (It was quite a feat to keep their elegant rearings in synch on what was a genuinely "live" show!) Also in the programme were the excellent dancers of the State Opera company and they performed (live again) in the grand reception rooms of the Schoenbrunn palace. So during the rehearsals I had the chance to wander round that magnificent building, which to my mind is preferable to Versailles, enlivened as it is by the special exhibition devoted to "Cissi", the tantalisingly beautiful wife of the Emperor Franz Joseph who was (according to which gossip you believe) a spoilt-brat princess or the first feminist. Turning back to Karajan for a moment: on the Ringstrasse opposite the Hotel Bristol you can find the Karajan Centre, devoted to music in general and to the maestro's manifold achievements in particular. Well worth a visit, as is the Haus der Musik, in nearby Seilerstaette, where the Vienna Philharmonic has installed the latest audio-visual technologies and interactive experiences to bring you closer to the holy art.

Waltzes and operetta melodies were also at the heart of an alternative New Year's programme I made a few years ago for an enterprising Canadian impresario; the show was taped in advance in Vienna and on January 1st screened simultaneously in big city cinemas all over North America. The music director, Peter Guth, had studied for three years with Oistrakh in Moscow and was a violinist-conductor in the Johann Strauss tradition. Peter is a man of the utmost charm as well as virtuosity and he's blessed with a viola-playing wife, Apollonia, who is not only a first-class musician in her own right but also a cook in a million. Her *Sacher-torte* and *apfel-struedel* are irresistible. The Guths live opposite the house where Schubert was born; it's now an excellent little museum. In recent years I have got them to play an exhilarating selection of *Wienermusik* – two violins, viola and double bass: dances by Lanner and the Strauss family in the museum's tiny concert hall, after which we all repair over the road to the Guth apartment and enjoy Apollonia's epic afternoon tea. That's just one example of how my Viennese experiences over half a century have spilled over into the itinerary for the week-long ACE tours I've been leading for the past few years. Hugh Barnes challenged me to devise my own programme, interlocking with prime events from the city's annual music festival. Of course there isn't the time to fit everything in, but we visit the opera houses and the Hofburg (the riding school is an option); we go out to the Vienna Woods for a meal and a stroll where Beethoven found inspiration for his Pastoral, and we visit the monastery of Heiligenkreuz, close to the shooting lodge, now a chapel, at Mayerling, where the Crown Prince shot his mistress and several hours later turned the gun on himself – perhaps you've seen Kenneth Macmillan's balletic version of that very disturbing tale! Art demands a place in our wanderings: in my opinion no visit is complete without an hour spent with the fabulous Breughels in the Kunsthistorisches Museum; others prefer the Belvedere, featuring Klimt and Schiele, or the drawings at the Albertina or the varied delights of the new Museum Quartier. We usually hear the Vienna Boys Choir in concert at the Musikverein and enjoy lunch at a secular temple called Café Demel. One morning is spent exploring the inner city and the Mozart museum, with maybe, on the way out to Heligenstadt, a visit to Joseph Haydn's town house; he added a second storey with the profits of his visit to London. Finally, on our way out to the airport for the return flight, we round things off by dropping in on the central cemetery so we can pay our respects to Vienna's musical greats in their final resting place.

Saint Petersburg

Colin Bailey

COLIN BAILEY gained his PhD in art history at Nottingham University and has held a succession of top posts: head librarian at the Barber Institute at Birmingham University, keeper of British art at Liverpool's Walker Art Gallery and head of the Department of Humanities at Edinburgh College of Art. A trained linguist, Colin is one of only two westerners to have been awarded a special permit to conduct tours in St Petersburg's Hermitage Museum.

Of all the many Study Tours I have had the privilege to lead for ACE over the past decade, no destination, I think, has quite the same variety or degree of magic as St Petersburg. Founded by Peter the Great in 1703 as his "Window on the West", it remains too European to be Russian and yet too Russian to be European, and in this paradox lies its great fascination. So enchanting is the city that many first-time visitors have expressed the desire to return. Accordingly, ACE now offers an entirely different Study Tour entitled *Unexplored St Petersburg*.

No trip to St Petersburg, of course, would be complete without at least one visit to the Hermitage, whose complex of buildings comprises Bartolomeo Rastrelli's Winter Palace, Vallin de la Mothe's Small Hermitage, the Large Hermitage by Yury Velten and the New Hermitage designed in the nineteenth century by Leo von Klenze. It ranks as one of the greatest and most famous museums in the world, with as many different departments as the Louvre and a collection of almost four million objects. In addition to the Gold Room, with its fabulous collection of Scythian artefacts, during three visits to the Hermitage we concentrate our attention on the old masters. These range from Simone Martini to Canaletto in Italy (there are two Leonardos and a splendid early Caravaggio), from Robert Campin to Rubens and Van Dyck in Flanders, and include an outstanding selection of works by Rembrandt and all of the most famous seventeenth-century Dutch and French masters. On a separate occasion we also study the celebrated Impressionist and Post-Impressionist pictures (including the so-called "Hidden Impressionists") and the unrivalled collection of early pictures by Picasso and Matisse purchased by the discerning and far-sighted Sergei Shchukin and Ivan Morozov. My treasured licence to guide in the Hermitage permits us to explore at our leisure.

The second great picture collection in St Petersburg is the State Russian Museum, housed in Carlo Rossi's Mikhailovsky Palace. Opened to the public in 1898, it boasts (along with the Tretyakov Gallery in Moscow) the finest array of Russian art in the world, from

The Hermitage, St Petersburg.

twelfth-century Novgorod icons to twentieth-century Constructivism. Perennially popular are the nineteenth-century works of the social realist Ilya Repin (famous for his *Barge-Haulers on the Volga),* the marine painter Ivan Aivasovsky (whose masterpiece is the epic *Ninth Wave),* and the landscapists Ivan Skiskin and Arkhip Kuindzhi. It is so rare to see so many Russian nineteenth-century pictures of such exceptional quality that a visit to the State Russian Museum is invariably a highlight.

St Petersburg is also justly celebrated for the splendour of its town and country residences, from the grand town houses of the Russian nobility to the spectacular Imperial summer palaces. The earliest of these to survive in the city itself, grander even than Peter's Summer Palace and the first of its kind on Vasilevsky Island, is the gabled yellow and white Menshikov Palace, built in the early eighteenth century by Tsar's favourite Alexander Menshikov. On the Moyka embankment not far away is the colonnaded Yusupov Palace, where Glinka's opera *Ivan Susanin* was premiered in 1836 in the intimate private theatre and Grigori Rasputin violently done to death in December 1916. In the Sheremetev Palace, home to a museum documenting this family's contribution to the musical life of the city, we regularly enjoy a private performance of largely eighteenth-century Russian court music (unperformed in Soviet times and therefore little known).

In the countryside to the south of the city is the opulent Catherine Palace at Tsarskoe Selo, designed by Rastrelli in 1752 for the Tsarina Elisabeth and named in honour of her mother Catherine I. Here are a reconstruction of the famous Amber Room by Andreas Schluter, a gift to Peter the Great from Friedrich Wilhelm I of Prussia; a hall of mirrors to rival Versailles; some of the finest eighteenth-century interiors; a mind-blowing enfilade; and one of Russia's very first landscaped gardens (complete with follies), commissioned by Catherine the Great in 1768.

Twenty minutes further south lies Pavlovsk, an elegant Palladian mansion by that most elusive of expatriate Scottish architects Charles Cameron. The lands were presented to Grand Duke Paul (Pavel in Russian) by Catherine the Great in 1777 and work on the house began in 1780. In 1789 wings were added to Cameron's central block by Vincenzo Brenna. The extensive grounds, where troika rides can be had in the winter, are in the style of the then fashionable English garden.

The third of the great palaces, commanding magnificent views of the Baltic, is Peterhof, built as "befitting the very highest of monarchs" by Peter the Great after his defeat of the Swedes at Poltava in 1709. It is here that St Petersburg families flock in good weather. Jean Baptiste Le Blond's original palace was completed in 1721 and was transformed first, in the reign of Elisabeth, by Rastrelli and afterwards, under Catherine the Great, by Velten, whose Throne Room provides the perfect setting for portraits of the Imperial family. The Grand Cascade leads down through a series of gilded bronze sculptures, fountains and water jets to the Gulf of Finland. The gravity-operated fountains are reckoned among the most spectacular in the world.

Scattered throughout the countryside and the city alike, countless monasteries, cathedrals and churches bear witness to the strength and resurgence of the Russian Orthodox faith. Of the churches, my personal favourite is the strawberry-pink and white Neo-Gothic fairy-tale confection of Chesma, designed by Velten and completed in 1780. Among the cathedrals, pride of place in my affections goes to "the sailors' church" of St Nicholas, built between 1753 and 1762 by Savva Chevakinsky (there is a memorial here to the victims of the *Kutsk* submarine disaster). Ice-blue and white with gleaming golden domes, it is as beautiful outside as within, especially seen against the snow of a Russian winter. The interior is divided into two churches, one above the other. The vaulted lower church, intended for everyday use, is festooned with icons and lit by flickering icon lamps, chandeliers and candles. Few things are as stirring as an evening service here, when the sonorous Orthodox liturgy is chanted and sung by the priests in an atmosphere heavy with incense.

At the south-eastern end of Nevsky Prospekt, close to the majestic Neva river, stands the imposing Alexander Nevsky Monastery, founded by Peter the Great. There are fewer than a dozen monks left here but the gardens are beautifully maintained and unforgettable services are guaranteed. Nearby are the Tikhvin and Lazarus cemeteries. The larger and more recent of these is the Tikhvin Cemetery, where many of Russia's most famous composers are buried. Elaborate and occasionally exotic gravestones mark the final resting place of Borodin, Glinka, Mussorgsky, Rimsky-Korsakov and Tchaikovsky. In the Lazarus Cemetery are buried some of St Petersburg's greatest architects, including Quarenghi, Rossi and Voronikhin.

Nevsky Prospekt itself (simply Nevsky to the locals) is arguably Russia's most famous avenue; it is certainly St Petersburg's major artery and shopping street. Laid out early in the eighteenth century, it stretches for three miles and connects the Alexander Nevsky Monastery with Andrey Zakharov's imposing Admiralty Building. Along the northwestern section alone there is enough of interest, in a profusion of architectural styles, to detain the curious visitor for days: the Literary Café (formerly Wolf and Beranger), where Pushkin dined before his fatal duel in 1837; the Stroganov Palace of 1753 (one of the oldest on the street – and, yes, connected with beef Stroganov); the tongue-twisting Beloselskiy-Belozerskiy Palace built by Andrey Stakenschneider from 1847 to 1848; the House of Books (formerly the Singer Sewing Machine Company building); Marian Lyalevich's Fashion House; and, last but not least, Voronikhin's Kazan Cathedral, partly inspired by St Peter's and especially by Bernini's colonnade. The presence nearby of a Dutch church, an Armenian church, a Lutheran church and the Catholic Church of Saint Catherine explains Nevsky's description in former times as the "Street of Tolerance".

There was a time not so very long ago when there were scarcely any recognisable shop signs the length of Nevsky. Nowadays, western designer names and restaurant chains proliferate. Even the Literary Café has partially sold out to Kentucky Fried Chicken! However, there are still many institutions that have retained their Russian identity and where one is unlikely to rub shoulders with too many tourists. These include the unbelievably vast department store of Gostiny Dvor (though this too now houses branches of a few foreign shops); Yesileev's food emporium, occupying Gavriil Baranovskiy's opulent Style Moderne building, complete with stained glass; and the perennially popular Passazh Arcade, first opened in 1848. Reliably good vodka and excellent caviar (including beluga and sevruga) are both to be had at reasonable prices at Yesileev's and at several places within Gostiny Dvor.

There is also a thriving café culture in St Petersburg and no shortage of excellent hotels and restaurants serving traditional Russian cuisine. Among the best in the modest price range are the 1913 Restaurant, the Behind the Scenes Restaurant, the Tchaikovsky Restaurant and the Austeria in the grounds of St Peter and St Paul Fortress. ACE visits them all. Russian food is very good: try *zakuski,* a variety of salty hors d'oeuvres; *borshch,* of course, but also *solyanka,* meat or fish soup with a decidedly spicy taste; *pelmeny* (my favourite), originally from Siberia and rather like Chinese wonton; and savoury *pirozhki,* small pastries typically stuffed with fried cabbage, curd cheese, meat and rice or mushrooms. Desserts are also good, though often very rich, and the best Russian ice-cream second only to Italian. Clear and flavoured vodkas (especially *pertsovka,* with red chilli pepper pods!) and old vodka (*starka*) should be sampled, as well as wines from Georgia and Moldova and *kvas,* a slightly alcoholic beverage made from rye and barley, which is also drunk by children. But I'm getting carried away! Revenons a nos moutons.

St Petersburg is also renowned for its world famous Mariinsky Theatre (also known as the Kirov). Presently Dominique Perrault's Mariinsky II is being built on the opposite bank of the Kryukov canal and will be connected to the original theatre by an elevated bridge. There is at least one visit on each ACE Study Tour to the Mariinsky to see either opera or ballet performances. Another unforgettable highlight for ballet aficionados is a visit to the Vaganova Ballet Academy, the world's finest ballet school in the classical tradition. Founded in 1738, it produced such famous dancers as Anna Pavlova, Vaslav Nijinsky, Galina Ulanova and Rudolf Nureyev and continues to supply the Mariinsky. ACE has recently awarded scholarships to two of the Vaganova's most promising and deserving young dancers and has presented encyclopaedias of ballet and dance to the Academy library. Through our friendship and connections with Olga Obramova, we are regularly granted the very rare privilege of attending dance classes taught by one or other of the Academy professors.

We are indebted to Olga for many things, not least for her great organisational skills and her provision of outstanding local guides who ensure that we see all the most important historical sights, from the city's origins with the Saints Peter and Paul Fortress to the Monument to the Heroic Defenders of Leningrad, a poignant reminder of the privations suffered during the siege of the Second World War. We make a point of paying our respects here (as do thousands of Russian newly-weds) on our way to Pulkov airport at the end of every tour. We carry home memories of a friendly and hospitable people, of an elegant city bearing the architectural hallmarks of Rossi and Rastrelli, of a metropolis rich in cultural traditions but courageously embracing change.

Belle Epoque Istanbul

Peter Clark

PETER CLARK is a Middle East specialist and former Cultural Attaché at the British Council in Damascus. He is a fluent speaker of Arabic. Peter has also recently edited a book with Michael Foot on the unsung heritage of Britain, entitled The Lefties' Guide to Britain.

I first went to Istanbul in 1962. I returned occasionally during the next three decades but my love affair with the city began only in 1993 when I took my son, Gabriel, then aged 12, to the city. We stayed at the Pera Palas. Gabriel was a fan of James Bond films and we toured the city locating sites that appeared in the film *From Russia with Love*. We found five, and enjoyed discovering one huge deception in the film: the Russian Consulate General is not, and never was, immediately above any of the Byzantine cisterns. That visit also deeply affected Gabriel. Eleven years later, in 2004, with a qualification in teaching English as a foreign language, he moved to Istanbul. He has lived there ever since, and is married to a Turkish girl to whom he says, most gallantly, "Coming to Istanbul was the second best thing I have done in my life." His parents are equally delighted for it gives us an excuse to spend time in the most wonderful city of the world.

Istanbul has outstanding monuments of two historic empires. I have constantly enjoyed visiting and revisiting St Sophia, Topkapi, the Sinan mosques, the City Walls and the smaller monuments. In more recent years I have been fascinated by the last years of the Ottoman Empire. We were taught that nineteenth-century Turkey was an oppressive regime, a civilisation in decline. The art and architecture was a bastard hotchpotch of styles. But as I have looked more closely at that period, I find that the art and architecture reflect the creative multiculturalism of the city.

Many of the most prominent buildings of the nineteenth century were the work of one remarkable Armenian family, the Balians. Over the years four generations built mosques, barracks, villas, churches and palaces. Their most amazing work was the Dolmabahce Palace, built in the 1850s by Garabed Balian, with his son, Nicogos, in charge of the interior decoration. Wrought iron gates facing the road are crowned, in the words of one architectural historian, Michael Levey, by "sugar-icing crenellations and urn-like protuberances, [and] have the fantasy height and effect of Hollywood-Oriental style, whether for a film or a film-star's home. Marble Arch and the Arc de Triomphe shrivel by comparison to insignificance. The Balian family appears almost inebriated by their opportunity…" (*The World of Ottoman Art*, London, 1975).

'Beethoven in the Harem', painted by the last Khalifa, Abdulmecid. The painting shows two women and a man playing a trio together. Abdulmecid paints himself into the picture as an observer of the central scene. A Beethoven score has been tossed carelessly onto the floor.

Architectural historians have been impressed by the showmanship, but have shown a barely suppressed disapproval of the Balians' eclecticism. They borrowed from everywhere. The Ortakoy Mosque (Nicogos Balian, 1854) has slender minarets that sprout Corinthian capitals immediately beneath the balconies. The Hamidiye Mosque outside the Yildiz Palace (Sarkis Balian, 1886) has Gothic windows. Nineteenth- and early twentieth-century Istanbul also attracted architects from the rest of Europe. From Britain came Charles Barry, the architect of the Houses of Parliament, who designed the British Embassy for the great nineteenth-century Ambassador, Stratford Canning. G. E. Street, who designed the Old Bailey, was the architect of the Crimean Memorial Church. An Italian, Raimondo D'Aronco, experimented with Art Nouveau, designing much of Sultan Abdulhamit's Yildiz Palace as well as villas along the Bosphorus. A Frenchman, Alexandre Vallaury, designed two buildings that symbolised the economic links between Istanbul and western Europe – the Ottoman Bank in Galata, and the Office of the Public Debt Administration, now a secondary school, near Topkapi. The German August Jachmund designed Sirkeci railway station.

Much of the most interesting urban development throughout the last century of the Ottoman Empire was between Taksim Square and the Galata Tower – on either side of the narrow pedestrianised road, now called Istiklal Caddesi but, in earlier times, the Grande Rue de Pera. In recent years there has been a new civic pride in the architectural and historical museum that this road represents. If we raise our eyes above the ground floor shop level we see a huge variety of styles and revived styles. Indeed one building, Elhamra Pasaji (built in 1923) blends three revived styles – Classical, Islamic and Lombardy Gothic. Some buildings have recently been lost. A few cinemas and theatres have gone, including the Saray theatre, where Louis Armstrong once played. Some have been sensitively restored, such as the Markiz Pastry Shop, that once served Sarah Bernhardt, with its Art Nouveau faience of the four seasons: it still serves sumptuous cakes and ice-creams. Others, such as D'Aronco's Botter Building, are badly in need of tender loving care. Just as a century ago the Grande Rue de Pera was architecturally an international street, so today Istiklal Caddesi is an international commercial mall. Some of the ground floor shop fronts could be in New York, Munich, Paris or London with such global brand names as Accessorize, Starbucks and McDonald's.

The cinemas, theatres, music halls and cake shops show how Istiklal Caddesi has been a highway of international hedonism. The internationalism did not exclude the people of the Empire. The owners of the property along Istiklal Caddesi were citizens of the Ottoman Empire. Suriye Pasaji (Syria Passage) and Halep Pasaji (Aleppo Passage) reflect the Syrian Arab provinces. Galatasaray school was the major secondary school for the upper classes of the Empire. Much of the property was owned by Muslim Turks. The royal family were patrons of the shops along the Grande Rue. One shop was of particular interest. In the nineteenth and early twentieth centuries the Istanbul elite were great lovers of Western classical music. Franz Liszt came to Istanbul and stayed with a family called Commendiger, who had a music store. The shop is gone but a plaque commemorates Liszt's time here, at 19 Nuruziya Sokak, just off Istiklal Caddesi.

The Commendigers supplied the Ottoman court with the instruments and sheet scores they wanted. Sultan Abdulaziz wrote marches and dances. In 1867 he was the first Sultan to pay a state visit to France and Britain. In London the Prince of Wales gave a reception at Marlborough House for the Sultan, during which the band of the Grenadier Guards, conducted by Dan Godfrey, played the Sultan's La Gondola Barcarolle.

The Ottoman Empire ended in stages. It suffered military defeat in the First World War. The head of the Imperial family had combined the political role of Sultan and the religious role of Khalifa (Caliph). These titles were stripped from them piecemeal. The Sultanate was abolished in 1923, but the Caliphate lingered on a further twelve months. The last Khalifa – Abdulmecid – was a son of the musical Sultan Abdulaziz. The son was politically liberal, a man of deep Islamic faith and intimately familiar with the languages and cultural developments of western Europe. In his youth and early manhood he was kept away from the city centres, and had a villa built by Raimondo D'Aronco at Camlica on the Asian side of the Bosphorus. Abdulmecid was a talented musician and an even more talented painter. One of his most fascinating paintings is in the National Painting and Sculpture Gallery at Besiktas, on the Bosphorus near Dolmabahce. It is called 'Beethoven in the Harem' and shows two women and a man playing a trio together. Abdulmecid paints himself into the picture as an observer of the central scene. A Beethoven score has been tossed carelessly onto the floor. In the background can be seen an equestrian statue of Sultan Abdulaziz – designed by an English sculptor, specially commissioned by Abdulmecid – which can now be seen in Beylerbey Palace. One of the political points Abdulmecid was making in the painting is gender equality. Both sexes participate in chamber music and there is no leader. The picture also illustrates the painter's devotion to German culture – he also did a painting of 'Goethe in the Harem'.

Enough has been said to show how an examination of what we may call Belle Epoque Istanbul undermines stereotypes of the last days of the Turkish Empire. One of the many pleasures of devising and leading tours for ACE Study Tours is the interaction with the participants. The latter are usually well travelled and well read. Often some participants have a specific expertise from which the tour director can draw. For the most part we have all been brought up with conventionally negative views of the "sick man of Europe", the "decline of the Ottoman Empire" and "the terrible Turk", but are ready to reconsider received views. And so the most enjoyable ACE tours I have been on, such as Belle Epoque Istanbul, have consisted of a shared intellectual adventure in which we all look at places, people and buildings with sceptical eyes, seeing things we may previously have overlooked, and interpreting anew what we see with independent judgements.

Museums: va va voom!

Marina Vaizey

MARINA VAIZEY, a native of
New York City, has lived in England
since 1959. She was formerly the
art critic for the Financial Times
and the Sunday Times and editor
of the Art Quarterly and Review.
Marina has curated numerous
exhibitions and has written several
books, including The Artist as
Photographer and Great Women
Collectors. She has also been a
judge for the Turner Prize and
a trustee of such institutions as
the Imperial War Museum and
the South Bank. She is currently
a trustee of the Association for
Cultural Exchange.

Louis Sullivan (1856-1924) the gifted, formidable, philosophical and troubled architect of Chicago's outstanding turn of the century skyscrapers also wrote extensively about architecture. His aphorism, form follows function, is his best known remark. Not that he necessarily followed it himself, as can be seen from his use of decoration. But just as pithy and thought provoking is his aphorism that "As you are, so are your buildings. And as your buildings, so are you." Sullivan always emphasised the spiritual and emotional content of architecture.

Buildings literally embody a view of how to live and work. Nowhere is this truer than in the multitudes of recent cultural buildings, which seem to encapsulate competitive aspirations on regional and national scales.

I have been following this phenomenon for decades, as a student, a visitor, a museum trustee, a traveller, an ACE passenger, and even an ACE lecturer. Should museums be spectacles, or reserved, austere guardians of high culture? Infotainment or secular cathedrals?

As in so much of the past half century, America started the trend. In 1959, a few blocks uptown from the Metropolitan Museum, on Fifth Avenue, facing Central Park, the oddest building opened in an area which is now known as Museum Mile: the most famous architect in America, Frank Lloyd Wright, had designed the new Guggenheim Museum. A coiled inverted building with an internal six-story ramp, with a greater circumference at the top than at its base, it was the first museum spectacular, and indeed first building spectacular, of the post-war period. To some it looked like a rather strange car park; to others, it was simply a great building, whatever it meant. Endlessly discussed, analysed and criticised, and endlessly photographed, it captured the public imagination.

The Guggenheim Museum, Bilbao.

It was no accident that this iconic building was a museum: cultural buildings, including at times those for universities, have for the past half century and more taken far more risks (which have not always worked) than commercial buildings. They, after all, do not have to rent their spaces out, or be constrained by wholly economic considerations. Although, to digress, occasionally developers and corporations will do the same – build an eyecatching building – such as the Gherkin (Norman Foster) and the Ark (Ralph Erskine) in London. And if cultural buildings do not rent themselves out as office space, museums and galleries are often for hire for commercial launches and private parties: the Metropolitan's wing that houses the Temple of Dendur is particularly popular, as is the Natural History Museum in London. And cultural buildings have to entice visitors. The unattended museum is unlikely to find the funding and the gifts that are needed to sustain its vitality. The public success of Tate Modern has changed the climate for modern art in Britain, and attracted the major funding and acquisitions that it needs, although, as both ambition and costs escalate, never enough. But, again, it is no accident that Tate Modern announced a £200 million extension to coincide with the London Olympics, for which it is confident it will find the funding.

Museums and galleries will have private and foundation subsidy, which they need on an ongoing basis; sometimes they immortalise individual backers and collectors (in Britain alone Ashmole, Fitzwilliam, Walker, Lever, Cartwright, Courtauld, Tate, Horniman, Barber, Hunter, to name but a few); and governments, both national and regional, will see them as loss leaders, enhancing the reputation of the host cities and bringing in tourists who will contribute to the economy.

Almost forty years later, in Bilbao, Spain, another Guggenheim opened (1997) designed by another American architect, Frank Gehry, and became an instant worldwide success, energising the art world but even more transforming a depressed post-industrial city into a major tourist destination, providing economic and social benefits.

And both Guggenheims of course have the added advantage of being strikingly photogenic, emblems of the host city.

Thus the post-war period has seen in the West, and now worldwide, an unprecedented outpouring of original, idiosyncratic, and striking buildings dedicated to culture. Yes, there are now new and amazing music halls and opera houses, but museums are a special case for several reasons. First, they house collections. These collections are themselves often identified with their surrounding culture. Indeed at times they define it: for example the Van Gogh Museum in Amsterdam, two post-war buildings joined together, the first by Gerrit Rietveld, the second by Kisho Kurosawa, 1999. Or the Renzo Piano/Richard Rogers Pompidou Centre (1977) in Paris, perhaps the most startling building of its decade.

Second, unlike opera houses and concert halls, museums are now multi-functional, even 18 hour-a-day buildings. They can be and often are open late, and are usually open at least six, if not seven days a week. They have auditoria; they run festivals, concerts, symposia, extensive educational programmes, and film seasons. They have cafés and restaurants which are often rated in restaurant guides (the Guggenheim Bilbao runs a gourmet restaurant where you can observe business people having long lunches who probably never visit the collections).

For a comparatively small fee, or even for no admission charge, you can spend the day: there was a very effective, even notorious, ad done by Saatchi's for the Victoria and Albert in the 1980s, describing the century-old museum as "an ace café with quite a nice museum attached". They have extensive programmes for Friends. A museum can become the 21st century equivalent of the market place, a centrally located gathering place, which also has some of the functions of a secular cathedral. We may be entertained. We may also worship at the altar of art, as we know art is supposed to be inspirational and uplifting at its highest, or at least just plain enjoyable.

Museums and galleries have become destination events, as well as economic catalysts. Guggenheim Bilbao and Tate Modern, housed in Southwark, one of London's poorer boroughs, publish economic analyses showing the positive effect the galleries have on their neighbourhood and city. Bilbao claims that the Guggenheim earned more than it cost to build in its very first year of operation. Tate Modern is now the leading cultural asset of Britain. Its visitor figures are greater than even the British Museum. Property developers are building as though there is no tomorrow in its immediate neighbourhood.

Perhaps one of the most extreme examples is the totally amazing engineering feat of the Quadracci Pavilion as an entrance for the medium rank Milwaukee Art Museum, Milwaukee, Wisconsin. Designed by the Valencian born engineer architect Santiago Calatrava, it featured on the cover of Time magazine in 2001 as the Building of the Year. Facing the vast Lake Michigan, it is a light-filled lobby with external wings, which raise and lower, as big as a Boeing airplane. It has been described as "a spectacular building that has nothing to do with the display of art and everything to do with getting crowds to come to the museum". I have an architecture fan friend who flew from New York to Milwaukee just for the day to see the Pavilion, and came back mightily impressed, but with no views on the Art Gallery and its collections. Is the architecture now more important than the art?

Well, yes and no. The MAM is a case in point. The galleries were upgraded, and a new shop, vital for its earning power, was encased in the new pavilion. Milwaukee has been able to attract more and better travelling exhibitions. Special exhibitions are vital for sustaining interest and visitor figures. Visitor figures in turn are persuasive in attracting public and private funding.

So everybody's doing it. Scores, hundreds, even perhaps thousands of museums have been and are being redone, renewed and newly created. Some are refurbishments and expansions of existing galleries. Others are adaptations of warehouses, factories, banks, post offices, libraries, railway stations.

The Asian Art Museum of San Francisco has been rehoused, in an adaptation by Gae Aulenti, in a building that was once the major library. Tate Modern is famously in a revamped defunct powerstation. The Baltic in Gateshead was once a Rank flour mill. The DIA Foundation in Beacon, New York is in a factory. Donald Judd's Chinati Foundation is an old Army base in West Texas; MassMoca is a series of adapted textile factories. The Geffen Contemporary in Los Angeles is a police car garage adapted by Frank Gehry. The Musée d'Orsay in Paris was once a railway station, as is the contemporary art space in Berlin, the Hamburger Bahnhof. Lyons has converted a slaughterhouse into a modern art complex.

And still others are new builds. The starriest are currently the 1997 Getty in Los Angeles (Richard Meier) and the Guggenheim Bilbao, and the de Young (Herzog and de Meuron) in San Francisco.

Overwhelmed as we might be by so much to see, so many places to visit, we might think enough is enough. Yet ever more new museums are on site, and on the planning board. We might soon be visiting Dubai and the Emirates to see museums of architectural distinction; Abu Dhabi is proposing a museum island to house new builds which will be branches of the Louvre and the Guggenheim. Arousing controversy in both the museum world and France, they are paying 600 million euros for the franchise. The Hermitage is doubling in size and has outposts in London, Amsterdam, Las Vegas and Berlin. China and Japan are building museums almost as though they have just discovered the very concept; several decades ago Japanese collections accessible to the public often were to be found housed in department stores. Now their finest architects have been designing exquisite dedicated buildings throughout the country. In the process of this museum explosion, homegrown architects have become international starchitects.

Culture is in, in a big way.

For the traveller, there is now hardly a great city or significant town without a collection of note in a building of interest, indeed often several. The critical dialogue which has increasingly surrounded these new manifestations is complicated with no clear answers. What do we want museums for, how populist should they be, how much does the building outshine its contents, how to balance the allure of the jewel box itself with the jewels it contains, how much is the museum an engine of social change, how to balance our notions of access and inclusion, and indeed education, with the need to care, preserve and display the actual collection, are all urgent questions for the staff of museums and their funders.

One thing is indisputable however. Museums and galleries are increasingly being used as windows on the world. This is typified by the British Museum, one of the three great universal museums in the world (the others being the Louvre and the Metropolitan). The British Museum is building on more than 250 years of international connections to increase alliances with other countries and cultures in co-operative ventures. Its archaeologists and specialists bravely went into war-torn Iraq to help their colleagues, and the museum has recently re-emphasised Islamic art, both ancient and contemporary, in an attempt to increase both appreciation and understanding.

We may travel to Barcelona for Catalan art, Picasso and Miro; but for Barcelona, the expansion of museums and exhibition spaces has meant an increasing internationalism. We now see the world of art coming to Barcelona in their new Museum of Contemporary Art (Richard Meier) and the superb Caixa Forum, a converted art nouveau textile factory.

In many ways, the health of museums reflects the health of the societies that house them. In this first decade there have been significant losses too: because they are treasure houses, they are the first to be looted and destroyed in war-torn areas, or altered for political purposes.

But in much of the world, through the astonishing and increasing wealth of museums and galleries, there are ever more possibilities for learning to appreciate our own culture, and those of the world around us. For the price of a trip to your nearest city, or London underground ticket, train to Liverpool, Manchester, Edinburgh, Glasgow, St Ives, Eurostar to Paris, flight to New York, Helsinki, Seattle, Shanghai, Madrid, Amsterdam, Toronto, Copenhagen, Vienna, Tokyo and scores and scores of other destinations, endless opportunities are ours.

We are living in a new museum age.

Danish Design

Paul Brooke Barnes

PAUL BROOKE BARNES is General Secretary of the Association for Cultural Exchange. After completing his PhD at University College London, he worked for a number of years as a strategic analyst for the Ministry of Defence, investigating the causes and resolution of conflict. In addition to his many scientific interests he has a passion for 20th century design and architecture.

I didn't realise it at the time, but, looking back, I first fell under the spell of Danish design when I was about eight or nine years old. My mother being a Dane, family holidays were often spent in Denmark and at some point during our stay we would make the journey from the surrounding towns and suburbs where most Danes live, our relatives being no exception, to the centre of Copenhagen. The walls may be gone, but the medieval heart of the city is still clear from a cursory glance at the map. Just look for the sequence of lakes, once marking the outer walls, running from Tivoli around the city to the Natural History Museum and National Gallery, not forgetting the Hirschprung Gallery, which houses a small but surprisingly comprehensive collection of Danish art, including a roomful of the most wonderful paintings by Skagen artist P. S. Krøyer. The museum was funded by one of the twin vices of tobacco and alcohol, in this case tobacco. The Danes remain copious consumers of both, but the results of all this indulgence are not at all bad, as anyone who has had the pleasure of visiting the Ny Carlsberg Glyptotek, one of the world's great art collections, will testify. Named after and funded by a scion of the brewing family, it is positioned next door to the famous Tivoli gardens, and both are built on space made available by the demolition of the old city walls. Opposite, you will see the city hall and square, and it is here that you will find the beginning of Strøget, Europe's longest pedestrian street. Halfway along you will come to Illums Bolighus, designed in 1961 by architect Kay Kørbing, not just a shop but a Danish institution, and an important port of call for any self-respecting Dane returning home from abroad in the 1960s and 1970s. The building was then, and remains to a lesser extent today, a treasure trove of Danish design. In its heyday, less a bastion of consumerism and more a temple of modern elegance, presenting the best of Danish-designed (and, in those days, -made) furniture, silver, glass, textiles, metalware and lighting.

The products were the work of a golden coterie of Danish designers including such luminaries as Arne Jacobsen, Finn Juhl, Børge Mogensen, Jørn Utzon, Poul Kjærholm and not least the uniquely gifted designer *and* craftsman, Hans Wegner. All eschewed ornamentation and instead concentrated on pure lines, paring all extraneous elements

The Round Chair, designed in 1949 by Hans Wegner (1914–2007), is an icon of the Danish Modern design movement. Originally made by Johannes Hansen, it is now produced by PP Møbler.

away until what remained was a beautiful synthesis of form *and* function. At the time the pool of talent seemed endless, just the normal everyday state of affairs; perhaps only in retrospect can we appreciate what an extraordinary period it was, when Danish design was feted across the globe from New York to Sydney. To consider its origins, we must look back to the rather less well known figure of Kaare Klint (1888-1954), a pivotal figure in Danish design, considered by some, including the author, to be a founder of the modern movement, by others, the last of the older generation. He was the son of P.V. Jensen-Klint (1853-1930), a leading architect of the time who worked in his own Arts & Crafts style, paying particular attention to craftsmanship, which was already perceived as being in decline (perhaps it always is). His magnum opus is the Grundtvig Church in the northern Copenhagen suburb of Bispebjerg, as much a paean to the bricklayer's craft as it is a panegyric to Grundtvig's religious vision. I have taken several ACE groups to the church and it always fascinating to witness individuals' reactions, whether of delight, curiosity or indifference. Such was the scale of the project that much of the work was not completed until after his death, his son Kaare taking over as architect and designing the furniture and interior fixtures. Kaare Klint was a student not only of his father but also of the neo-classical architect Carl Petersen, who designed the Faaborg Museum on the island of Fyn. Completed in 1915, it is a jewel-like masterpiece housing a collection of local islanders' art. Kaare Klint was commissioned to design the furniture and came up with the seminal Faaborg chair, that remains in production to this day at Rud Rasmussen's workshop. It is a timeless design which signals the future whilst paying tribute to the masters of 18th-century English furniture. Constructed to the highest standards in mahogany with a simple leather seat and cane back, it is resolutely traditional; with its fluid sculptural form, lack of decoration, and seamlessly integrated back and arms, it is a harbinger of things to come.

In 1924, Klint was appointed lecturer in "Interior & Furniture Art" in the School of Architecture at the Royal Academy in Copenhagen, becoming Professor in 1944. This inspired appointment had two far-reaching outcomes: firstly, it made interior and furniture design integral elements of architecture, increasing the intellectual and professional status of these disciplines; secondly, Klint developed objective design principles that were to influence both his own students and other designers in Denmark. These principles were to form the basis of what became known as the "Klint School", in which Klint emphasised the importance of measurement and analysis in the design process. The starting point was the human body and its movement, which were measured in detail, then the required tasks were examined, followed by analysis of the available material technology and construction methods, and, finally, aesthetics could be considered and pen put to paper. Klint was a pioneer in rational design and ergonomics but he retained a love of traditional craftsmanship, and it was this combination that distinguished Danish (and more generally Scandinavian) design from the international Modernist movement as epitomised by Le Corbusier and the Bauhaus.

Of the many talented Danish designers who emerged in the 1950s, it is Hans Wegner who, for me, has a special place as the creator of some of the most beautiful and timeless pieces of 20th-century design. Wegner was born in 1914 in the southern Jutland town of Tønder, which was then under German control, having been lost in the Schleswig-Holstein wars and not returned to Denmark until the conclusion of World War I. Son of a master cobbler, he left school early and served a four-year apprenticeship before qualifying as a cabinetmaker. Keen to develop his skills further, at the age of 22 he enrolled at Copenhagen's School of Arts & Crafts. In 1938 his talent was spotted by the architects Arne Jacobsen and Erik Møller, who immediately hired him to design furniture for Aarhus town hall. From this point on Hans Wegner was in continuous demand as a designer, his combination of technical knowledge and mastery of line and proportion being unrivalled. He designed for both large-scale manufacturers and fellow master cabinetmakers, such as Johannes Hansen, his own craftsman's skills being reserved for individual pieces and delightful 1:5 scale models of prototype designs.

Hans Wegner's designs for large-scale production provided a significant contribution to the Danish furniture industry in the post-war period and helped shape the popular view of Scandinavian design – light, airy, functional, good value. But, like Kaare Klint before him, he retained a particular affection for craftsman-made pieces of the highest quality. Inevitably such pieces are expensive. That is not to suggest that all buyers are wealthy, for in Denmark there is a reassuring number of people on more modest incomes who are prepared to save enough to purchase a few high quality items designed to last a lifetime. Nevertheless, Hans Wegner (like William Morris) recognised the threat to craftsmen in an industrial, high-wage economy. He was determined that not only should craftsmen survive into the 21st century, but that they should prosper, that they should be pioneers of the future rather than symbols of the past. His approach was twofold: first, he created determinedly modern designs that combined grace and function; second, as a skilled craftsman himself, he was able to devise innovative construction methods and incorporate new materials. At a stroke, Hans Wegner moved beyond the limitations of Arts & Crafts philosophy and established the craftsman at the forefront of developments in design and manufacture. An early example of his genius is the Round Chair from 1949. The design is striking in the way the back and the arms flow into each other with a beautiful fluidity, the vertical emphasis of the back turning almost imperceptibly into the horizontal of the arms. Look more closely and you will see the back and arms are carved from three solid piece of wood and joined with an exquisite fingerjoint that is curved in both the horizontal and vertical planes. The chair was, and remains, modern in its pure form and lack of ornamentation, but to make it requires craftsmanship of the highest order. Wegner continued to innovate for the next forty years or more and it was a privilege for the author to meet him to discuss his work a few years before his death in 2007. It remains to be seen whether Denmark will be able to re-establish its preeminence in design, but visitors to the country can continue to enjoy a distinct body of work that represents a major contribution to 20th-century applied art.

By motorcycle to Bucharest:
an ACE Reconnaissance Trip

Mark Powell

MARK POWELL is a graduate of Durham University in French and German. He has lectured on landscape, art and architecture at Durham, Oxford and Buckingham. He is extremely well-travelled and has led many tours for ACE, including trips to Finland, Prague, Eastern Europe and the Baltic States. Mark also contributes articles to the Architectural Review.

In late April 1995 two British motorcyclists met at a prearranged spot on the Hungarian-Romanian border, having set out separately, as chance would have it, from Cambridge and Oxford respectively. My friend John was riding a BMW R100RS to Istanbul where he would visit an ex-pat sister. I was on a two month exploration of Eastern Europe on a rugged BMW R80GS, a sort of "Two-Wheeled Land Rover".

Biking in Romania was an unpredictable adventure then, so we had stuffed our panniers with useful things. I was carrying old guide-books and inaccurate maps (there *were* no accurate maps) and John, fearing famine, had packed a huge stock of pot noodles and our only contact address: of a journalist in Bucharest neither of us had met. He was head of the Reuters office there and, we feared, would probably be too grand to receive us.

A sardonic border guard warned us of bandits and appalling road surfaces. The bandits we were to meet later, but the disintegrating roads hit us from the start.

Gingerly circumnavigating potholes, we entered Oradea, our first Transylvanian city, along a road whose verges were rigged with huge lagged hot water pipes from which insulation fell off in lumps. They ran from a powerstation to the estates of concrete and brick high-rise blocks. I later found the "bricks" were tiles, stuck on to enliven the concrete, but with inadequate adhesive, and they too were falling off. Once past these outskirts the centre revealed the grandest of public buildings in Hungarian Art Nouveau style. It was a contrast we soon became accustomed to.

Beyond this city of the plain we came to the foothills of Transylvania's downland where our plodding straight highway looped into whiplash curves over sheep-grazed slopes. It might have stood in for pastoral Wiltshire or Thomas Hardy's Wessex. The villages, Romanian, Hungarian or German, were gabled fronts enclosing farmyards full of animals and carts, one house deep either side of the road, with barns beyond.

Bran Castle, Brasov, Romania.

In the centre was the house of the village policeman and often a tiny post office, which I later learned had the *only* telephone in the village.

What we saw on our route began to resonate with the many travelogues I had read about the country. We passed a Hungarian-Transylvanian market town, Huedin, once known as Banffyhunyad. The Banffys were one of the great political families of the Austro-Hungarian Empire, and we were passing their ancestral lands, lost in 1918 to the new Greater Romania. I had read about it in *Raggle Taggle* by Walter Starkie. In the city of Cluj we passed the old hotel where Patrick Leigh Fermor drank cocktails in the 1930s, which he described in *Between The Woods And The Water*.

The campsite in Cluj was closed and we tried to pitch our tents a few miles to the south, on a meadow in Copaceni, a village in the mouth of a gorge. Aurel, a local man who spoke German, warned us not to, for fear of the bears living in caves nearby. A local family took us in and we had our first experience of Romanian hospitality at the simple brick and mud home of Gheorge, mechanic, shepherd and smith. The second night we stayed with Aurel's family. Aurel was Romanian for "Aurelius", and among the proudly Latin-cultured Romanians the humblest peasant might be called after a Roman emperor or poet. I was to meet many called Trajan or Ovid.

All the houses in the village had a little menagerie of free-range animals. At dusk the housewives simultaneously came to their gates and whistled to the mass of ducks and geese on the common. The gabbling fowl answered the calls, separating into their several platoons, each of which waddled to its allocated pen through the opened gate.

On the third day we left and that afternoon, turning off the tarmac onto a beaten stone track, came to another village, the formerly Transylvanian German settlement of Magherus. Its medieval German church was opened for us by the last German family. All the others had moved to the distant fatherland. The church's plate and chalices had been moved for safekeeping to their home, and sat incongruously on the sideboard with their everyday crockery.

The local Romanian schoolmaster was excited to meet strangers. He asked us:

"Where are you from?"

We told him.

"Oxford and Cambridge!" he echoed.

Pelisor Castle, Sinaia, Romania.

He shook our hands in a fit of enthusiastic wonder at the distant spires, which to a provincial dominie were mythically sacred.

"I shall not wash my hand now I have touched yours!" he whispered in awe.

To add to our embarrassment he gave me a tattered old atlas from his school stock. It was published before the First World War. At home in Oxford a month later the page with a map of the Kingdom of Hungary fell from the binding and now hangs framed on my wall like an icon.

The high point of the day's architectural exploration was riding up to the citadel of Sigisoara. We rode up a steep lane and under an arch only to stall at the sight of the most beautiful tower in Transylvania. At the far end of the cobbled street a vast glittering Baroque pavilion of multi-coloured tiles sat on top of a Hansel and Gretel medieval gate tower. To the right was the modest house where Vlad the Impaler was born. The street was empty but for a parked Soviet-built motorcycle and sidecar. For a motorcycling art historian, no scene could have appeared more romantic.

That night we climbed the Carpathian hairpins but found no food or shelter. The few restaurants and hotels were dark and empty. To add to the sinister atmosphere, pairs of gendarmes armed with AK47s loomed at regular intervals in the pines. No doubt a night exercise was in progress. Exhausted, we pitched a tent in a dark glade heaped with snow, lit a camping stove and ate the worst meal of the entire trip: a mess of those pot noodles scooped with our fingers as neither of us had remembered to bring a spoon. We were undoubtedly in bear country again and I recalled a hiking rule that food had to be hung in a tree. The noodle pot dangled like a Christmas decoration. The bears were not tempted.

It was on the outskirts of Bucharest that we met our bandits. We had stopped to puzzle over a plan of the city when the driver of a battered BMW saloon racing towards us on the other side of the road saw us, initiated a handbrake turn and spraying us with shards of broken tarmac slewed to a halt in front of us and his passenger told us to follow them in the shiftiest manner. We disengaged ourselves and decided to look up our contact from Reuters. Asking a taxi driver for directions to the address, he insisted on leading us there and would take no recompense.

As we stood in front of the door of a mansion next door to the Egyptian embassy, unwashed, unshaven and smelling of bear and spicy noodles, we didn't reckon our chances of admission were high. But Peter, the Reuters boss, was an unfussy New Zealander and former motorcyclist himself. He invited us to use the shower and share his dinner table and offered us beds for an indefinite stay. Our bikes were parked on the street outside, but the entertainment they provided for the bored soldiers guarding the embassy meant that they were happy to protect them. A chain and padlock deters some thieves. A pair of armed guards with AK47s takes care of the rest.

John had to continue to Turkey but I stayed to research the city. I was made to feel at home in the Reuters office and was given invaluable help by the journalists.

Bucharest in the mid 1990s was as disorganised, disreputable and exciting as 1920s Berlin. No maintenance or cleaning had been done for years, but investigating the fine architecture of this "Paris of the East" was like coming across an open treasure chest covered with cobwebs. There were Beaux Arts villas swallowed by their own gardens, colossal university buildings freighted with political graffiti like the Sorbonne in 1968 and modernist flats, which had once been gleaming white, lurking under tangled telephone cables, dusty persiennes and washing lines stretched on the balconies.

To explore this on a nimble motorcycle, sharing an uneven road surface with erratically driven cars, which would fail any MOT, and lurching buses with blown shock absorbers was an adrenalin-pumping treat. To be pursued at night by feral packs of dogs while dodging open manholes on unlit streets was adventure of a high order.

I had two urgent tasks: to find out about the National Monuments Commission (equivalent to our English Heritage) and to replace the brake pads on my front wheel, which had been worn wafer thin by hot work on the Carpathian passes. Radu, a press photographer, took me deep into a drab part of town close set with blocks of flats and into a square which was an unscheduled miniature industrial zone. Carcasses of vehicles were piled up in the centre, while all around in cavernous workshops at the ground floor level of the flats men were panel-beating and dismantling or repairing machines in a cacophony of sharp metallic resonance. It was like an artisans' quarter in an Ottoman Balkan town. For a mere 6 dollars, a workman shaved the brake material off a car's pads and riveted them onto my bare metal plates. Refitted onto my bike, the bodge worked well all the way back to the UK a month later.

As for contacting the Monuments organization, what the resourceful Reuters staff set up for me could not have been better. I was accorded a half hour interview with the director, Razvan Teodorescu, soon to become Minister of Culture. He had not heard of ACE Study Tours, but visitors from the West were rare and a curiosity. The professor's office was in a Ceaucescu period building opposite the gargantuan Palace of the People. This was ironic justice as Teodorescu had been instrumental in saving many churches and other buildings from destruction in Ceaucescu's remodelling of the centre. He had moved them entire off the site on rails or hidden the most important carved stone fragments in stores and churchyards around the city.

He answered all my questions and then finally offered me a coffee, which he said his secretary would bring from the adjoining office. But there was no intercom. Instead, the professor looked up at a corner of the room, cupped his mouth in his hands and shouted the order. I then noticed the gap between the partition wall and the ceiling.

I eventually left the city in tandem with a Reuters photographic expedition and after many more adventures arrived home deeply affected by Romania. Radu used the word "infected". It meant that for the rest of the decade I went out by bike nearly every spring for a month or so of exhilarating travel. I was never disappointed.

En route between Mosna and Pelisor.

Law Department of Sucre University.

Bolivian Baroque

Michael Jacobs

A graduate of the Courtauld Institute, MICHAEL JACOBS works as a writer and tour leader. His many books on art and travel include The Good and Simple Life: Artists' Colonies in Europe and America, Andalucía, Between Hopes and Memories: A Spanish Journey, The Factory of Light: Tales from my Andalucían Village, and Ghost Train through the Andes: On my Grandfather's Trail in Chile and Bolivia. A Senior Honorary Research Fellow in the Hispanics Department of Glasgow University, and an honorary member of various Spanish Gastronomic Societies, he is currently writing a book chronicling a journey the whole length of the Andes, from Venezuela to Tierra del Fuego.

Bolivia has always struck me as the ideal destination for an ACE tour. Within a relatively manageable area (for South America), it combines spectacular scenery, major pre-Columbian sites, and outstandingly preserved colonial towns and monuments. Moreover, it remains a country far less commercialised than its Andean neighbours. Sometimes it is easy to understand why. In June 2005, only days before our first tour exclusively devoted to Bolivia was due to begin, protests against the then government of Carlos Mesa had threatened to paralyse the city of La Paz. In any place other than Bolivia, this would have been serious cause for concern. But, as I would later tell my group, if you waited for the moment when the political situation in Bolivia was entirely calm then you would never visit the country. In any case, the consensus of expert opinion was that the crisis would have resolved itself long before we had reached La Paz, near the end of the two week tour.

We started off in the lowland city of Santa Cruz. The small group, remarkably cosmopolitan in its make-up, comprised the sort of people who make working for ACE such a pleasure. Enthusiastic and informed, they also seemed likely to share my soon-to-be-severely-tested philosophy of tour leading as an activity requiring considerable flexibility and the ability to improvise. And if everything did start going wrong, I had the additional support of a disproportionately large team of assistants, including a Bolivian tour manager (known as Tito) who filled me with instant confidence. Hugely knowledgeable and experienced, Tito was also so contagiously optimistic that I felt immediately relieved of my worries, and able to enjoy an untroubled first night's sleep. This would turn out to be my last such sleep in Bolivia.

On my way early the next morning to breakfast, Tito took me aside to warn me of a "little problem" we might be facing later in the day. The unrest in La Paz appeared to be spreading, and there were rumours that our road to the Jesuit missionary churches of the Chiquitos was going to be blocked by agitators. He told me not to say a word about this to the clients, as we would be probably be "worrying them unnecessarily". About three hours later, our progress was suddenly halted by a chaos of parked vehicles and shouting people.

We paid a boy to guide us around the blockade along a series of country tracks; but an open pick-up truck immediately rushed to block our path. "And now we are about to witness a traditional Bolivian festive welcome", I announced unconvincingly to the group, as some drunken men advanced towards us wielding sticks. Tito got out to try and bribe them, and got back in ashen-faced just in time to avoid the sticks beating against the bus's windows. Our driver turned around as hastily as he could.

The tour might well have ended there and then had it not been for Tito's and my refusal to admit defeat. Numerous calls on Tito's cell-phone finally revealed to the relief of everyone that we could drive to our intended destination of San Javier by an entirely different route. Though this would not get us there by lunch, as in the original itinerary, it would entail us passing through most of the major Jesuit settlements of Bolivia. The group cheered, delighted by the prospect of seeing far more than had been promised in the ACE brochure.

All that worried me now was the timing. If I am someone notoriously optimistic in this respect, Tito was even more so. With the light fading, and with many miles yet to go before even arriving at the first of the Jesuit settlements, he still tried to persuade me that we would be in San Javier in time for a late supper. The road surface was by now rapidly deteriorating, and a huge expanse of jungle lay ahead. We were also running out of petrol. But miraculously we managed to keep going. In the middle of nowhere we tracked down a man who sold us petrol in two-litre plastic bottles of Coca-Cola; we enjoyed an atmospheric nocturnal visit to the grand and evocatively decayed church of San José de Chiquitos; and we averted the prospect of an all-night bus-ride by breaking the journey at an incongruous luxury hotel in a colonial style. When we eventually got to San Javier, twenty-five hours behind schedule, the group was in remarkably high spirits, oblivious that our adventures had only just begun.

The owner of the hotel here thought it madness that we should even attempt to return the next day to Santa Cruz, where vast crowds of protesters were apparently about to gather. His proposal that we should stay relaxing in his lushly gardened establishment until the crisis was over was a briefly tempting one, especially as the road blockade of the previous day was still in force, and no one was keen on going back the same way we had come. However, clients of ACE do not normally travel just to hang around sunning themselves in hammocks and loungers.

In the end Tito proposed a means of pressing ahead that appeared comparatively free of risk and hardships. A public bus, according to him, was heading the next morning

The Salar de Uyuni salt flats.

to Santa Cruz by way of a vast tract of agricultural land belonging to the Mennonites - an Amish-like Germanic sect whose pacifist views meant we would be safe at least from political protest. All we had to do was to stay closely behind this other bus, the driver of which was one of the few people who knew his way round this confusingly monotonous area. We succeeded in following the bus through jungle before losing sight of it forever at the entrance to the endless flat fields and near-identical parallel dirt tracks constituting the Mennonite domain. The handful of Mennonites we came across - in pony-and-traps and speaking High German - proved no help at all, and only gave us misleading directions. But then, in the penumbral gloom, we stumbled by chance upon the right track, and made it back to Santa Cruz in time for a few hours sleep.

At five in the morning Tito woke me up to tell me that I should assemble the group as rapidly as possible. Barricades were being set up all around the town. Within half an hour we were all on the bus, being driven recklessly towards the airport. We were among the last passengers to make it there. Together with a man whom we would later see installed as Bolivia's interim new president, we flew to the country's political capital of Sucre, on the lower slopes of the Andes.

The whole of Bolivia was now paralysed; but I was no longer so worried. We had three scheduled nights in a charming colonial hotel in Sucre, during which time President Mesa and his government would surely be forced to resign. Moreover, of all places in South America to weather political storm, Sucre could hardly be bettered. With its quiet small town atmosphere, lively university life, and wonderful mix of Andalucían and French Empire-style architecture, it was one of my favourite towns anywhere. And, as Tito perhaps unwisely pointed out, its inhabitants were famously peace-loving, in contrast to those of volatile La Paz.

Mesa did indeed resign as anticipated; but his much-hated vice-president surprised everyone by trying at first desperately to hold on to power. What was worse and even less expected was his decision to hold the necessary emergency meeting of Parliament not in La Paz but in Sucre. We were about to be among the few foreign witnesses to a key moment in Bolivia's recent political history.

Thousands of miners from Potosí began advancing towards Sucre armed with dynamite; water cannons were being placed on the main square; and journalists in combat gear were taking over the computer room of our hotel. In the meantime the governments of France, Spain, Germany and the United States were busily helping with the evacuation of their citizens. The British government had clearly no such intention; and, in any case, every plane out of the country was already completely full. For my first time as a tour leader, I felt solely responsible not simply for the success of people's holidays, but for their lives.

Matters were made worse for me by a stranded German guide who told everyone in my group not to listen to me, and that they should be leaving Bolivia before the "inevitable blood-bath" ensued. It became a matter of personal and national pride to prove him wrong. But circumstances were not initially on my side. Warned by the hotel management to stay put in the building, I tried to distract the group with a lecture on the Bolivian Baroque, and found myself talking to the accompaniment of explosions, the smashing of glass, and, finally, tear gas. When, later that day, news came that the vice-president had gone into hiding, and that a miner had been fatally injured almost on our doorstep, one of my clients nearly broke down completely. "Michael", she said, "It's a tragedy, an absolute tragedy! We're going to miss the Weaving Museum".

However, we did not miss the Weaving Museum, or almost anything else on our itinerary. Just as Tito and I had predicted, the country went back to normal literally overnight. We went on to see a Bolivia devoid of tourists, and could enjoy undisturbed the colonial treasures of Potosí (the source of Spain's Golden Age wealth), the haunting whiteness of the Great Salt Flat of Uyuni, and the powerful carvings of Tiwanaku, South America's most important pre-Incan civilisation. As a final recompense for all that we had gone through, we looked forward to a last day visiting Lake Titicaca and the Incan monuments on the Island of the Sun. But, at this stage of the tour, it would have been almost an anti-climax had everything gone to plan.

A ferry strike led to an on-the-spot complete change of schedule. Rather than go back disappointed to La Paz, Tito and I suggested a night stop at the small town of Coroico, idyllically situated at a point where the high Andes fall precipitously down into the jungles of the Yungas. A newly opened road was said to make the journey to this once barely accessible place "almost too easy". No one warned us that this road had just been closed because of landslides, forcing us to drive in rain and darkness down the old one – a narrow track clinging to the edge of a void into which buses and lorries once fell with notorious regularity.

The general mood at supper that night was not good; but improved noticeably the next morning on seeing the sun light up a panorama of distant snowy peaks rising over the dense and colourful tropical vegetation. Clients whom I thought would never talk to me again now began wondering whether I would lead a tour to somewhere really problematical such as Colombia. Probably none of them would ever forget their time in Bolivia. In an age when group tourism is becoming ever more standardised, there is certainly something to be said for the wholly unexpected, and for offering people a glimpse of what is truly the sublime – "beauty tinged with terror".

The Yungas.

Ethiopia

Richard Snailham

RICHARD SNAILHAM is
Honorary Foreign Secretary of
the Royal Geographical Society.
He worked for twenty-five years
as Senior Lecturer at the Royal
Military Academy at Sandhurst
and has visited Ethiopia
regularly since the mid 1960s.
As well as being a seasoned
traveller, Richard has written a
number of books, including The
Blue Nile Revealed: The Story of
the Great Abbai Expedition and,
with John Blashford-Snell,
East to the Amazon: In Search
of the Great Paititi and the
Trade Routes of the Ancients.

Some people are astonished that travel companies run tours to Ethiopia. Surely the country is full of stick-thin children with distended bellies; the risk of being taken hostage or caught up in riots is high; you'll have to lodge in some flea-infested hut and eat rubbish; there isn't much to see there anyhow?

The truth is that intermittent droughts followed by times of starvation are now, almost certainly, things of the past. The work of international aid agencies and the local Disaster Prevention and Preparedness Commission has meant that emergency supplies of foodstuffs are dotted about in the habitually drought-stricken regions (only about half of just two of the provinces, Tigre and Wollo). No ACE tour has ever met evidence of starvation even while travelling in these parts of the country.

Hostage taking only befalls groups which stray well off the beaten track and although ACE goes within twenty miles or so of the Eritrean border and used to visit the eastern, predominantly Muslim, half of Ethiopia, no group has experienced anything other than warm friendliness in places like Harar and Dire Dawa. There has been some civil tumult (police crackdowns nearly interrupted our November 2005 tour) but it is rare.

The hotels are adequate to good and the food is Western-style, fairly wholesome if somewhat unvarying. There are opportunities to sample the local fare – *injera* and *wat* – and in most groups there are some brave souls who express a liking for it.

As for what there is to see, there is variety in plenty: the rambling, organic muddle and colour of Addis Ababa, the 2000-year-old stelae of Axum, Lalibela's ancient rock-hewn hypogea, the Blue Nile river and falls, the strange and brilliant imagery on the walls of numerous Orthodox Christian churches, the majesty of the Simien mountains, Gondar's impressive stone castles, the rich bird life of Bahir Dar and Lake Tana, the Rift Valley lakes and hot springs. And that's only the World Heritage sites and other top places.

The Church of St. George, Lalibela, carved from solid rock in the shape of a cross in the early thirteenth century.

This is not to say that touring in Ethiopia is without its problems. One of the most prevalent is the irregularity of Ethiopian Airlines' domestic flights. While it is one of the safest of airlines – it trains aircrew for many other African systems – it seems unable to maintain its internal flight schedules. Axum and Lalibela have both proved difficult places to get into and out of. Weight restrictions, on one occasion, caused a group to have to leave all its hold baggage on the Axum tarmac. Another time, the pilot wouldn't fly to Lalibela unless he was guaranteed a room in the already full Roha hotel. In the early days the Historic Route was flown by 19-seater Britten-Norman Islanders. Our groups were 20 or 21 strong, plus myself and Solomon, our local manager. So we often had to split the group and play catch-you-later. Now Fokker 50s do it, but are still constantly retimed.

We have also travelled miles by battered springless buses and minibuses, by cross-lake ferryboats and on muleback – several times, with great intrepidity, to the heights above Lalibela and the rock-hewn church of Asheton Mariam. Once I had to carry several members of the group piggy-back across a river on the way to the Blue Nile falls.

I have enjoyed recounting to participants the experiences of Scots explorer James Bruce, whilst they sit on the steps, outside the very room he stayed in at the palace of the Empress Mentuab in Gondar in the 1770s, overlooked by vultures in the trees above. Another bizarre experience is giving talks in the swimming pool at the Tana Hotel in Bahir Dar. Every hotel on the Historic Route was given a swimming pool by its Russian builders in the 1970s. None is ever filled with water. The deep end at the Tana is a quiet place in which to Blu-Tack up some maps and outline the Italian invasions of 1935.

One of the regular excitements has been the drive from Addis Ababa, via Awash station and the long ridge of the Chercher mountains to Harar. In the days when the road was gravel all the way the journey called for a very early start and took over thirteen hours. Gradually the Chinese and South Koreans have produced an excellent tarmac road and, jumping off these days from Nazret and the last decent hotel on the way east, we can crack it in eight hours or so. And that includes the evocative stop at the Buffet d'Aouache (Ethiopia's now nearly defunct railway is still residually French). Haile Selassie always overnighted here between Addis and the coast, and Evelyn Waugh spent idle hours on his way with colourful members of the international diplomatic corps to Addis and the Emperor's coronation in 1930.

We have had a few thrills and spills. Three or four unfortunate falls have led to bruises, sprains and an occasional fracture, but there has almost always been a doctor or a vet in the party and Ethiopian hospitals and clinics have proved adequate. Once Charles Goodhart got stuck inside an Ethiopian army tank, abandoned on the roadside after the rout of Mengistu's Marxists in 1991. We got him out somehow.

There have been some interesting and valuable spin-offs. Maria-José Friedlander has organised her own tours to enable her friends to explore little-known rock churches in Tigre. Several members have joined the Anglo-Ethiopian Society and attend its meetings at the School of Oriental and African Studies. Perhaps most significantly Professor Richard Beard and his wife Irène were appalled, as we all are, at the ill-equipped schools we sometimes visit – no books, only primitive desks, a blackboard, chalk and talk. After seeing such a school they discussed the possibility of securing some of the superseded and redundant textbooks which are regularly pulped by educational publishers in Britain and getting them out to Ethiopian schools, where English is the medium of instruction from an early age.

A scheme had already formulated in their minds by the time we were all waiting on the runway at Bahir Dar airport on the way back to Addis Ababa. The plane was held up for some minutes until two VIPs arrived and occupied the front seats alongside the Beards. One of them, a lady, got into conversation with Irène and she turned out to be Ethiopia's Minister of Education! I could not conceive of a more extraordinary and happy coincidence. All the way to Addis they talked. Next evening the Beards and I met the Minister and her colleague the Minister of Information at her house.

Discussions led to the setting up of Book-Link and since this fortuitous meeting in November 2002 Book-Link has despatched seventeen containers, totalling almost a million books, to schools in Ethiopia. ACE has adopted Book-Link as one of the charities it supports. To send a container from Britain to Djibuti and thence by rail or road to Addis is not cheap. Money is raised by Book-Link's energetic Director, Irène Beard, and by its trustees, and systems have been developed in Ethiopia to ensure that only the right sort of books are sent, that they are properly received and despatched to needy schools and carefully protected and used when they get there. It is a remarkable, ongoing by-product of just another ACE tour to Ethiopia.

الامبراطور لوكيوس سبتميوس سيفروس

Libya: land of contrasts and surprises

Philip Kenrick

PHILIP KENRICK is a freelance classical archaeologist, specialising in the study of Hellenistic and Roman pottery. He read Classics at Oxford University, where he also completed his doctorate on pottery from British excavations at Benghazi in Libya. He has travelled widely in Libya and has worked at Lepcis Magna and Cyrene and has produced a major volume on Sabratha. He has worked also on excavations in Italy, Sicily, Turkey and Jordan. Philip has held research posts at Reading and Oxford and is a research associate of the Oxford University Institute of Archaeology.

I first visited Libya in 1971, on a small archaeological expedition to investigate Roman farming in the hinterland of Tripolitania and tiny medieval mosques in the Jebel Nefusa. Over the following five years, my wife and I returned numerous times, mainly in connection with a big rescue excavation near the centre of Benghazi, from which I was studying part of the Hellenistic and Roman pottery. Those years gave us the opportunity to travel widely (in our own Land Rover) and they led to bonds of affection for both the country and its people, which have lasted ever since. Over the last few years it has been my privilege, through leading tours for ACE, to share that affection with others. I enjoy leading these tours because Libya remains off the beaten track: people are attracted out of curiosity, but don't know quite what to expect. I know that they will be fascinated by what they see and will enjoy the trip, and I make it my business to ensure that they do!

Part of the fascination for me lies in the contrasts and paradoxes which one constantly encounters. What tends to be advertised in the travel brochures is the splendour of the Classical (i.e. Greek and Roman) sites – and justifiably so: Lepcis Magna is just about the most impressive Roman city that you can see anywhere! Yet modern Libya sees itself essentially as an Arab and an Islamic nation. Rather as British historians used to consider that we were not truly English before the Norman conquest in 1066, so Libyan officialdom has always been ambivalent about the great monuments which predate the Arab conquest in the seventh century AD. This ambivalence was exacerbated by the presence of the Italians as a colonial power between 1911 and 1943: the Italians used the Roman antiquities shamelessly as propaganda to justify their presence in the country. The Fascists under Mussolini constantly proclaimed themselves as the inheritors and revivers of the ancient Roman Empire. It is not therefore surprising that the Libyan state tends to regard the material remains of its Classical past as an unattractive reminder of past oppression and subjection by foreign powers.

The Roman Emperor Septimius Severus presides over tourists at Lepcis Magna.

Yet this is, of course, an over-simplification, which you might compare with our attitude towards Roman Britain. We know that very few of its inhabitants were Italians, and that over time "Roman" civilisation was embraced by the British population and enriched our heritage. The two coastal regions of Libya (Tripolitania and Cyrenaica, only joined together as a political entity for the first time in the twentieth century) became part of the Roman Empire a hundred years before Britannia. Tripolitania in particular was of enormous importance to the economy of Rome as a source of grain and oil, and many of its citizens became very wealthy and sat in the senate in Rome. One consequence of this was that, towards the end of the second century AD and following the death of the emperor Commodus (did you see the film *Gladiator*?), a native of Lepcis Magna succeeded in securing for himself the title of Emperor of Rome. He was able to do this because he had grown up within the Roman system and was at the time in command of Roman legions in the Balkans. His name was Septimius Severus and we have a special association with him: he died in AD 211 at York, while directing military operations against Scotland. The Italians set up a bronze statue of Severus in the main square in Tripoli, in front of the castle. After Ghaddafi's revolution in 1969, among many other emblems of foreign domination, he was swept from his plinth and hidden away. Maybe someone eventually pointed out to the Leader that Severus was not a symbol of a foreign power, but arguably the most successful and famous Libyan in history. That would still not have endeared him, of course, to his twentieth-century rival, but at least he has been restored to public view and he now stands in front of the museum in his native city!

There is another symbol of empire which is visited by ACE tours, providing a welcome break on the long road journey back from Benghazi towards Tripoli, and which I find equally fascinating in its own way. One of the great engineering achievements of the Italian colonial period between the wars was the completion of an asphalt road running all the way from the Tunisian to the Egyptian frontier. The Fascists were so pleased with this that they published a book, *La strada litoranea della Libia*, which tells the reader how many millions of cubic metres of rock were moved, and how the noble *nazionali* worked tirelessly in the midday heat of the desert while the feckless *indigeni* (so much more sensible) slunk away! The extraordinary arrogance of Fascist Italy is displayed on the title page: the date of publication is given as "Anno XV E.F. – Primo dell'impero", Year 15 of the Fascist Era [counting from 1922], Year 1 of the [restored] Empire! The achievement of the New Romans was also immortalised (or so they thought) by the construction of a monumental arch, over 100 feet high, straddling the road in the middle of the most arid tract around the Syrtic Gulf. On either face across the top were set bronze figures of the Philaeni, alluding to an ancient legend concerning the fixing at this spot of the boundary between the spheres of influence of Carthage and Cyrene. The legend relates that a race was arranged between two pairs of runners, who would set off simultaneously from their mother cities, with the intention that the boundary should be fixed at the point where they met. A glance at the map will show that the Carthaginians (the Philaeni or "Lovers of fame") travelled rather more than twice as far as the two Greeks (whose names we are not told), and it is not surprising that they were accused of cheating. They were therefore challenged either to admit their deceit and to draw back, or to prove their good faith by being buried alive on the spot in defence of their territory. They chose the latter course – an example of extreme patriotism, which appealed greatly to the Fascists. The figures were portrayed gruesomely writhing within their open graves, each with one arm raised to shield his face against the earth falling from above. On the inner faces of the arch were carved travertine panels, illustrating on one side the re-establishment of the Empire, and on the other the construction of the road; above the crown, in huge letters, was a Latin quotation from a hymn written by the poet Horace in 17 BC: *Alme Sol possis nihil urbe Roma visere maius* ("O fostering Sun, may you never see anything greater than the City of Rome!").

When the Allies came across this extraordinary structure during the North African campaign, they of course immediately christened it "Marble Arch", and so it is still shown on some maps. It survived the early years of Libyan independence (with an altered inscription), but fell an early and justifiable casualty to the new nationalism of Ghaddafi: it had fairly recently been demolished when I first travelled past the spot in 1973. However, with a laudable sense of history, the principal carvings and the two huge bronze figures of the Philaeni were first taken down and they are now conserved in the Antiquities Department compound some miles to the west at Medinat Sultan, where they may be seen. The bronzes – each about 15 feet long – have been set up on low plinths, but the slabs of the commemorative reliefs lie scattered nearby on the ground, where the sand and the wild flowers are gradually encroaching upon them, silently vanquishing their vain militarism. One cannot escape the echo of Shelley's *Ozymandias*:

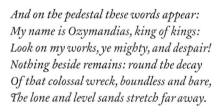

And on the pedestal these words appear:
My name is Ozymandias, king of kings:
Look on my works, ye mighty, and despair!
Nothing beside remains: round the decay
Of that colossal wreck, boundless and bare,
The lone and level sands stretch far away.

From *Ozymandias* by Percy Byshhe Shelley,
first published 1818.

Figures in the sand: Mussolini, with his helmeted soldiers behind him and Roman legionary standards above their heads, salutes the King-Emperor Vittorio Emanuele III on the occasion of the foundation of the New Roman Empire in 1937.

An Illustrated history of an ACE Study Tour
Manor Houses of Southern Sweden, 1967

David Medd

DAVID and MARY MEDD were both awarded OBEs for their work in school architecture and travelled widely in Scandinavia in the 1930s and after World War II. The Medds liked to keep detailed diaries of their journeys, which they illustrated with delightful drawings. David's account of their visit to Southern Sweden 40 years ago is therefore partly told by his drawings. David and Mary went on to enjoy many more tours with ACE and David is our longest serving trustee.

We aim to go north whenever we can, so it caught our attention when, in 1967, we saw a little advertisement in the National Trust magazine offering a study tour in Skåne. What is ACE and where is Skåne? It was time to learn some history, and it turned out that Philip and Inger Barnes were not only just the people for the job, but that we are still learning from them today. All for £75.

The tour was arranged with the co-operation of the Swedish Institute for Foreign Relations. We were 33 participants and the course was held at Önnestad Folk High School, in a small village a few miles from the Baltic Coast, surrounded on all sides by ripening fields of wheat and barley and, overhead, an almost perpetual blue sky.

Skåne, we learnt, gives it name to Scandinavia, and was for 800 years part of Denmark, until conquered by Sweden in 1658. It has a gentle undulating agricultural landscape once covered in deciduous forest, similar to Denmark and unlike the lakes and coniferous landscape of Sweden proper. Sandstone abounds and the red brick, a popular building material for manor houses in Skåne, originates from the twelfth century when brick was first introduced to Denmark.

We visited 18 manor houses or castles, many of which are not normally open to the public, and a number of churches. These included Romanesque village churches like Lyngsjö, with its thirteenth century golden altar and twelfth century granite font showing the murder of Thomas à Becket; the Romanesque cathedral at Lund, once the cathedral of the archbishop of Denmark; King Christian IV's seventeenth century Dutch Renaissance church of Kristianstad; the Norrviken Gardens at Båstad and two open-air museums, Kulturen at Lund and Broby. The Folk High School was built in 1871, one of the first in Sweden, for 190 students over the age of 18. We were there in the summer vacation. The High School Principal, Mr Söderquist, also invited us to tea at his summer house by the beach at Åhus. At the Folk High School there was also a group of 65 pensioners on a

Church gate at Lyngsjö.

two month's long English course. In the evenings they sang Swedish songs for us, led by the Principal's wife dressed in folk costume. The evening meal was served at five.

Believing that we should also see something recent on an ACE tour, we went to a modern old people's home at Fårlöv, built two years previously in 1965. The individual rooms were well planned and furnished, with attractive modern furniture and private bathrooms. Modern prints furnished the walls, including works by Paul Klee.

The manor houses, which were the main object of our attention, fell broadly into three groups. The first consisted of fortified tower houses from the fifteenth and early sixteenth centuries, of which the oldest was Glimminge Hus dating from 1499, built by Jens Holgersen Ulfstand, governor of Gotland and admiral of the Danish fleet. A four-storied building with shooting gallery on the top floor, Glimminge Hus was considered to be a safe retreat from peasant uprisings. Bollerup and Tosterup were similar constructions of this period, the Romanesque church adjacent to Tosterup, rebuilt in 1598, containing two Lucius Cranach paintings.

The second group included manor houses, such as Vittskövle, from the last hundred years of the Danish period, built in the Dutch Renaissance style in red brick with ornamental gables. Vittskövle dates from 1553 and is home to the Stjernswärd family, only the third family to own this moated manor. A fine liriodendron was in full flower, but the hornbeam hedges remained untrimmed as the chauffeur was on holiday. Trolle Ljungby, with its Dutch-influenced curvilinear gables, is also from this period, as is Svenstorp, built by the Gyllenkrok family in the 1590s. The wings of Svenstorp are vernacular in character with whitewash between the granite blocks.

The third and final group of houses are those dating from the Swedish Baroque or Rococo period. Some of these houses have fine Swedish eighteenth century furniture in a Louis XVI style, such as Övedskloster and Rosendal. Övedskloster, a monastery until the reformation in 1536, was taken over by King Christian III. In 1753 it was bought by the Ramel family who commenced a major rebuild. An unforgettable aspect of the Rosendal visit was the chilled elderflower cordial, served by our host Baron Bennet. Swedes with Scottish names like Sinclair, MacLean, Hamilton and Bennet are descendants of Scottish soldiers of fortune who took part in the Thirty Years War and were rewarded by the protestant Swedish king, Gustav Adolphus, with property in Sweden.

We visited Ovesholm, owned by a Countess Hamilton who preferred to be called "Mrs" and whose father had been prime minister of Sweden. Another highlight was Maltesholm, originally dating from 1630 but rebuilt in 1730 by the Ramels and now owned by the Palmstierna family, which featured a wide moat, mansard roof and sash windows, all unusual features in Sweden, as was the clipped privet used as ground cover.

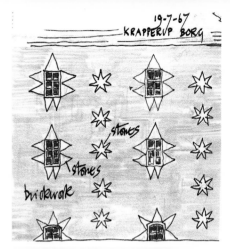

Krapperup Castle. Seven-pointed star of the Gyllenstierna family (Shakespeare's Guildenstern in Hamlet) is set in stone on the brick wall.

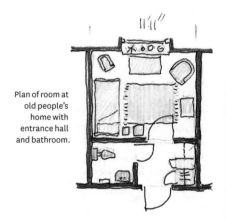

Plan of room at old people's home with entrance hall and bathroom.

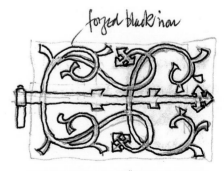

Rococo ironwork on door of Önnestad Church tower.

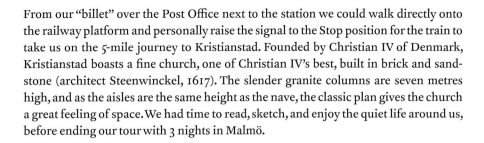

From our "billet" over the Post Office next to the station we could walk directly onto the railway platform and personally raise the signal to the Stop position for the train to take us on the 5-mile journey to Kristianstad. Founded by Christian IV of Denmark, Kristianstad boasts a fine church, one of Christian IV's best, built in brick and sandstone (architect Steenwinckel, 1617). The slender granite columns are seven metres high, and as the aisles are the same height as the nave, the classic plan gives the church a great feeling of space. We had time to read, sketch, and enjoy the quiet life around us, before ending our tour with 3 nights in Malmö.

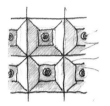

In 1985 Philip Barnes took us to the heart of Sweden, Dalarna. Then there were more ACE visits to Jylland, Fyn and Bornholm. Nor should we forget the more recent visits to Finland, to experience how poetry, art and architecture, and music have released a nation from the alternative grips of Sweden and Russia.

So we have much to thank Önnestad and ACE for.

And finally it has been a privilege to have been associated with ACE for 40 years, from which we have learnt so much and made so many friends.

Village of Önnestad, drawing by Mary Medd.

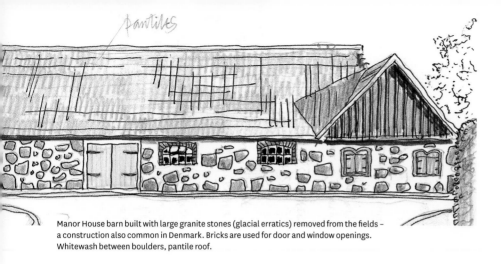

Manor House barn built with large granite stones (glacial erratics) removed from the fields – a construction also common in Denmark. Bricks are used for door and window openings. Whitewash between boulders, pantile roof.

The summer house belonging to the Principal of the Foll High school, Mr Söderquist, who invited the party to tea

Baroque freestanding bedstead with cupboards and drawers. Note overhead rope to pull one up. Broby Open Air Museum.

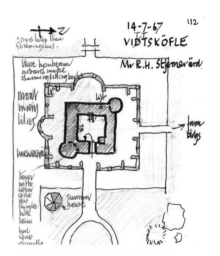

Ground plan of Vittskövle, 1553, with round staircase towers, moat and hornbeam hedges, large Liriodendron Tulipfera in the grounds.

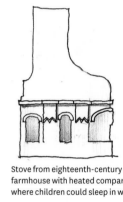

Stove from eighteenth-century farmhouse with heated compartment where children could sleep in winter.

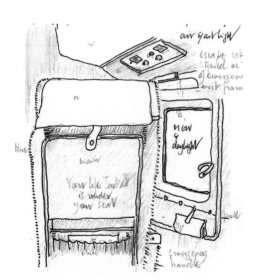

The ACE party flew on a DC6 charter plane from Manston, Kent to Copenhagen, then travelled by ferry and bus to Önnestad.

Shaped wooden box similar to those of the Shakers.

16 buildings moved in
grounds of vicarage to
show old buildings, tools
etc. of NE Skane
last ho. moved here 1926

BROBY
16-7-67

1730

Curate's house, 1730, of Northern Swedish timber construction. Broby Open Air Museum.

Village garden with picket fence and
traditional Swedish red painted barn, Önnestad.

Önnestad churchyard.

Detail showing typical construction of village churches.

AN ILLUSTRATED HISTORY OF AN ACE STUDY TOUR

Clockwise from top left: Vittskövle, seen from the north; Maltesholm, showing the moat to the south; Bollerup, members of the group by the southeast entrance; Lynsjö church seen from the south; (centre) Traditional farmhouse interior at Lund.

Part 3

The Tours

Facts and Figures: The first 50 years of cultural travel

82,000
Total number of participants

Total number of study tours
3871

90
Number of countries visited

Top twenty course directors (years of service, number of courses)	
1 PHILIP B BARNES (1958–2001)	229
2 DENIS MORIARTY (1992–)	181
3 MARK POWELL (1988–)	180
4 TONY CROWE (1958–1988)	173
5 DOUGLAS FERGUSON (1962–1998)	172
6 IAN LOWSON (1959–2004)	166
7 CHRISTIE ARNO (1975–2003)	128
8 MALCOLM OXLEY (1991–)	112
9 RUPERT SCOTT (1998–)	94
10 COLIN BAILEY (2000–)	90
11 JOE ACHESON (1958–1994)	89
12 PATRICIA BAKER (1982–2008)	85
13 ALEX KOLLER (1999–)	74
14 ROLAND RANDALL (1989–)	73
15 KEVIN HAND (1993–)	72
16 ROGER WHITE (1995–)	66
17 ANDREW WILSON (1994–)	64
18 BARRIE SINGLETON (1985–2000)	63
19 FRANCIS CHEETHAM (1993–2006)	59
20 GERALD RANDALL (1987–2007)	53

Most popular towns and cities

Venice

Rome

St Petersburg

Prague

Dresden

Paris

Santiago de Compostela

Salzburg

Berlin

Vienna

Most popular countries by number of study tours	
1 England	1142
2 Italy	427
3 France	309
4 Spain	188
5 Scotland	153
6 Germany	131
7 Austria	89
8 Greece	83
9 USA	77
10 Russia	74
11 Turkey	74
12 Wales	57
13 Ireland	56
14 India	49
15 Portugal	51
16 Belgium	45
17 Mexico	43
18 Czech Republic	38
19 Holland	37
20 Denmark	35

Complete tour listing

1958
Round Britain Art Tour · *Joe Acheson*
Education Tour to Copenhagen · *Philip B Barnes*
Clare Summer School, Scandinavians & Germans,
    English Literature · *Philip B Barnes*
Oxford Summer School, SSTS Scandinavians,
    English Lit · *Philip B Barnes*
Oxford Summer School, Exeter College,
    English Literature · *Tony Crowe*

1959
Clare Summer School, Scandinavians & Germans, English
    Literature · *Ian Lowson*
European Art & Architecture Tour · *Joe Acheson*
British Education the Leicester Plan · *Philip B Barnes*
Oxford Summer School, New College, American Students ·
    Tony Crowe
Oxford Summer School, New College, Scandinavians · *Tony Crowe*

1960
Clare Summer School, Scandinavians, English Literature ·
    Ian Lowson
European Art & Architecture Tour, Italy, France, Netherlands ·
    Joe Acheson
Comparative Education Tour, Bremen & Copenhagen ·
    Philip B Barnes
Oxford Summer School English Literature & Institutions ·
    Tony Crowe

1961
Drew University Oxford Programme · *Ian Lowson*
Summer School for Scandinavians · *Ian Lowson*
English Language & Literature, Lampeter Oxford · *Ian Lowson*
Lampeter Summer School, Language & Literature · *Ian Lowson*
European Inheritance · *Joe Acheson*
European Art & Architecture, Italy, France, Netherlands ·
    Joe Acheson
Celts, Saxons & Vikings Study Tour · *Philip B Barnes*
Oxford Language & Literature for Scandinavians · *Tony Crowe*
Oxford Summer School, Lincoln College for American Students ·
    Tony Crowe
Structure & the Human Spirit · *Tony Crowe*
Studies in British Education · *Tony Crowe*

1962
Summer School for Scandinavians · *Douglas Ferguson*
Lampeter Summer School, Language & Literature ·
    Douglas Ferguson
English Language & Literature, Lampeter · *Ian Lowson*
Oxford Language & Literature for Scandinavians · *Ian Lowson*
Shakespeare Studies · *Ian Lowson*

European Art & Architecture Study Tour · *Joe Acheson*
Folklore in the Castile · *Ned Thomas*
Scandinavian Civilisation · *Philip B Barnes*
Twentieth Century European Tour · *Philip B Barnes*
English Language & Literature, Lincoln College · *Tom Fletcher*
English Language & Literature, Lampeter · *Tom Fletcher*
European Inheritance Seminar Lincoln College · *Tony Crowe*
The European Inheritance, Lincoln College & London ·
    Tony Crowe
British & Irish Landscape · *Tony Crowe*

1963
Summer School for Scandinavians · *Douglas Ferguson*
Lampeter Summer School, Language & Literature · *Douglas
    Ferguson*
Oxford Language & Literature for Scandinavians · *Ian Lowson*
European Art & Architecture Study Tour · *Joe Acheson*
English Summer School Guernsey · *Tom Fletcher*
International Seminar at Elsinore · *Tony Crowe*
European Inheritance Seminar Lincoln College · *Tony Crowe*
Oxford Summer School, Lincoln College for American Students ·
    Tony Crowe

1964
Geographical Study Tour of England, Scotland & Wales ·
    Adrian Harvey
Mount St Scholastica College Tour of Britain · *Denis Lowson*
Lampeter Summer School, Scandinavians · *Douglas Ferguson*
SKALK Archaeology Tour · *Hugo Blake*
Cambridge Seminar · *Ian Lowson*
Oxford Language & Literature for Scandinavians · *Ian Lowson*
European Art & Architecture Tour · *Joe Acheson*
European Art & Architecture Seminar · *Tony Crowe*
University of Pittsburg Seminar · *Tony Crowe*

1965
Rhone Valley & Provence Archaeology Tour · *David Whitehouse*
British Archaeology Seminar Westminster College Oxford ·
    Desmond Collins
English Literature, Oxford & Guernsey · *Douglas Ferguson*
English Language & Literature · *Douglas Ferguson*
Summer School Lampeter · *Douglas Ferguson*
English, Westminster College · *Ian Lowson*
Oxford Language & Literature for Scandinavians · *Ian Lowson*
Shakespeare Studies · *Ian Lowson*
Art & Architecture Tour · *Joe Acheson*
Geographical Study Tour of England, Scotland & Wales ·
    Peter Cumming
Art & Architecture Seminar, Lincoln College · *Peter Draper*
WEA Summer School in Sweden · *Philip B Barnes*
The English Country House & its Garden · *Tony Crowe*

1966
Handa Island & the Northern Highlands · *Anthony Haslam*
Ornithology Tour in Scotland & Wales · *Anthony Haslam*
Birdwatching Bardsey Island · *Anthony Haslam*
British Archeology Seminar Westminster College Oxford · *Bernard Wailes*
Torquay & London · *D A Rigg*
Liberal News Tour of Sweden · *David Brown*
The Normans, Southern England & Northern France Tour ·
    David Whitehouse
Edinburgh, Scarborough & London · *Douglas Ferguson*
Swedish Group in Scarborough & Oxford · *Douglas Ferguson*
Lampeter & Oxford · *Douglas Ferguson*
Pre-Seminar European Tour · *George Thomas*
Weymouth & London · *Harry Shutt*
SKALK Archaeology of Northumbria · *Hazel Wheeler*
English Literature, Oxford · *Ian Lowson*
Oxford Language & Literature for Scandinavians · *Ian Lowson*
English Literature Westminster College · *P T Armistead*
WEA Summer School in Denmark · *Philip B Barnes*
Canterbury School of Architecture Visit to Denmark & Sweden ·
    Philip B Barnes
English Castles & Manors · *Philip B Barnes*
English Country Houses · *Philip B Barnes*
Garden Tour 1 for Danish Horticultural Society · *Philip B Barnes*
Garden Tour 2 for Danish Horticultural Society · *Philip B Barnes*
SSTS at Winchester · *Philip B Barnes*
Scottish Castles · *Philip B Barnes*
TBV Brighton · *Tom Fletcher*
TBV Torquay · *Tom Fletcher*
TBV Weymouth · *Tom Fletcher*
History & Literature · *Tony Crowe*
History on the Ground · *Tony Crowe*
The Normans in Southern England & Northern France · *Tony Crowe*

1967
British Archaeology Seminar Westminster College Oxford · *Bernard Wailes*
English Language & Literature 2 weeks · *Douglas Ferguson*
English language & Literature 3 weeks · *Douglas Ferguson*
English Language & literature, Edinburgh · *Douglas Ferguson*
English Language & Literature, Lampeter · *Douglas Ferguson*
Fact & Artefact Tour · *George Thomas*
Oxford Language & Literature for Scandinavians · *Ian Lowson*
Shakespeare Studies Lincoln College · *Ian Lowson*
Summer School for Scandinavians II · *Ian Lowson*
The Age of Elegance · *Ian Lowson*
The Age of Elegance Tour · *Ian Lowson*
European Art & Architecture Tour · *Joe Acheson*
The Uses of Imagery · *Peter Sulston*
German Baroque · *Philip B Barnes*
Manor Houses in Sweden · *Philip B Barnes*
Welsh Castles & Gardens · *Philip B Barnes*

Landscape & Literature Tour · *Timothy Pearce*
European Art & Architecture · *Tony Crowe*
Fact & Artefact · *Tony Crowe*
Field Research Projects · *Tony Crowe*

1968
Summer School for Scandinavians · *Douglas Ferguson*
English Language & Literature Lampeter · *Douglas Ferguson*
Practical Archaeology in Southampton/King's Lynn · *Eric Talbot*
English Language & Literature Brighton · *H Rump*
SKALK Tour of Orkney & Shetland · *Hugo Blake*
The Vikings in Norway & Denmark · *Hugo Blake*
Oxford Language & Literature for Scandinavians · *Ian Lowson*
Antikvitetsrejse FOF · *Karl Poulsen*
London FOF · *Karl Poulsen*
Det Skønne Wales FOF · *Karl Poulsen*
British Archaeology Seminar Queen's College Oxford · *Paul Mellars*
Early Renaissance in Florence · *Peter Draper*
Houses & Gardens in Denmark · *Philip B Barnes*
Baroque Architecture & Art in Southern Germany · *Philip B Barnes*
Castles & Country Houses in Central Sweden · *Philip B Barnes*
SKALK Archaeology Tour of Southern Ireland · *Stephen Briggs*
Architecture & Gardens in Southern Ireland · *Tony Crowe*
Irish Gardens & Houses · *Tony Crowe*

1969
SSTS Summer School Oxford for Swedes · *Chas Osborne*
Music in England · *Denis Stevens*
Oxford Language & Literature for Scandinavians · *Douglas Ferguson*
Summer School for Scandinavians · *Douglas Ferguson*
Lampeter Summer School Scandinavians · *Douglas Ferguson*
SKALK Archaeology Tour Wales · *Eric Talbot/Jørgen Ilkjær*
European Sightseeing Tour · *George Thomas*
European Art & Architecture Seminar & Study Tour · *Joe Acheson*
FOF Antiques, Gardens & Houses Tour · *Karl Poulsen*
Sprog og Music · *Karl Poulsen*
FOF Garden Tour of Ireland · *Karl Poulsen*
Irish Gardens Tour FOF · *Karl Poulsen*
Morley College Tour Sweden & Denmark · *M M Green*
Uses of Imagery · *Noel Purdon*
Huntingdonshire Historic Towns · *P M G Dickinson*
British Archaeology Seminar Merton College Oxford · *Paul Mellars*
Copenhagen · *Philip B Barnes*
Houses & Gardens in Denmark & Sweden · *Philip B Barnes*
Bury St Edmunds · *Philip B Barnes*
York Summer School · *Philip B Barnes*
European Art & Architecture · *Philip Conisbee*
Theatre Workshop · *Roger Jerome*
SKALK Ireland Tour · *Stephen Briggs/Olaf Jørgensen*
Nova Britannia · *Tony Crowe*
Petworth Historic Town · *Tony Crowe*
Stamford Historic Town · *Tony Crowe*
Wells Historic Town · *Tony Crowe*
Dublin · *Tony Crowe*
Dublin Historic Town · *Tony Crowe*
Venice & the Veneto · *William Collier*

1970
Music in England Seminar Oxford · *Denis Stevens*
Oxford Language & Literature for Scandinavians · *Douglas Ferguson*
Summer School in Lampeter for Scandinavians · *Douglas Ferguson*
SKALK Archaeology Tour of Wales & Wessex · *Eric Talbot/Vivi Jensen*
European Sightseeing Tour · *George Thomas*
Brighton Summer School for Scandinavians · *H Rump*
Archaeology Tour of Northumbria · *Hugo Blake*
SSTS Course for Swedes Merton College · *Jennifer French*
City of Florence · *Joe Acheson*
Archaeology in Malta · *John Evans*
SSTS Course for Swedes Lincoln College · *Malcolm Golding*
Northern Portugal · *Martin Blake*
Quintas in Northern Portugal · *Martin Blake*
Furniture in English Houses · *Michael Kirkby*
The English Country House & its Contents Tour · *Michael Kirkby*
Uses of Imagery seminar Oxford · *Noel Purdon*

Fenland Abbeys · *P M G Dickinson*
Scottish Castles · *P M G Dickinson*
British Archaeology Seminar Merton College Oxford · *Paul Mellars*
Renaissance in Florence · *Peter Draper*
European Art & Architecture Seminar Oxford · *Philip and Susan Conisbee*
Danish Manor Houses & Gardens · *Philip B Barnes*
King's Lynn · *Philip B Barnes*
Sicilian Cities · *Philip B Barnes*
Scottish Tower Houses · *Philip B Barnes*
Swedish Castles & Country Houses · *Philip B Barnes*
Music in English Cathedrals · *Richard Andrews*
British Theatre Seminar Oxford · *Roger Jerome*
SKALK Archaeology Tour of Northumbria · *Stephen Briggs/Olaf Jørgensen*
European Art & Architecture Tour · *Thomas Cross*
Bruges · *Tony Crowe*
Farnham · *Tony Crowe*
Lewes · *Tony Crowe*
Nova Britannia Seminar Oxford · *Tony Crowe*
Stamford · *Tony Crowe*
Edinburgh · *Tony Crowe*

1971
Music in Oxford · *Denis Stevens*
Oxford Language & Literature for Scandinavians · *Douglas Ferguson*
Summer School for Scandinavians · *Douglas Ferguson*
Palladio · *Frances Vivian*
European Art & Architecture Tour · *Joe Acheson*
Nuneham Courtenay · *Mavis Batey*
Uses of Imagery · *Noel Purdon*
East Anglian Abbeys · *P M G Dickinson*
East Anglian Castles · *P M G Dickinson*
Fenland Abbeys · *P M G Dickinson*
British Archaeology Seminar Merton College Oxford · *Paul Mellars*
Eastern Sicily · *Peter Draper*
Scandinavian Manors & Churches · *Philip B Barnes*
Northern Portugal · *Philip B Barnes*
European Art & Architecture Seminar Oxford · *Philip Conisbee*
Bruges · *Tony Crowe*
Bath · *Tony Crowe*
Canterbury · *Tony Crowe*
Furniture in English Houses · *Tony Crowe*
King's Lynn & Wisbech · *Tony Crowe*
Lewes · *Tony Crowe*
Ludlow, Stourport & Bewdley · *Tony Crowe*
Stamford · *Tony Crowe*
Winchester & Southampton · *Tony Crowe*
Edinburgh · *Tony Crowe*

1972
Norwich · *Alan Carter*
Lampeter Summer School Scandinavians · *Douglas Ferguson*
The Orkney & Shetland Islands · *Eric Talbot*
Palladio · *Frances Vivian*
Oxford Language & Literature for Scandinavians · *Ian Lowson*
European Art & Architecture Study Tour · *Joe Acheson*
English Furniture · *Michael Kirkby*
Uses of Imagery · *Noel Purdon*
Cotswold Manors · *P M G Dickinson*
East Anglian Manors · *P M G Dickinson*
Fenland Abbeys · *P M G Dickinson*
Lincoln · *P M G Dickinson*
Saffron Walden · *P M G Dickinson*
Saxon Churches · *P M G Dickinson*
Wiltshire Churches · *P M G Dickinson*
Brittany · *P M G Dickinson*
British Archaeology Seminar Merton College Oxford · *Paul Mellars*
Early Renaissance · *Peter Draper*
Sicily · *Peter Draper*
Belgian Chateaux · *Philip B Barnes*
Copenhagen · *Philip B Barnes*
Scandinavian Manors & Churches · *Philip B Barnes*
Portugal · *Philip B Barnes*

European Art & Architecture · *Philip Conisbee*
Bruges · *Tony Crowe*
Bath · *Tony Crowe*
Canterbury · *Tony Crowe*
Lewes · *Tony Crowe*
Petworth · *Tony Crowe*
The Normans · *Tony Crowe*
Edinburgh · *Tony Crowe*

1973
Timber, Stone & Brick · *A S Ireson*
Norwich · *Alan Carter*
Cotswold Manors · *Douglas Ferguson*
Hebrides & Highlands · *Eric Talbot*
Palladio · *Frances Vivian*
Rome & the Grand Tour · *Frances Vivian*
Pottery & Porcelain · *Fred Sumner*
Chaucer's England · *Ian Lowson*
Lincoln College Language & Shakespeare · *Ian Lowson*
European Art & Architecture Study Tour · *Joe Acheson*
English Furniture · *Michael Kirkby*
Uses of Imagery · *Noel Purdon*
Fenland Abbeys · *P M G Dickinson*
Kentish Manors · *P M G Dickinson*
Norfolk Churches · *P M G Dickinson*
Norfolk Country Houses · *P M G Dickinson*
Saxon Minsters & Norman Churches · *P M G Dickinson*
Yorkshire Minsters & Monasteries · *P M G Dickinson*
French Gothic · *P M G Dickinson*
British Archaeology Seminar Merton College Oxford · *Paul Mellars*
European Art & Architecture Seminar in Oxford · *Philip and Susan Conis...*
Central European Baroque · *Philip B Barnes*
Portugal · *Philip B Barnes*
Folklore in the Castile · *Philip B Barnes*
Bruges · *Tony Crowe*
Ghent · *Tony Crowe*
Cinque Ports · *Tony Crowe*
Farnham · *Tony Crowe*
Lincoln · *Tony Crowe*
Oxford · *Tony Crowe*
Petworth · *Tony Crowe*
The Normans · *Tony Crowe*
Edinburgh · *Tony Crowe*
Scottish Tower Houses · *Tony Crowe*
Châteaux of the Loire · *Vivian Rowe*

1974
Kentish Manors · *Douglas Ferguson*
Summer Course in English Lincoln College Oxford · *Douglas Ferguson*
The Cotswolds · *Douglas Ferguson*
West Country Manors · *Douglas Ferguson*
Castles of North Wales · *Douglas Ferguson*
Shetland & Aberdeen · *Eric Talbot*
Genoa & Venice - Rival Republics · *Frances Vivian*
Rome & the Grand Tour · *Frances Vivian*
Venice & the Veneto · *Frances Vivian*
Pottery & Porcelain · *Fred Sumner*
East Anglian Churches · *George Winkley*
Chaucer's England · *Ian Lowson*
Shakespeare's Imagery · *Ian Lowson*
Mexico · *Ian Lowson*
European Art & Architecture Study Tour · *Joe Acheson*
Italian Renaissance · *Joe Acheson*
Italian Renaissance · *Joe Acheson*
Furniture in Country Houses · *Michael Kirkby*
Yorkshire Houses · *Michael Kirkby*
Fenland Abbeys · *P M G Dickinson*
West Country Abbeys · *P M G Dickinson*
French Gothic · *P M G Dickinson*
Byzantium · *Paul Hetherington*
British Archaeology Seminar Merton College Oxford · *Paul Mellars*
Church Arts · *Philip B Barnes*
East Anglian Manors · *Philip B Barnes*
Norwich · *Philip B Barnes*

Timber, Stone & Brick · *Philip B Barnes*
Yorkshire Minsters & Monasteries · *Philip B Barnes*
Central European Baroque · *Philip B Barnes*
Castles of Holland & Belgium · *Philip B Barnes*
Portugal · *Philip B Barnes*
European Art & Architecture Seminar in Oxford · *Philip Conisbee*
Provence · *Philip Conisbee*
British Theatre - Shakespeare's Imagery · *Roger Jerome*
British Theatre, Oxford, London, Edinburgh · *Roger Jerome*
Hebrides & Highlands · *Sara Erskine*
Cheltenham · *Tony Crowe*
Hadrian's Wall & Northumbria · *Tony Crowe*
Lewes · *Tony Crowe*
Petworth · *Tony Crowe*
Salisbury · *Tony Crowe*
Châteaux of the Loire · *Tony Crowe*
Normans · *Tony Crowe*

1975
Northern Portugal with Santiago de Compostela · *Alan Tait*
Portugal for US students · *Alan Tait*
Byzantine Monasteries of Southern Yugoslavia · *Bernard Cox*
Monasteries of Southern Yugoslavia · *Bernard Cox*
French Gothic · *Christie Arno*
Shakespeare's England · *Christopher Oprey*
Cotswolds · *Douglas Ferguson*
Lake District · *Douglas Ferguson*
West Country Abbeys · *Douglas Ferguson*
Chateaux of the Loire for US students · *Douglas Ferguson*
Athens & the Peloponnese · *Douglas Ferguson*
Castles of North Wales · *Douglas Ferguson*
Archaeology of Wales · *Eric Talbot*
Palladio Winter Lecture · *Frances Vivian*
Corsica · *Frances Vivian*
Italian Renaissance in Tuscany & Umbria · *Frances Vivian*
Palladio · *Frances Vivian*
Palladio for US students · *Frances Vivian*
Norfolk Churches · *George Winkley*
Chaucer's England · *Ian Lowson*
Mexico · *Ian Lowson*
Decorative Tradition in France · *Joe Acheson*
French Taste in the 18th Century · *Joe Acheson*
European Art & Architecture Study Tour · *Joe Acheson*
Castles & Country Houses of Northumbria · *Michael Kirkby*
Georgian Yorkshire · *Michael Kirkby*
Georgian Yorkshire for US students · *Michael Kirkby*
Northumbria for US students · *Michael Kirkby*
British Archaeology, Seminar & Excavations · *Paul Mellars*
Denmark & Southern Sweden · *Philip B Barnes*
Scandinavian Manors & Churches · *Philip B Barnes*
Cambridge · *Philip B Barnes*
Church Arts · *Philip B Barnes*
Cornwall · *Philip B Barnes*
East Anglia · *Philip B Barnes*
Fenland Abbeys · *Philip B Barnes*
Suffolk Manors · *Philip B Barnes*
The Victorian Achievement · *Philip B Barnes*
West Country Manors · *Philip B Barnes*
Bavarian & Austrian Baroque · *Philip B Barnes*
Persia · *Philip B Barnes*
Portuguese Art & Architecture · *Philip B Barnes*
European Art & Architecture, Lincoln College, Oxford ·
   Philip Conisbee
From Renaissance to Romanticism · *Philip Conisbee*
British Theatre · *Roger Jerome*
Hebrides & Highlands · *Sara Erskine*
Hebrides & Highlands for US students · *Sara Erskine*
Hadrian's Wall & Northumbria · *Tony Crowe*
Lewes · *Tony Crowe*
Petworth · *Tony Crowe*
Flemish Cities · *Tony Crowe*
Edinburgh, The Athens of the North · *Tony Crowe*
Chateaux of the Loire · *Vivian Rowe*

1976
Italian Art & Architecture · *Alan Windsor*
Russia · *Bernard Cox*
Monasteries of Southern Yugoslavia · *Bernard Cox*
Norman Romanesque · *Christie Arno*
Provence · *Christie Arno*
East Anglian Houses · *Douglas Ferguson*
Greece Winter Lecture · *Douglas Ferguson*
Hereford & the Welsh Borders · *Douglas Ferguson*
Lake District · *Douglas Ferguson*
Peak District · *Douglas Ferguson*
The Isle of Wight · *Douglas Ferguson*
Vernacular Architecture in Worcester · *Douglas Ferguson*
Athens, Crete & the Peloponnese · *Douglas Ferguson*
Archaeology of Southern Ireland · *Eric Talbot*
Palladio · *Frances Vivian*
Rome & the Grand Tour · *Frances Vivian*
Church Arts · *George Winkley*
Shakespeare · *Ian Lowson*
Mexico · *Ian Lowson*
French Gothic · *Joe Acheson*
Castles & Country Houses of Northumbria · *Michael Kirkby*
Roehampton · *P R Gilfillan*
Romania · *P R Gilfillan*
British Archaeology Seminar Merton College Oxford · *Paul Mellars*
Cornwall · *Philip B Barnes*
East Anglian Monasteries · *Philip B Barnes*
Georgian Yorkshire - John Carr & His Circle · *Philip B Barnes*
Glastonbury & Wells · *Philip B Barnes*
Medieval House · *Philip B Barnes*
Mexico Winter Lecture · *Philip B Barnes*
Norfolk · *Philip B Barnes*
Persia · *Philip B Barnes*
London Theatre · *Roger Jerome*
Archaeology of Wales · *Stephen Briggs*
Flemish Cities: Veurnes, Bruges, Ghent · *Tony Crowe*
Cinque Ports · *Tony Crowe*
Guildford · *Tony Crowe*
Edinburgh & the Scottish Borders · *Tony Crowe*
Tunisia · *Tony Crowe*
Roman Colchester · *V White*

1977
Portugal · *Alan Tait*
Italian Renaissance · *Alan Windsor*
Russia · *Bernard Cox*
Norman Romanesque · *Christie Arno*
Kent · *David Wickham*
A Country House Weekend · *Douglas Ferguson*
Greece Lectures · *Douglas Ferguson*
Hereford & the Welsh Borders · *Douglas Ferguson*
Lake District · *Douglas Ferguson*
Lincolnshire · *Douglas Ferguson*
Peak District · *Douglas Ferguson*
West Country Gothic · *Douglas Ferguson*
Athens, Crete & the Peloponnese · *Douglas Ferguson*
Crete · *Douglas Ferguson*
Scottish Houses · *Douglas Ferguson*
Caithness & Orkney · *Eric Talbot*
French Taste · *Frances Vivian*
Etruscans & Romans · *Frances Vivian*
Palladio · *Frances Vivian*
Rome & the Grand Tour · *Frances Vivian*
East Anglian Houses · *George Winkley*
Yorkshire Minsters & Monasteries · *George Winkley*
Chaucer's England · *Ian Lowson*
Mexico · *Ian Lowson*
Peru · *Ian Lowson*
Dutch & Flemish Art · *Joe Acheson*
Northumbrian Houses · *Michael Kirkby*
Norman Chateaux · *Michael Kirkby*
Romania · *Paul Hetherington*

Cornwall · *Philip B Barnes*
Dorset · *Philip B Barnes*
Georgian Craftsmen · *Philip B Barnes*
Medieval House · *Philip B Barnes*
Norfolk · *Philip B Barnes*
Persia Lectures · *Philip B Barnes*
Roman Colchester · *Philip B Barnes*
Stone Buildings · *Philip B Barnes*
West Country Houses · *Philip B Barnes*
Worcester Houses · *Philip B Barnes*
German Baroque · *Philip B Barnes*
Persia · *Philip B Barnes*
Palladianism & the English Country House · *Philip Conisbee*
London Theatre · *Roger Jerome*
Hadrian's Wall & Northumbria · *Tony Crowe*
Petworth · *Tony Crowe*
Roehampton · *Tony Crowe*
Rome Lectures · *Tony Crowe*
Surrey House · *Tony Crowe*
Plantagenets · *Tony Crowe*
Tunisia · *Tony Crowe*

1978
Portugal · *Alan Tait*
Surrey House · *Alan Windsor*
Russia · *Bernard Cox*
Norman Romanesque · *Christie Arno*
Romania · *Christie Arno*
Medieval House in Kent · *David Wickham*
A Country House Weekend · *Douglas Ferguson*
Cotswolds · *Douglas Ferguson*
Fenland Abbeys · *Douglas Ferguson*
Greece Lectures · *Douglas Ferguson*
Lincolnshire · *Douglas Ferguson*
Northamptonshire Stone Buildings · *Douglas Ferguson*
West Country Gothic · *Douglas Ferguson*
Minoan & Mycenaean Greece · *Douglas Ferguson*
Scottish Castles · *Douglas Ferguson*
English Furniture · *E T Joy*
Isle of Man · *Eric Talbot*
South West Scotland · *Eric Talbot*
Chateaux of the Ile de France · *Frances Vivian*
Etruscans & Romans · *Frances Vivian*
Mantua, Urbina & Vicenza · *Frances Vivian*
Norfolk · *George Winkley*
Mexico · *Ian Lowson*
Peru · *Ian Lowson*
Roman Sights in Southern Britain · *Lawrence Carter*
Northumbrian Houses · *Michael Kirkby*
Norman Chateaux · *Michael Kirkby*
Roehampton · *Peter Gerhold*
Denmark & Southern Sweden · *Philip B Barnes*
Archaeology of Wessex · *Philip B Barnes*
Cornwall · *Philip B Barnes*
Hereford & the Welsh Borders · *Philip B Barnes*
Persia Lecture Weekend · *Philip B Barnes*
Worcester Houses · *Philip B Barnes*
Yorkshire Minsters & Monasteries · *Philip B Barnes*
German Baroque · *Philip B Barnes*
Persia · *Philip B Barnes*
London Theatre · *Roger Jerome*
Flemish & Dutch Art · *Timothy Hyman*
Flemish Cities · *Tony Crowe*
Egypt · *Tony Crowe*
Alternative Design · *Tony Crowe*
Egypt Lectures · *Tony Crowe*
Greenwich · *Tony Crowe*
Hadrian's Wall & Northumbria · *Tony Crowe*
Rome Lectures · *Tony Crowe*
West Country Houses · *Tony Crowe*
Plantagenets · *Tony Crowe*
Tunisia · *Tony Crowe*

1979

Portugal · *Alan Tait*
Isle of Man · *Alistair Gordon*
Russia & the Caucasus · *Bernard Cox*
Yugoslavia & the Adriatic Coast · *Bernard Cox*
English Romanesque · *Christie Arno*
French Gothic · *Christie Arno*
Cinque Ports · *David Wickham*
Jane Austen & Late 18th Century Taste · *David Wickham*
Norfolk · *David Wickham*
Cotswolds · *Douglas Ferguson*
Greece Lectures · *Douglas Ferguson*
Lincolnshire · *Douglas Ferguson*
Shropshire · *Douglas Ferguson*
Staffordshire Houses · *Douglas Ferguson*
Suffolk Manors · *Douglas Ferguson*
West Country Gothic · *Douglas Ferguson*
Crete · *Douglas Ferguson*
Greek Islands · *Douglas Ferguson*
Northern Greece · *Douglas Ferguson*
North Wales · *Douglas Ferguson*
English Furniture · *E T Joy*
Caithness & Orkney · *Eric Talbot*
Ravenna & Venice · *Frances Vivian*
Sicily · *Frances Vivian*
Dorset · *George Winkley*
Bali & South-East Asia · *Ian Lowson*
Mexico · *Ian Lowson*
Peru · *Ian Lowson*
Italian Renaissance in Tuscany & Umbria · *Joe Acheson*
Bristol · *Michael Stanford*
Roehampton · *Peter Gerhold*
Cambridge · *Philip B Barnes*
Cornwall · *Philip B Barnes*
Vale of Evesham · *Philip B Barnes*
Wiltshire Houses · *Philip B Barnes*
Aachen & Cologne · *Philip B Barnes*
Moghul India · *Philip B Barnes*
London Theatre · *Roger Jerome*
Theatre in the Midlands · *Roger Jerome*
Burgundy · *Timothy Hyman*
Flemish Cities · *Tony Crowe*
Egypt · *Tony Crowe*
Dartmoor & South Devon · *Tony Crowe*
Egypt Lectures · *Tony Crowe*
Greenwich · *Tony Crowe*
Stamford · *Tony Crowe*
The Borders · *Tony Crowe*
The Weald · *Tony Crowe*
Plantagenets · *Tony Crowe*
Tunisia · *Tony Crowe*

1980

Portugal · *Alan Tait*
North Wales · *Alistair Gordon*
Romania · *Bernard Cox*
Russia & Soviet Central Asia · *Bernard Cox*
English Gothic · *Christie Arno*
English Romanesque · *Christie Arno*
French Gothic · *Christie Arno*
Cinque Ports · *David Wickham*
Jane Austen & Late 18th Century Taste · *David Wickham*
Staffordshire Houses · *David Wickham*
Greece Lecture Weekend · *Douglas Ferguson*
Hampshire · *Douglas Ferguson*
Lake District · *Douglas Ferguson*
Lincolnshire · *Douglas Ferguson*
Northamptonshire Houses · *Douglas Ferguson*
Oxford · *Douglas Ferguson*
Normandy · *Douglas Ferguson*
Athens & the Peloponnese · *Douglas Ferguson*
Crete & Santorini · *Douglas Ferguson*
Galloway & Dumfries · *Douglas Ferguson*
English Furniture · *E T Joy*

South Wales Castles · *Eric Talbot*
Palladio · *Frances Vivian*
Palladio (2) · *Frances Vivian*
Sicily · *Frances Vivian*
Bali & South-East Asia · *Ian Lowson*
Peru & Bolivia · *Ian Lowson*
Burgundy · *Joe Acheson*
Italian Renaissance in Tuscany & Umbria · *Joe Acheson*
Shetland · *Noel Fojut*
China · *Philip B Barnes*
Cambridge · *Philip B Barnes*
China Lecture Weekend · *Philip B Barnes*
Cornwall · *Philip B Barnes*
Medieval Suffolk · *Philip B Barnes*
Suffolk Manors · *Philip B Barnes*
Thameside Villas · *Philip B Barnes*
William Morris & the Arts & Crafts Movement · *Philip B Barnes*
Yorkshire Minsters & Monasteries · *Philip B Barnes*
Moorish Spain · *Philip B Barnes*
London Theatre · *Roger Jerome*
Theatre in the Midlands · *Roger Jerome*
Flemish Cities · *Tony Crowe*
Cheshire · *Tony Crowe*
Egypt Lecture Weekend · *Tony Crowe*
Farnham · *Tony Crowe*
Hereford & the Welsh Borders · *Tony Crowe*
India lecture weekend · *Tony Crowe*
Mendips · *Tony Crowe*
The Borders · *Tony Crowe*
West Country Houses · *Tony Crowe*
Moghul India · *Tony Crowe*

1981

Portugal · *Alan Tait*
Aberdeenshire · *Alistair Gordon*
North Wales · *Alistair Gordon*
Georgia & Armenia · *Bernard Cox*
Yugoslavia & the Adriatic Coast · *Bernard Cox*
English Gothic · *Christie Arno*
French Gothic · *Christie Arno*
Poland · *Christie Arno*
Cornwall · *David Wickham*
Horace Walpole & the Gothick Imagination · *David Wickham*
Jane Austen & Late 18th Century Taste · *David Wickham*
Medieval House in Kent · *David Wickham*
Cumbria & Hadrian's Wall · *Douglas Ferguson*
Normandy · *Douglas Ferguson*
English Furniture · *E T Joy*
Southwest Scotland · *Eric Talbot*
Italian Renaissance · *Frances Vivian*
Sicily · *Frances Vivian*
Southern Italy · *Frances Vivian*
Norfolk · *George Winkley*
Yorkshire Minsters & Monasteries · *George Winkley*
Yorkshire Houses · *Ian Lowson*
Bali, Java & Sumatra · *Ian Lowson*
Mexico · *Ian Lowson*
Mexico (2) · *Ian Lowson*
Mayas, Mexico & Guatemala · *Ian Lowson*
Peru & Bolivia · *Ian Lowson*
Hatchments, Heraldry & Country Houses · *J H Cordingley*
Athens & the Peloponnese · *Joe Acheson*
Eastern United States · *Joe Acheson*
Mendips · *Marian Barraclough*
Wiltshire Houses · *Marian Barraclough*
China · *Philip B Barnes*
Cambridge · *Philip B Barnes*
China Lecture Weekend · *Philip B Barnes*
Fenland Abbeys · *Philip B Barnes*
Suffolk Manors · *Philip B Barnes*
William Morris & the Arts & Crafts Movement · *Philip B Barnes*
Rhine & Moselle · *Philip B Barnes*
Country Houses of Flanders & Holland · *Philip B Barnes*
Moorish Spain 1 · *Philip B Barnes*

Moorish Spain 2 · *Philip B Barnes*
Edinburgh Festival Theatre · *Roger Jerome*
London Theatre · *Roger Jerome*
Burgundy · *Timothy Hyman*
Flemish Cities · *Tony Crowe*
Egypt · *Tony Crowe*
Egypt (2) · *Tony Crowe*
Egypt Lecture Weekend · *Tony Crowe*
Hampshire · *Tony Crowe*
India Lecture Weekend · *Tony Crowe*
Stamford · *Tony Crowe*
Sussex · *Tony Crowe*
The North West in the Age of Gladstone · *Tony Crowe*
Tudor Essex · *Tony Crowe*
Plantagenets · *Tony Crowe*
Moghul India & Nepal · *Tony Crowe*
Edinburgh · *Tony Crowe*

1982

Portugal · *Alan Tait*
Aberdeenshire · *Alistair Gordon*
Fife & Angus · *Alistair Gordon*
The Steppes of Central Asia · *Bernard Cox*
Yugoslavia · *Bernard Cox*
English Gothic · *Christie Arno*
English Romanesque · *Christie Arno*
French Gothic · *Christie Arno*
Romania · *Christie Arno*
Jane Austen & Late 18th Century Taste · *David Wickham*
Strawberry Hill Gothick · *David Wickham*
The Cinque Ports · *David Wickham*
Cornwall · *Douglas Ferguson*
Greece Lecture Weekend · *Douglas Ferguson*
Normandy · *Douglas Ferguson*
Crete · *Douglas Ferguson*
Normans & Welsh · *Eric Talbot*
Chateaux of the Ile de France · *Frances Vivian*
Sicily · *Frances Vivian*
Norfolk & King's Lynn Festival · *George Winkley*
English Furniture · *H J Scott Hutchinson*
Dorset · *Ian Lowson*
Mexico & Peru Lecture Weekend · *Ian Lowson*
Yorkshire Houses · *Ian Lowson*
Bali, Java & Sumatra · *Ian Lowson*
Mexico · *Ian Lowson*
The Mayas, Mexico & Guatemala · *Ian Lowson*
The Mayas, Mexico & Guatemala II · *Ian Lowson*
Peru & Bolivia · *Ian Lowson*
Architecture of Bohemia & Moravia · *J H Cordingley*
Norfolk Hatchments · *J H Cordingley*
Burgundy · *Joe Acheson*
Venice & the Veneto · *Joe Acheson*
Lake District · *Marian Barraclough*
Hereford & the Welsh Borders · *Michael Tomkins*
Vale of Evesham · *Michael Tomkins*
Yorkshire Minsters & Monasteries · *Michael Tomkins*
Egypt · *Patricia Baker*
Chinese Civilisation · *Philip B Barnes*
Cambridge · *Philip B Barnes*
China Lecture Weekend · *Philip B Barnes*
Fenland Abbeys · *Philip B Barnes*
Medieval Suffolk · *Philip B Barnes*
Renaissance House · *Philip B Barnes*
Provence · *Philip B Barnes*
Rhine & Moselle · *Philip B Barnes*
Country Houses of Flanders & Holland · *Philip B Barnes*
Moorish Spain · *Philip B Barnes*
Sri Lanka · *Philip B Barnes*
Edinburgh Festival Theatre · *Roger Jerome*
Oxford · *Ron Brown*
Italian City Republics · *Timothy Hyman*
Flemish Cities · *Tony Crowe*
Egypt Lecture Weekend · *Tony Crowe*
Hampshire · *Tony Crowe*

India Lecture Weekend · *Tony Crowe*
Moghul India & Nepal · *Tony Crowe*
Weald Downland · *Tony Crowe*
Plantagenets · *Tony Crowe*
Edinburgh · *Tony Crowe*
Tunisia · *Tony Crowe*
California & the American Experience · *Tony Crowe*

1983

Fife & Angus · *Alistair Gordon*
The Steppes of Central Asia · *Bernard Cox*
Split & Central Dalmatia · *Bernard Cox*
English Gothic · *Christie Arno*
English Romanesque · *Christie Arno*
French Gothic · *Christie Arno*
Romania · *Christie Arno*
Road to Compostela · *Christie Arno*
Devon · *David Wickham*
East Kent · *David Wickham*
Strawberry Hill Gothick · *David Wickham*
Cornwall · *Douglas Ferguson*
Greece Lecture Weekend · *Douglas Ferguson*
Normandy · *Douglas Ferguson*
Crete · *Douglas Ferguson*
Northern Greece · *Douglas Ferguson*
North Wales · *Eric Talbot*
Chateaux of the Ile de France · *Frances Vivian*
Palladio · *Frances Vivian*
Southern Italy · *Frances Vivian*
Norfolk & King's Lynn festival · *George Winkley*
Moorish Spain · *Gerald Crowson*
Tunisia · *Gerald Crowson*
Chinese Civilisation · *Graham Hutt*
Dorset & Thomas Hardy · *Ian Lowson*
Georgian Yorkshire · *Ian Lowson*
Bali Java & Lombok · *Ian Lowson*
Kenya · *Ian Lowson*
Mexico · *Ian Lowson*
Bohemia & Moravia · *J H Cordingley*
Warwickshire Houses & Hatchments · *J H Cordingley*
English Furniture · *Jan Scott Hutchman*
Surrey House · *Joe Acheson*
Italian Renaissance · *Joe Acheson*
Sicily · *Joe Acheson*
Lake District · *Marian Barraclough*
Mendips · *Marian Barraclough*
Shropshire · *Michael Tomkins*
Yorkshire Minsters · *Michael Tomkins*
Provence · *Michael Tomkins*
Orkney & Caithness · *Noel Fojut*
ACE 25th Anniversary RIBA · *Philip B Barnes*
Cambridge · *Philip B Barnes*
China Lecture Weekend · *Philip B Barnes*
Fenland Abbeys · *Philip B Barnes*
Medieval Suffolk · *Philip B Barnes*
Renaissance House · *Philip B Barnes*
Suffolk Houses · *Philip B Barnes*
German Baroque · *Philip B Barnes*
Rhine & Moselle · *Philip B Barnes*
Edinburgh Festival Theatre · *Roger Jerome*
Oxford · *Ron Brown*
Aegean Turkey · *Rowland Mainstone*
Burgundy · *Timothy Hyman*
Flemish Cities · *Tony Crowe*
Colonial America Lecture Weekend · *Tony Crowe*
Hampshire · *Tony Crowe*
India Lecture Weekend · *Tony Crowe*
Somerset · *Tony Crowe*
Edinburgh · *Tony Crowe*
Colonial America · *Tony Crowe*

1984

Thomas Hardy & Wessex · *A G Berrisford*
Portugal · *Alan Tait*
Aberdeenshire · *Alistair Gordon*
Fife & Angus · *Alistair Gordon*
Monasteries of Southern Yugoslavia · *Bernard Cox*
English Gothic · *Christie Arno*
English Romanesque · *Christie Arno*
Burgundy · *Christie Arno*
French Gothic · *Christie Arno*
Road to Compostela · *Christie Arno*
Tunisia · *Christie Arno*
Architecture of the Weald · *David Wickham*
Cheshire & Merseyside · *David Wickham*
Cinque Ports · *David Wickham*
Leicestershire Houses · *David Wickham*
Cornwall · *Douglas Ferguson*
Greece Lecture Weekend · *Douglas Ferguson*
Nottingham · *Douglas Ferguson*
Staffordshire Houses · *Douglas Ferguson*
Chateaux of the Loire · *Douglas Ferguson*
Rouen & the Seine Valley · *Douglas Ferguson*
Northern Greece · *Douglas Ferguson*
Normans & Welsh · *Eric Talbot*
North Wales · *Eric Talbot*
Southern Italy · *Frances Vivian*
Sri Lanka · *Gerald Crowson*
Edinburgh · *Gordon Steele*
Chinese Civilisation · *Graham Hutt*
Historic York · *Ian Lowson*
Bali & Java · *Ian Lowson*
Mexico · *Ian Lowson*
Mexico (2) · *Ian Lowson*
Peru · *Ian Lowson*
Peru II · *Ian Lowson*
Thailand & Burma · *Ian Lowson*
Derbyshire Houses · *J H Cordingley*
Somerset · *J H Cordingley*
English Furniture · *Jan Scott Hutchman*
Surrey House · *Joe Acheson*
Victorian Heritage · *Joe Acheson*
Crete & Santorini · *Joe Acheson*
Art of the Netherlands · *Joe Acheson*
Italian Renaissance · *Joe Acheson*
Hong Kong, Macau & Taiwan · *John Edge*
Kenya · *John Edge*
Lake District · *Marian Barraclough*
Quantocks · *Marian Barraclough*
Switzerland · *Maurice Jarrett*
Shropshire · *Michael Tomkins*
Three Choirs Festival · *Michael Tomkins*
Provence · *Michael Tomkins*
Shetlands · *Noel Fojut*
Egypt · *Patricia Baker*
American Inheritance · *Patrick Davies*
Denmark · *Philip B Barnes*
Annual Reunion (Royal Society of Art) · *Philip B Barnes*
Cambridge · *Philip B Barnes*
China Lecture Weekend · *Philip B Barnes*
Fenland Abbeys · *Philip B Barnes*
Medieval Suffolk · *Philip B Barnes*
Renaissance House · *Philip B Barnes*
Suffolk Houses · *Philip B Barnes*
Rhine & Moselle · *Philip B Barnes*
Moorish Spain · *Philip B Barnes*
Sri Lanka · *Philip B Barnes*
Italian Theatre · *Roger Jerome*
London Theatre · *Roger Jerome*
Edinburgh Festival Theatre · *Roger Jerome*
Oxford · *Ron Brown*
Central & Eastern Turkey · *Rowland Mainstone*
Flemish Cities · *Tony Crowe*
Egypt Lecture Weekend · *Tony Crowe*
India Lecture Weekend · *Tony Crowe*
Northumbria · *Tony Crowe*
Brittany · *Tony Crowe*
Moghul India & Nepal · *Tony Crowe*

1985

Thomas Hardy & Wessex · *A G Berrisford*
Portugal · *Alan Tait*
Orkney & Caithness · *Andrew Foxon*
Anglo-Saxon England · *Barrie Singleton*
French Gothic · *Barrie Singleton*
Rhineland Romanesque · *Barrie Singleton*
Road to the Pyrenees · *Christie Arno*
Sicily · *Christie Arno*
Road to Compostela · *Christie Arno*
Tunisia · *Christie Arno*
Cheshire & Merseyside · *David Wickham*
Jane Austen · *David Wickham*
Marsh & Downland · *David Wickham*
Cornwall · *Douglas Ferguson*
Isle of Wight · *Douglas Ferguson*
Chateaux of the Loire · *Douglas Ferguson*
Picardy & Artois · *Douglas Ferguson*
Greek Islands & Asia Minor · *Douglas Ferguson*
Northern Greece · *Douglas Ferguson*
Isle of Man · *Eric Talbot*
Corsica · *Frances Vivian*
Provence · *Frances Vivian*
East Anglian Houses · *George Winkley*
Scottish Art & Architecture · *Gordon Steele*
Chinese Civilisation · *Gregor Benton*
Chinese Civilisation · *Gregor Benton*
Bali & Java · *Ian Lowson*
Mexico · *Ian Lowson*
Peru · *Ian Lowson*
Peru II · *Ian Lowson*
Bohemia & Moravia · *J H Cordingley*
Hatchments & Houses · *J H Cordingley*
Adam Family in Scotland & Northern England · *J H Cordingley*
Renoir · *Joe Acheson*
William Morris & the Arts & Crafts Movement · *Joe Acheson*
Art of the Netherlands · *Joe Acheson*
Italian Renaissance · *Joe Acheson*
Kenya · *John Edge*
Georgian Bristol · *Marian Barraclough*
Welsh Marches · *Marian Barraclough*
Wiltshire Landscape · *Marian Barraclough*
Norfolk & King's Lynn Festival · *Michael Tomkins*
Three Choirs Festival Hereford · *Michael Tomkins*
Egypt · *Patricia Baker*
Egypt (2) · *Patricia Baker*
Moghul India & Nepal · *Patricia Baker*
American Inheritance · *Patrick Davies*
Annual Reunion · *Philip B Barnes*
Cambridge · *Philip B Barnes*
Fenland Abbeys · *Philip B Barnes*
Medieval Suffolk · *Philip B Barnes*
Celle · *Philip B Barnes*
Moorish Spain · *Philip B Barnes*
Sri Lanka · *Philip B Barnes*
Sri Lanka II · *Philip B Barnes*
Sweden · *Philip B Barnes*
Norwich · *Robin Emmerson*
Theatre in Vienna · *Roger Jerome*
London Theatre · *Roger Jerome*
Edinburgh Festival Theatre · *Roger Jerome*
Oxford · *Ron Brown*
Fife & Angus · *Ross Samson*
Flemish Cities · *Tony Crowe*
Northumbria · *Tony Crowe*
Somerset · *Tony Crowe*
Brittany · *Tony Crowe*
Russia · *Venetia Cross*

1986

Kilvert · *A G Berrisford*
Portugal · *Alan Tait*
Burgundy · *Barrie Singleton*
French Gothic · *Barrie Singleton*
Rhineland Romanesque · *Barrie Singleton*
Auvergne · *Christie Arno*
Provence · *Christie Arno*
Sicily · *Christie Arno*
Route to Compostela · *Christie Arno*
Tunisia · *Christie Arno*
Cinque Ports · *David Wickham*
Cornwall · *David Wickham*
Gothick Revival · *David Wickham*
Painting in Italy · *Denis Lowson*
Cambridge · *Douglas Ferguson*
English Imagination · *Douglas Ferguson*
Greece Lecture Weekend · *Douglas Ferguson*
King's Lynn Festival · *Douglas Ferguson*
Crete & Santorini · *Douglas Ferguson*
Greek Islands & Asia Minor · *Douglas Ferguson*
Romania · *Douglas Ferguson*
Sri Lanka · *Douglas Ferguson*
Corsica · *Frances Vivian*
Southern Italy & Rome · *Frances Vivian*
Scottish Art & Architecture · *Gordon Steele*
Chinese Civilisation · *Gregor Benton*
Peru · *H Strand Jones*
Road to Tibet · *Hugh Baker*
Chinese Civilisation · *Ian Lowson*
Mexico Lectures · *Ian Lowson*
Bali, Java & Sumatra · *Ian Lowson*
Mexico · *Ian Lowson*
Mexico (2) · *Ian Lowson*
Peru · *Ian Lowson*
Adam Family in Scotland & Northern England · *J H Cordingley*
William Morris & the Arts & Crafts Movement · *Joe Acheson*
Flemish & Dutch Art · *Joe Acheson*
Italian Renaissance · *Joe Acheson*
Venice & the Veneto · *Joe Acheson*
High Aragon · *John Boucher*
Hatchments, Houses & Churches · *John Cordingley*
Georgian Bristol · *Marian Barraclough*
Lake District · *Marian Barraclough*
Welsh Marches · *Marian Barraclough*
Shetlands · *Noel Fojut*
Egypt (2) · *Patricia Baker*
Sri Lanka · *Patricia Baker*
Berlin, Potsdam & Dresden · *Patrick Davies*
Pavia & Genoa · *Patrick Davies*
Frank Lloyd Wright's America · *Patrick Davies*
Annual Reunion (Art Workers Guild) · *Philip B Barnes*
China Lecture Weekend · *Philip B Barnes*
East Anglia in the 18th Century · *Philip B Barnes*
Fenland Abbeys · *Philip B Barnes*
Iceland · *Philip B Barnes*
Norway · *Philip B Barnes*
Norfolk Churches · *Robin Emmerson*
London Theatre · *Roger Jerome*
Theatre in Vienna · *Roger Jerome*
Edinburgh Festival Theatre · *Roger Jerome*
Oxford · *Ron Brown*
Fife & Angus · *Ross Samson*
Ghent, Veurnes & Bruges · *Tony Crowe*
Domesday Book · *Tony Crowe*
Hampshire · *Tony Crowe*
London's Historic Buildings · *Tony Crowe*
Northumbria · *Tony Crowe*
Plantagenets · *Tony Crowe*
Russia · *Venetia Cross*

1987

Portugal · *Alan Tait*
Highland Scotland · *Alistair Gordon*
Scottish Tower Houses · *Alistair Gordon*
Garden Cities · *Andrew Saint*
Durham · *Barrie Singleton*
Lincoln · *Barrie Singleton*
French Gothic · *Barrie Singleton*
Medieval Burgundy · *Barrie Singleton*
Rhineland Romanesque · *Barrie Singleton*
Auvergne · *Christie Arno*
Provence · *Christie Arno*
Road to the Pyrenees · *Christie Arno*
Sicily · *Christie Arno*
Route to Compostela · *Christie Arno*
Swaziland · *David Price Williams*
Cinque Ports · *David Wickham*
Egypt · *Delia Pemberton*
Tunisia · *Delia Pemberton*
Cambridge · *Douglas Ferguson*
English Imagination · *Douglas Ferguson*
Greece Lecture Weekend · *Douglas Ferguson*
King's Lynn Festival · *Douglas Ferguson*
Three Choirs Festival · *Douglas Ferguson*
Greece: Corinth & Argos · *Douglas Ferguson*
Romania · *Douglas Ferguson*
North Wales · *Eric Talbot*
Fenland Abbeys · *Gerald Randall*
Chinese Civilisation · *Gregor Benton*
Nepal & Tibet · *Gregor Benton*
Walking in High Aragon · *Hugh Barnes*
Mexico · *Ian Lowson*
Peru · *Ian Lowson*
Peru II · *Ian Lowson*
Georgian Yorkshire · *J H Cordingley*
William Morris & Victorian Art & Design · *Joe Acheson*
Italian Renaissance · *Joe Acheson*
High Aragon · *John Boucher*
Bristol · *Marian Barraclough*
Cotswold Landscape · *Marian Barraclough*
Quantocks · *Marian Barraclough*
Welsh Marches · *Marian Barraclough*
Iceland · *Noel Fojut*
Orkney · *Noel Fojut*
Silk Road · *Patricia Baker*
Egypt (2) · *Patricia Baker*
Southern India · *Patricia Baker*
Ottoman Turkey · *Patricia Baker*
Le Corbusier · *Patrick Davies*
Berlin · *Patrick Davies*
American Architecture · *Patrick Davies*
London Theatre · *Paul Ranger*
Edinburgh Festival Theatre · *Paul Ranger*
Chateaux of the Loire · *Peter Dovell*
Albania & Macedonia · *Philip B Barnes*
Bulgaria · *Philip B Barnes*
Copenhagen · *Philip B Barnes*
Annual Reunion · *Philip B Barnes*
China Lecture Weekend · *Philip B Barnes*
East Anglian Houses · *Philip B Barnes*
German Baroque · *Philip B Barnes*
Dutch Castles · *Philip B Barnes*
Moghul India & Nepal · *Philip B Barnes*
Leningrad · *Philip B Barnes*
Castile · *Philip B Barnes*
Moorish Spain · *Philip B Barnes*
East Anglia in the 18th Century · *Robin Emmerson*
Norwich - England's Second City · *Robin Emmerson*
Oxford · *Ron Brown*
The Black Forest · *Ross Samson*
Fife & Angus · *Ross Samson*
Hampshire · *Tony Crowe*
London's Historic Buildings · *Tony Crowe*
Northumbria · *Tony Crowe*
Plantagenets · *Tony Crowe*
Scottish Borders · *Tony Crowe*
Russia · *Venetia Hill*

1988

Portugal · *Alan Tait*
Glasgow's Treasures · *Alistair Gordon*
Scottish Tower Houses · *Alistair Gordon*
Canterbury · *Barrie Singleton*
Wells & Glastonbury · *Barrie Singleton*
Age of Chivalry · *Barrie Singleton*
Gothic France · *Barrie Singleton*
Medieval Burgundy · *Barrie Singleton*
Charlemagne's Kingdom · *Barrie Singleton*
Walking in High Aragon · *Charis Boucher/Hugh Barnes*
Sicily · *Christie Arno*
Namib Desert · *David Price Williams*
Swaziland · *David Price Williams*
Ancient Cities of the Turquoise Coast · *David Price Williams*
Ancient Cities of the Turquoise Coast (2) · *David Price Williams*
Malta · *David Trump*
Midland Themes · *David Wickham*
Albania & Macedonia · *Delia Pemberton*
Tunisia · *Delia Pemberton*
Painting in Corsica · *Denis Lowson*
Arabia Felix · *Dennis Sykes*
Geology of the Dorset Coast · *Diana Smith*
Cambridge · *Douglas Ferguson*
English Imagination · *Douglas Ferguson*
Three Choirs Festival · *Douglas Ferguson*
Timber, Stone & Brick · *Douglas Ferguson*
Normandy · *Douglas Ferguson*
Northern Greece · *Douglas Ferguson*
Romania · *Douglas Ferguson*
Cyprus · *Eric Talbot*
Brecon Beacons · *Eric Talbot*
Corsica · *Frances Vivian*
Bulgaria · *Gerald Randall*
Fenland Abbeys · *Gerald Randall*
Yorkshire Minsters & Monasteries · *Gerald Randall*
Nepal & Tibet · *Gregor Benton*
Silk Road · *Hugh Baker*
Walking in the Cevennes · *Hugh Barnes*
Chinese Civilisation · *Ian Lowson*
China Lecture Weekend · *Ian Lowson*
Guatemala · *Ian Lowson*
Mexico · *Ian Lowson*
Mexico (2) · *Ian Lowson*
Peru · *Ian Lowson*
Peru II · *Ian Lowson*
Castile · *Ian Lowson*
New York Experience · *Ian Lowson*
Russian Churches & Literature · *Irina Kirilova*
Classical Architecture · *J H Cordingley*
Paris des Peintres · *Joe Acheson*
Italian Renaissance · *Joe Acheson*
Venice & the Veneto · *Joe Acheson*
High Aragon · *John Boucher*
Pompeii & Paestum · *Lorna Kellett*
Industrial Archaeology of the Peak District · *Marian Barraclough*
Lake District · *Marian Barraclough*
Somerset Landscape · *Marian Barraclough*
Bohemia & Moravia · *Mark Powell*
Leningrad · *Mark Powell*
Iceland · *Noel Fojut*
Shetland Islands · *Noel Fojut*
Anatolia · *Patricia Baker*
Imperial Istanbul · *Patricia Baker*
Finnish Architecture · *Patrick Davies*
Gothick England · *Paul Ranger*
London Theatre · *Paul Ranger*
Chateaux of the Loire · *Peter Dovell*
Annual Reunion (Hinchingbrook) · *Philip B Barnes*
Faroe Islands · *Philip B Barnes*
Moghul India & Nepal · *Philip B Barnes*
Moorish Spain · *Philip B Barnes*
Provence · *Philip Conisbee*
Norfolk Churches · *Robin Emmerson*

Tudor & Stuart Norfolk · *Robin Emmerson*
Oxford · *Ron Brown*
Archaeology Summer School · *Stephen Briggs*
Flemish Cities · *Tony Crowe*
Egypt · *Tony Crowe*
Northumbria · *Tony Crowe*
Edinburgh & the Borders · *Tony Crowe*
Arabia Felix · *Vivienne Sharpe*

1989

Hadrian's Wall · *Alan Tait*
Portugal · *Alan Tait*
Highland Scotland · *Alistair Gordon*
Gloucester & Tewkesbury · *Barrie Singleton*
Sherborne & Salisbury · *Barrie Singleton*
Loire Romanesque · *Barrie Singleton*
Medieval Burgundy · *Barrie Singleton*
Medieval Burgundy · *Barrie Singleton*
German Romanesque · *Barrie Singleton*
Three Choir's Festival · *Brian Richardson*
Stained Glass · *Carola Hicks*
The Grandmontines · *Carole Hutchinson*
Sicily · *Christie Arno*
Road to Compostela · *Christie Arno*
Flowers & Wine of the Cape · *David Paton*
Namib Desert · *David Price Williams*
Swaziland & Botswana · *David Price Williams*
Lycia · *David Price Williams*
Cyprus · *David Trump*
English Vineyards · *David Wickham*
Christian & Islamic Egypt · *Delia Pemberton*
Egypt (2) · *Delia Pemberton*
New Kingdom Thebes · *Delia Pemberton*
New Kingdom Thebes · *Delia Pemberton*
Tunisia · *Delia Pemberton*
Geology of Pembrokeshire · *Diana Smith*
English Imagination · *Douglas Ferguson*
Greece Lecture Weekend · *Douglas Ferguson*
Herefordshire & the Welsh Borders · *Douglas Ferguson*
Athens · *Douglas Ferguson*
Crete · *Douglas Ferguson*
Peloponnese · *Douglas Ferguson*
Peloponnese · *Douglas Ferguson*
Romania · *Douglas Ferguson*
Galloway & Dumfries · *Douglas Ferguson*
Palladio · *Frances Vivian*
Bulgaria · *Gerald Randall*
Fenland Abbeys · *Gerald Randall*
Yorkshire Minsters & Monasteries · *Gerald Randall*
Mongols · *Gregor Benton*
Thailand, Unnan & Burma · *Gregor Benton*
Natural History of the Seychelles · *Heather Goudie*
Natural History of the Seychelles · *Heather Goudie*
Ecuador & the Galapagos · *Ian Lowson*
Guatemala · *Ian Lowson*
Mexico · *Ian Lowson*
Mexico (2) · *Ian Lowson*
Peru · *Ian Lowson*
Peru II · *Ian Lowson*
Castile · *Ian Lowson*
Russian Churches & Literature · *Irina Kirilova/Venetia Hill*
William Morris & Victorian Art & Design · *Joe Acheson*
Paris des Peintres · *Joe Acheson*
Italian Renaissance · *Joe Acheson*
Rome & the Campagna · *Joe Acheson*
High Aragon · *John Boucher*
High Aragon Revisited · *John Boucher*
Lady Anne Clifford · *Joseph Cordingley*
Pompeii & Paestum · *Lorna Kellett*
Peak District · *Marian Barraclough*
Quantocks · *Marian Barraclough*
Provence · *Mark Powell*
Leningrad · *Mark Powell*
Faroe Islands · *Noel Fojut*

Orkney · *Noel Fojut*
Eastern Anatolia · *Patricia Baker*
Ottoman Turkey · *Patricia Baker*
Steppes of Central Asia · *Patricia Baker*
Frank Lloyd Wright's America · *Patrick Davies*
Romantic Age · *Paul Ranger*
French Chateaux · *Peter Dovell*
Annual Reunion (St Paul's Cathedral) · *Philip B Barnes*
Annual Reunion (St Paul's Cathedral) · *Philip B Barnes*
Travel Themes · *Philip B Barnes*
Aquitaine · *Philip B Barnes*
India & Nepal · *Philip B Barnes*
Moorish Spain · *Philip B Barnes*
Albania · *Raymond Hutchings*
Georgian Norfolk & Suffolk · *Robin Emmerson*
Norwich – England's Second City · *Robin Emmerson*
London Theatre · *Roger Jerome*
Dublin Theatre Festival · *Roger Jerome*
Algarve, Portugal · *Roland Randall*
Cotswold Ways · *Ron Brown*
Italian Lakes & Gardens · *Simon Ditchfield*
Cevennes · *Tim Gardiner & Hugh Barnes*
Morocco · *Vivienne Sharpe*
Arabia Felix · *Vivienne Sharpe*

1990

Hadrian's Wall & Northumbria · *Alan Tait*
Portugal · *Alan Tait*
London's Docklands · *Alex Werner*
Glasgow's Treasures · *Alistair Gordon*
Highland Scotland · *Alistair Gordon*
Scottish Tower Houses · *Alistair Gordon*
Gloucester & Tewkesbury · *Barrie Singleton*
Medieval Devon · *Barrie Singleton*
Medieval Lincoln · *Barrie Singleton*
Sherborne & Salisbury · *Barrie Singleton*
French Romanesque, Poitou & Saintonge · *Barrie Singleton*
Medieval Burgundy · *Barrie Singleton*
German Baroque · *Barrie Singleton*
Natural History of the Seychelles · *Betty Becket*
Prague Music Festival · *Brian Richardson*
Lake District · *Brian Richardson*
Three Choirs Festival · *Brian Richardson*
Stained Glass · *Carola Hicks*
Sicily · *Christie Arno*
Barcelona & Tarragona · *Christie Arno*
Road to Compostela · *Christie Arno*
Flowers & Wine of the Cape · *David Paton*
Flowers & Wine of the Cape (2) · *David Paton*
Namib Desert · *David Price Williams*
Zimbabwe & Botswana · *David Price Williams*
Lycia Cruises · *David Price Williams/Peter Reynolds*
Lycia Cruises (2) · *David Price Williams/Peter Reynolds*
Lycia Cruises (3) · *David Price Williams/Peter Reynolds*
Falkland Islands · *David Rootes*
Mallorca & Minorca · *David Trump/Roland Randall*
English Vineyards · *David Wickham*
Coptic & Islamic Egypt · *Delia Pemberton*
Egypt · *Delia Pemberton*
New Kingdom Thebes · *Delia Pemberton*
Geology of the Cotswold · *Diana Smith*
Geology of the Cotswolds · *Diana Smith*
Geology of Pembrokeshire · *Diana Smith*
Cambridge · *Douglas Ferguson*
English Imagination · *Douglas Ferguson*
Greece Lecture Weekend · *Douglas Ferguson*
Hereford & the Welsh Borders · *Douglas Ferguson*
Medieval Suffolk · *Douglas Ferguson*
Shropshire · *Douglas Ferguson*
Yorkshire Dales · *Douglas Ferguson*
Greek Islands · *Douglas Ferguson*
Galloway & Dumfries · *Douglas Ferguson*
South-West Scotland · *Douglas Ferguson*
Australia · *Douglas Paine*

Bulgaria · *Gerald Randall*
Fenland Abbeys · *Gerald Randall*
Yorkshire Minsters & Monasteries · *Gerald Randall*
Adventure in Mongolia · *Gregor Benton*
Mongols · *Gregor Benton*
Eastern Anatolia · *Gulbikem Ronay*
Ecuador & the Galapagos (2) · *Ian Lowson*
Guatemala · *Ian Lowson*
Mexico · *Ian Lowson*
Peru · *Ian Lowson*
Castile · *Ian Lowson*
Russian Churches & Literature · *Irina Kirilova*
William Morris & Victorian Art & Design · *Joe Acheson*
French Painting · *Joe Acheson*
Paris des Peintres · *Joe Acheson*
Vincent van Gogh · *Joe Acheson*
Glory of Venice · *Joe Acheson*
Venetian Paintings · *Joe Acheson*
High Aragon · *John Boucher*
High Aragon (2) · *John Boucher*
High Aragon Revisited · *John Boucher*
In the Steps of Lady Anne Clifford · *Joseph Cordingley*
Athens · *Lorna Kellet*
Pompeii & Paestum · *Lorna Kellett*
Classical Greece · *Lorna Kellett & David Trump*
Natural History of the Seychelles · *Malcolm Coe*
Peak District · *Marian Barraclough*
Quantocks · *Marian Barraclough*
New Zealand · *Mark Hanger*
New Zealand (2) · *Mark Hanger*
Austria · *Mark Powell*
Provence · *Mark Powell*
Leningrad · *Mark Powell*
Greek Islands · *Martin Sands*
Iceland · *Noel Fojut*
Orkney · *Noel Fojut*
Shetland · *Noel Fojut*
Steppes of Central Asia · *Patricia Baker*
Ottoman Turkey · *Patricia Baker*
Road to Samarkand · *Patricia Baker*
Edinburgh Festival Theatre · *Paul Ranger*
Syria & Jordan · *Peter Parr & David Price Williams*
Church Towers & Hunky Punks · *Peter Poyntz-Wright*
Castles of North Wales · *Peter Poyntz-Wright*
Denmark · *Philip B Barnes*
Annual Reunion (Thomas Coram) · *Philip B Barnes*
Aquitaine · *Philip B Barnes*
India · *Philip B Barnes*
India & Nepal · *Philip B Barnes*
Moorish Spain · *Philip B Barnes*
Albania · *Raymond Hutchings*
Hungary · *Raymond Hutchings*
Romania · *Raymond Hutchings*
Georgian Norfolk & Suffolk · *Robin Emmerson*
Norwich - England's Second City · *Robin Emmerson*
Chichester Festival Theatre · *Roger Jerome*
Coventry Miracle Plays · *Roger Jerome*
London Theatre · *Roger Jerome*
Algarve, Portugal · *Roland Randall*
Cotswold Ways · *Ron Brown*
Oxford · *Ron Brown*
Private Wealth, Public Riches · *Simon Ditchfield*
Hill Towns of Tuscany · *Simon Ditchfield*
Italian Lakes & Villas · *Simon Ditchfield*
Rome Triumphant · *Simon Ditchfield*
Turin & the Italian Alps · *Simon Ditchfield*
Tuscan Villas & Gardens · *Simon Ditchfield*
Brittany · *Tim Gardiner*
Cevennes · *Tim Gardiner*
Greek Islands · *Tim Tatton Brown*
Arabia Felix · *Vivienne Sharpe*

1991

Hadrian's Wall & Northumbria · *Alan Tait*
Portugal · *Alan Tait*
London's Dockland · *Alex Werner*
Cyprus · *Alistair Gordon*
Glasgow's Treasures · *Alistair Gordon*
Highland Scotland – Pitlochry · *Alistair Gordon*
Oban & the West Highlands · *Alistair Gordon*
The Potteries · *Arnold Mountford*
Durham · *Barrie Singleton*
Norwich & Norfolk · *Barrie Singleton*
The Age of Bede · *Barrie Singleton*
French Romanesque – The South West · *Barrie Singleton*
German Romanesque, Trier & Speyer · *Barrie Singleton*
Upper Rhine · *Barrie Singleton*
Ravenna & its Neighbours · *Barrie Singleton*
Natural History of the Seychelles · *Betty Becket*
Prague Music Festival · *Brian Richardson*
Flowers & Wine of the Cape · *Bryn Joliffe*
Zimbabwe & Botswana · *Bryn Joliffe*
Bulgaria · *Christie Arno*
Sicily · *Christie Arno*
Road to Compostela · *Christie Arno*
Poland's Green Lung · *Christopher Hadley*
Poland's Green Lung II · *Christopher Hadley*
Aegean Turkey & Greek Island Cruise · *David Price Williams*
Falkland Islands · *David Rootes*
Falkland Islands · *David Rootes*
Namib Desert · *David Thomas*
Sardinia - Archaeology · *David Trump*
India · *Delia Pemberton*
Flemish Cities · *Douglas Ferguson*
Jersey · *Douglas Ferguson*
Isle of Wight · *Douglas Ferguson*
Medieval Suffolk · *Douglas Ferguson*
Yorkshire Dales · *Douglas Ferguson*
Seine Valley · *Douglas Ferguson*
Northern Greece · *Douglas Ferguson*
South West Scotland · *Douglas Ferguson*
Australia · *Douglas Paine*
Wild Flowers of Crete · *Franklyn Perring*
Birdwatching on the Bosphorus · *Franklyn Perring*
Fenland Abbeys · *Gerald Randall*
Lincolnshire · *Gerald Randall*
Norfolk Houses & Gardens · *Gerald Randall*
French Gardens · *Gerald Randall*
Burma & Thailand · *Gregor Benton*
Ecuador & the Galapagos · *Ian Lowson*
Ecuador & the Galapagos (2) · *Ian Lowson*
Aquitaine · *Ian Lowson*
Guatemala · *Ian Lowson*
Mexico · *Ian Lowson*
Bolivia & Peru · *Ian Lowson*
Palaces of St Petersburg · *Irina Kirilova*
The Japanese Print · *Joe Acheson*
Victorian Art & Design · *Joe Acheson*
French Painting · *Joe Acheson*
Paris des Peintres · *Joe Acheson*
Florentine Renaissance · *Joe Acheson*
Venetian Painting 1450–1750 · *Joe Acheson*
Venice · *Joe Acheson*
High Aragon · *John Boucher*
High Aragon (2) · *John Boucher*
High Aragon Revisited · *John Boucher*
Bulgaria · *John Snodgrass*
In the Steps of Lady Anne Clifford · *Joseph Cordingley*
Classical Rome · *Lorna Kellet & David Tristam*
Pompeii & Paestum · *Lorna Kellett & David Trump*
Andrea Mantegna · *Malcolm Oxley*
New Zealand · *Mark Hanger*
New Zealand (2) · *Mark Hanger*
Czechoslovakia · *Mark Powell*
Ducal Burgundy · *Mark Powell*
Provence · *Mark Powell*

Hungary · *Mark Powell*
Moscow · *Mark Powell*
Iceland · *Noel Fojut*
Central Anatolia · *Patricia Baker*
Ottoman Turkey · *Patricia Baker*
Road to Samarkand · *Patricia Baker*
Edinburgh Festival theatre · *Paul Ranger*
Somerset Churches · *Peter Poyntz-Wright*
Castles of South Wales · *Peter Poyntz-Wright*
Lycia Cruises · *Peter Reynolds*
Lycia Cruises (2) · *Peter Reynolds*
Lycia Cruises (3) · *Peter Reynolds*
Annual Reunion (St Paul's Cathedral) · *Philip B Barnes*
German Baroque · *Philip B Barnes*
India Revisited · *Philip B Barnes*
Moorish Spain · *Philip B Barnes*
Isles of Scilly · *Roland Randall*
Sardinia – Natural History · *Roland Randall*
Oxford · *Ron Brown*
Birmingham · *Rudi Herbert*
Monasteries of Southern Yugoslavia · *Ruth Macrides*
Private Wealth, Public Riches · *Simon Ditchfield*
Hill Towns of Tuscany · *Simon Ditchfield*
Hill Towns of Tuscany · *Simon Ditchfield*
Italian Lakes, Villas & Gardens · *Simon Ditchfield*
Tuscan Villas & Gardens · *Simon Ditchfield*
Chichester Festival Theatre · *Susan Friesner*
Brittany · *Tim Gardiner*
Cevennes · *Tim Gardiner*
Zululand & Drakensberg · *Tony Williams*

1992

Portugal · *Alan Tait*
The Hansa · *Alex Werner*
Burgundy · *Barrie Singleton*
French Romanesque - Anjou & Normandy · *Barrie Singleton*
German Gothic · *Barrie Singleton*
Ravenna & its Neighbours · *Barrie Singleton*
Coto Donana & Sierra Ronda · *Bob Gibbons/David Knight*
Musical Prague · *Brian Richardson*
Prague Music Festival · *Brian Richardson*
Musical Venice · *Brian Richardson*
Romanesque & The Pyrenees, Adorra, Catalonia, Rousillon · *Christie Arno*
Sicily · *Christie Arno*
Southern Italy · *Christie Arno*
Western Sicily · *Christie Arno*
Asturias · *Christie Arno*
Road to Compostela · *Christie Arno*
Poland's Green Lung · *Christopher Hadley*
Kalahari & Okevango Delta · *David Price Williams*
Namibia · *David Price Williams*
Ephesus & the Hellenistic World · *David Price Williams*
Archaeology of Malta · *David Trump*
Northern India · *Denis Moriarty*
Flemish Cities · *Douglas Ferguson*
Mani & Medieval Greece · *Douglas Ferguson*
Burma & Thailand · *Gregor Benton*
Vermilion Bird - Cultures of South China · *Gregor Benton*
Bird Migration in Thrace & the Bosphorus · *Guy Kirwan*
Ecuador & the Galapagos · *Ian Lowson*
Aquitaine · *Ian Lowson*
Guatemala · *Ian Lowson*
Mexico · *Ian Lowson*
Olmecs to Aztecs · *Ian Lowson*
Castile · *Ian Lowson*
Switzerland · *Ian Lowson*
Hawaii · *Ian Lowson*
Russian Ballet · *Irina Kirilova*
Russian Churches & Literature · *Irina Kirilova*
Rembrandt & His Contemporaries · *Joe Acheson*
Venice & the Veneto · *Joe Acheson*
High Aragon · *John Boucher*
High Aragon - a shorter visit · *John Boucher*

High Aragon (2) · *John Boucher*
Swaziland & Kruger National Park · *John Drennan*
Zimbabwe - with the Victoria Falls · *Justin Grant*
Pompeii & Paestum · *Lorna Kellet & David Tristam*
Renaissance Florence · *Malcolm Oxley*
New Zealand · *Mark Hanger*
New Zealand (2) · *Mark Hanger*
Bulgaria · *Mark Powell*
Alsace, Lorraine & the Rhine · *Mark Powell*
Autumn in Paris · *Mark Powell*
Provence · *Mark Powell*
Habsburg Lands · *Mark Powell*
Towns & Palaces of Poland · *Mark Powell*
St Petersburg · *Mark Powell*
Silk Road · *Patricia Baker*
Ottoman Turkey · *Patricia Baker*
1066 & All That – Bayeux & Caen · *Peter Poyntz-Wright*
Ancient Lycia · *Peter Reynolds*
Bornholm · *Philip B Barnes*
Annual Reunion (St Bartholomew) · *Philip B Barnes*
India Revisited · *Philip B Barnes*
Southern India · *Philip B Barnes*
Moorish Spain · *Philip B Barnes*
Sweden · *Philip B Barnes*
Falkland Islands · *Rana Bound*
West of Ireland · *Sara Champion*
Hill Towns of Tuscany · *Simon Ditchfield*
Italian Lakes, Villas & Gardens · *Simon Ditchfield*
Marvels of Rome: the Eternal City at Christmas · *Simon Ditchfield*
Tuscan Villas & Gardens · *Simon Ditchfield*
Umbria & the Marches · *Simon Ditchfield*
Brittany · *Tim Gardiner*
Cevennes · *Tim Gardiner*
Dutch Gardens · *Will van de Wiel*

1993

Alnwick · *Alan Tait*
Spring in Portugal · *Alan Tait*
Highland Scotland - Pitlochry · *Alistair Gordon*
Kilvranock · *Alistair Gordon*
Geology of Pembrokeshire · *Allan Insole*
Lombard Art · *Barrie Singleton*
Ravenna, Venice & Cividale · *Barrie Singleton*
Haydn at Eisenstadt · *Brian Richardson*
Salzburg - City of Music · *Brian Richardson*
Prague Music Festival · *Brian Richardson*
Musical Venice · *Brian Richardson*
Stained Glass - Cambridge · *Carola Hicks*
Durham - English Romanesque · *Christie Arno*
Dordogne · *Christie Arno*
Road to the Pyrenees · *Christie Arno*
Sicily at Easter · *Christie Arno*
Southern Italy · *Christie Arno*
Road to Compostela · *Christie Arno*
Renaissance England · *David Bostwick*
Archaeology of Cyprus · *David Trump*
Australia · *Denis Carlisle*
Berwick & the Borders · *Denis Moriarty*
Devon - Brixham · *Denis Moriarty*
Northern India & Nepal · *Denis Moriarty*
Flemish Cities · *Douglas Ferguson*
Robert Adam · *Douglas Ferguson*
Oban & the West Highlands · *Douglas Ferguson*
Scottish Castles · *Douglas Ferguson*
Pompeii & Paestum · *Edward Herring*
English Alabasters · *Francis Cheetham*
Norfolk in Tudor & Jacobean Times · *Francis Cheetham*
Italian Lakes, Villas & Gardens · *Francis Cheetham*
Tuscan Villas & Gardens · *Francis Cheetham*
Moorish Spain · *Francis Cheetham*
East Anglian Houses & Gardens · *Gerald Randall*
Fenland Abbeys · *Gerald Randall*
The Mongols · *Gregor Benton*
Guatemala · *Ian Lowson*

Mayas in Guatemala · *Ian Lowson*
Mexico · *Ian Lowson*
Castile · *Ian Lowson*
Switzerland · *Ian Lowson*
Russian Ballet · *Irina Kirilova*
Russian Ballet at Christmas · *Irina Kirilova*
Ben Nicholson · *Joe Acheson*
Camille Pissarro · *Joe Acheson*
Sickert · *Joe Acheson*
Sir Edward Burne-Jones · *Joe Acheson*
Sir Edward Burne-Jones · *Joe Acheson*
Sir Edward Burne-Jones · *Joe Acheson*
The Surrey House · *Joe Acheson*
William Morris & The Arts & Crafts Movement · *Joe Acheson*
Golden Age of Amsterdam · *Joe Acheson*
Golden Age of Amsterdam · *Joe Acheson*
Golden Age of Amsterdam · *Joe Acheson*
Venice & the Veneto · *Joe Acheson*
Poland's Green Lung · *John Akeroyd*
High Aragon · *John Boucher*
High Aragon - a shorter visit · *John Boucher*
High Aragon (2) · *John Boucher*
Zimbabwe - with the Victoria Falls · *Justin Grant*
Winter Birdlife in Norfolk · *Kevin Hand*
Crete - Flowers, Birds & Minoans · *Kevin Hand*
Namibia · *Leyanne Wahl*
Barbizon & Fontainebleau · *Louise Leates*
French Chateaux · *Louise Leates*
Renaissance Florence · *Malcolm Oxley*
Wildlife in India · *Mark Crocker*
New Zealand · *Mark Hanger*
New Zealand (2) · *Mark Hanger*
Christmas in Vienna · *Mark Powell*
Bulgaria · *Mark Powell*
Bohemia & Moravia · *Mark Powell*
Baltic States · *Mark Powell*
Alsace, Lorraine & the Rhine · *Mark Powell*
Provence · *Mark Powell*
Towns & Palaces of Poland · *Mark Powell*
Renaissance House · *Mary Stoyle*
Persia · *Patricia Baker*
Syria & Jordan · *Patricia Baker*
Central Anatolia · *Patricia Baker*
Ottoman Turkey · *Patricia Baker*
Hill Towns of Tuscany · *Paul Gwynne*
Umbria: Power, Piety an Patronage · *Paul Gwynne*
Chichester Festival Theatre · *Paul Ranger*
Abbeys & Cathedrals of the North · *Peter Poyntz-Wright*
Church Towers & Hunky Punks · *Peter Poyntz-Wright*
Castles & Abbeys of the Welsh Borders · *Peter Poyntz-Wright*
Aegean Turkey & the Greek Islands · *Peter Reynolds*
Ancient Lycia · *Peter Reynolds*
Denmark · *Philip B Barnes*
Annual Reunion (Chenies) · *Philip B Barnes*
Annual Reunion (Chenies) · *Philip B Barnes*
Stained Glass in York · *Philip B Barnes*
Charleston & the Carolinas · *Philip B Barnes*
Charleston & the Carolinas (2) · *Philip B Barnes*
Isles of Scilly · *Roland Randall*
Iona & Mull · *Roland Randall*
Wild Flowers of High Aragon · *Roland Randall*
Oxford · *Ron Brown*
West of Ireland · *Sara Champion*
Hill Towns of Tuscany · *Simon Ditchfield*
Tuscan Villas & Gardens · *Simon Ditchfield*
Cevennes · *Tim Gardiner*
Corsica · *Tim Gardiner*
Islamic Art & Architecture · *Tim Stanley*
Orkney · *Val Turner*
Etruscans · *Valerie Higgins*
Umbria: Power, Piety an Patronage · *Valerie Higgins*

1994

Northumbria & Hadrian's Wall · *Alan Tait*
Northern Portugal · *Alan Tait*
Spring in Portugal · *Alan Tait*
Georgian Scotland · *Andrew Clark*
Highland Scotland - Pitlochry · *Andrew Wilson*
Scottish Tower Houses · *Andrew Wilson*
Aegean Shore · *Andrew Wilson*
Ravenna & its Neighbours · *Barrie Singleton*
Eisenstadt · *Brian Richardson*
Salzburg - City of Music · *Brian Richardson*
Music in Bohemia · *Brian Richardson*
Budapest Spring Festival · *Brian Richardson*
Musical Venice · *Brian Richardson*
Victorian Cambridge · *Carola Hicks*
Mallorca · *Catherine Barnes*
Durham - English Romanesque · *Christie Arno*
Medieval World · *Christie Arno*
Medieval Languedoc · *Christie Arno*
Sicily at Easter · *Christie Arno*
Sicily in Autumn · *Christie Arno*
Southern Italy · *Christie Arno*
Road to Compostela · *Christie Arno*
The Smythsons & Elizabethan England · *David Bostwick*
Cradle of Mankind · *David Price Williams*
Cradle of Mankind · *David Price Williams*
The Cradle of Mankind · *David Price Williams*
Peloponnese · *David Trump*
Devon - Brixham · *Denis Moriarty*
Rajasthan · *Denis Moriarty*
Rajasthan II · *Denis Moriarty*
Southern India · *Denis Moriarty*
In the Steps of St Francis · *Denis Moriarty*
Charleston & the Carolinas · *Denis Moriarty*
Charleston & the Carolinas (2) · *Denis Moriarty*
Lincolnshire Houses · *Douglas Ferguson*
Pompeii & Paestum · *Edward Herring*
English Alabasters · *Francis Cheetham*
Georgian Norfolk · *Francis Cheetham*
Gunton Park - a private visit · *Francis Cheetham*
Industrial Archaeology of the Peak District · *Francis Cheetham*
Italian Lakes, Villas & Gardens · *Francis Cheetham*
Tuscan Villas & Gardens · *Francis Cheetham*
Historic Malta · *Francis Cheetham*
Moorish Spain · *Francis Cheetham*
Moorish Spain · *Francis Cheetham*
East Anglian Houses & Gardens · *Gerald Randall*
Fenland Abbeys · *Gerald Randall*
Chinese Civilisation · *Gregor Benton*
The Mongols · *Gregor Benton*
Thomas Hardy's Dorset · *Ian Lowson*
Mayas in Guatemala · *Ian Lowson*
Sumatra, Bali & Java · *Ian Lowson*
Mexico · *Ian Lowson*
Castile · *Ian Lowson*
Switzerland · *Ian Lowson*
Palladio · *Joanna Saurin*
Art in Cornwall · *Joe Acheson*
Salvador Dali · *Joe Acheson*
Salvador Dali · *Joe Acheson*
Surrey House · *Joe Acheson*
William Morris & The Arts & Crafts Movement · *Joe Acheson*
Florence · *Joe Acheson*
Glories of the Serenissima · *Joe Acheson*
Glories of the Serenissima · *Joe Acheson*
Burren & Dingle · *John Akeroyd*
Flowers of the Swiss Alps · *John Akeroyd*
High Aragon · *John Boucher*
High Aragon - a shorter visit · *John Boucher*
High Aragon (2) · *John Boucher*
Honiton Lace · *John Yallop*
Wildlife in Norfolk · *Kevin Hand*
Crete - Flowers, Birds & Minoans · *Kevin Hand*
Poland's Green Lung · *Kevin Hand*

Namibia · Leyanne Wahl
Arts of 19th Century Paris · *Louise Leates*
French Chateaux · *Louise Leates*
The Arts of 19th Century Paris · *Louise Leates*
Renaissance Courts · *Malcolm Oxley*
Venice Renaissance Models Exhibition · *Malcolm Oxley*
New Zealand · *Mark Hanger*
New Zealand (2) · *Mark Hanger*
Bulgarian Monasteries · *Mark Powell*
Baltic States · *Mark Powell*
Alsace & Lorraine · *Mark Powell*
Provence · *Mark Powell*
Provence II · *Mark Powell*
Berlin & Brandenburg · *Mark Powell*
Christmas in Vienna · *Mark Powell*
Towns & Palaces of Poland · *Mark Powell*
Ruthenians & Ruritania · *Mark Powell*
Hill Towns of Tuscany · *Mark Pritchard*
Syria · *Patricia Baker*
Lost Kingdoms of Eastern Turkey · *Patricia Baker*
Ottoman Turkey · *Patricia Baker*
Chichester Festival Theatre · *Paul Ranger*
Stained Glass in Oxford · *Pauline Barnes*
Flemish Cities · *Peter Poyntz-Wright*
Abbeys & Cathedrals of the North · *Peter Poyntz-Wright*
Castles & Abbeys of the Welsh Borders · *Peter Poyntz-Wright*
Norman Legacy · *Peter Poyntz-Wright*
Ancient Lycia · Peter Reynolds
Dronninglund - a Queen's Manor · *Philip B Barnes*
Annual Reunion (Chichely Hall) · *Philip B Barnes*
Stained Glass in York · *Philip B Barnes*
Faroe Islands · *Philip B Barnes*
Armagnac · *Philip B Barnes*
Music in Vienna · *Roger Rayner*
Barbados · *Roland Randall*
Isles of Scilly · *Roland Randall*
In the Steps of St Francis (2) · *Roland Randall*
Wildlife of Algarve · *Roland Randall*
Flowers & Birds of the Pyrenees · *Roland Randall*
Oxford · *Ron Brown*
Isle of Man · *Sara Champion*
West of Ireland · *Sara Champion*
Italian Lakes, Villas & Gardens · *Simon Ditchfield*
Russian Churches & Palaces · *Simon Franklin*
Cevennes · *Tim Gardiner*
Plantagenets · *Tim Gardiner*
Ottoman Turkey · *Tim Stanley*
Shetland Islands · *Val Turner*
Christmas in Rome · *Valerie Higgins*
Classical Rome · *Valerie Higgins*
Classical Rome · *Valerie Higgins*
Classical Rome · *Valerie Higgins*
Etruscans · *Valerie Higgins*
Hill Towns of Tuscany · *Valerie Higgins*
Morocco · *Vivienne Sharpe*

1995

Glasgow's Treasures · *Aileen Smart*
Hadrian's Wall & the Borders · *Andrew Wilson*
Road to Damascus · *Andrew Wilson*
Ancient Lycia · *Andrew Wilson*
French Gothic · *Barrie Singleton*
Gothic in Saxony · *Barrie Singleton*
Ravenna, Venice & Cividale · *Barrie Singleton*
Haydn at Eisenstadt · *Brian Richardson*
Salzburg - City of Music · *Brian Richardson*
Prague Music Festival · *Brian Richardson*
Budapest Spring Festival · *Brian Richardson*
Musical Venice · *Brian Richardson*
Chopin in Poland · *Brian Richardson*
Victorian Cambridge · *Carola Hicks*
French Pyrenees · *Catherine Barnes*
Land of the Cathars · *Catherine Barnes*
Land of the Cathars · *Catherine Barnes*

Dagali & the Hardanger Vidda · *Catherine Barnes*
Hardangervidde · *Catherine Barnes*
Mallorca · *Catherine Barnes*
Transmuntana · *Catherine Barnes*
Georgian Architecture · *Charles Hind*
Forest of Dean · *Christie Arno*
Medieval Burgundy · *Christie Arno*
Sicily at Easter · *Christie Arno*
Southern Italy · *Christie Arno*
Catalonia · *Christie Arno*
Road to Compostela · *Christie Arno*
Renaissance England · *David Bostwick*
The Green Man · *David Bostwick*
Archaeology of Sardinia · *David Trump*
William Morris & The Arts & Crafts Movement · *Denis Moriarty*
Northern India · *Denis Moriarty*
Northern India (2) · *Denis Moriarty*
Southern India · *Denis Moriarty*
Moghul India & Nepal · *Denis Moriarty*
Sri Lanka · *Denis Moriarty*
Charleston & the Carolinas · *Denis Moriarty*
New England · *Denis Moriarty*
Belgian Chateaux & Parks · *Douglas Ferguson*
Penwith & the Lizard · *Douglas Ferguson*
Pompeii & Paestum · *Edward Herring*
Private Wealth, Public Riches · *Elizabeth Newell*
English Alabasters · *Francis Cheetham*
The Future of the English Country House · *Francis Cheetham*
Italian Lakes, Villas & Gardens · *Francis Cheetham*
Magic of Umbria · *Francis Cheetham*
Tuscan Villas & Gardens · *Francis Cheetham*
Historic Malta · *Francis Cheetham*
Portugal · *Francis Cheetham*
Moorish Spain · *Francis Cheetham*
Moorish Spain (2) · *Francis Cheetham*
Semana Santa in Seville · *Francis Cheetham*
Toledo & Madrid · *Francis Cheetham*
East Anglian Houses & Gardens · *Gerald Randall*
Fenland Abbeys · *Gerald Randall*
Follies & Grottoes · *Gerald Randall*
Yorkshire Minsters & Monasteries · *Gerald Randall*
French Gardens · *Gerald Randall*
Chinese Civilisation · *Gregor Benton*
Thailand · *Gregor Benton*
Vienna at Christmas · *Ian Lowson*
Writers & Artists of Dorset · *Ian Lowson*
Aquitaine · *Ian Lowson*
Guatemala · *Ian Lowson*
Sumatra, Bali & Java · *Ian Lowson*
Mexico · *Ian Lowson*
Castile · *Ian Lowson*
Villas of the Veneto · *Joanna Saurin*
Poland's Green Lung · *John Akeroyd*
Steppe, Marsh & Mountain · *John Akeroyd*
High Aragon · *John Boucher*
High Aragon (2) · *John Boucher*
High Aragon with the Ordesa National Park · *John Boucher*
Hill Towns of Tuscany · *Jonna Saurin*
Stained Glass in Canterbury · *June Osborne*
Northern Wildlife · *Kevin Hand*
Wildlife in Norfolk · *Kevin Hand*
Gambia & Senegal · *Kevin Hand*
North Queensland & Papua New Guinea · *Kevin Hand*
Tenerife - Whales, Flowers & Birds · *Kevin Hand*
Arts of 18th Century France · *Louise Leates*
Autumn in Anjou & Touraine · *Louise Leates*
Cezanne Exhibition in Paris I · *Louise Leates*
Cezanne Exhibition in Paris II · *Louise Leates*
Paris - 17th & 18th Centuries · *Louise Leates*
Paris Cezanne Exhibition · *Louise Leates*
Sculpture in Paris · *Louise Leates*
Victorian Achievement – Leeds & Saltaire · *Malcolm Oxley*
Italian Renaissance · *Malcolm Oxley*
Renaissance Florence · *Malcolm Oxley*

New Zealand · *Mark Hanger*
New Zealand (2) · *Mark Hanger*
Art Nouveau in Belgium · *Mark Powell*
Bulgarian Monasteries · *Mark Powell*
Splendours of Prague · *Mark Powell*
Alsace & Lorraine · *Mark Powell*
Cote d'Azur · *Mark Powell*
Provence · *Mark Powell*
Berlin & Brandenburg · *Mark Powell*
Teutonic Knights · *Mark Powell*
Cracow at Christmas · *Mark Powell*
Ruthenians & Ruritania · *Mark Powell*
Romania · *Mark Powell*
Oxford Today · *Miriam Curtis*
Persia · *Patricia Baker*
Syria · *Patricia Baker*
Ottoman Turkey · *Patricia Baker*
Chichester Festival Theatre · *Paul Ranger*
Shakespeare at Stratford · *Paul Ranger*
Flemish Cities · *Peter Poyntz-Wright*
Castles of South Wales · *Peter Poyntz-Wright*
Bornholm · *Philip B Barnes*
Annual Reunion (Layer Marney) · *Philip B Barnes*
Pepys in London & Cambridge · *Philip B Barnes*
Music in Lucerne · *Roger Rayner*
Georgian Ireland · *Roger White*
Lesbos & Chios · *Roland Randall*
Madeira - Flowers & Gardens · *Roland Randall*
Inner Hebrides · *Roland Randall*
Dingle Peninsula · *Sara Champion*
Zimbabwe - Animals, Art & Archaeology · *Sara Champion*
Islamic Art · *Tim Stanley*
Ottoman Turkey · *Tim Stanley*
Shetland Islands · *Val Turner*
Abruzzo - Mountains, Bears & Samnites · *Valerie Higgins*
Etruscans · *Valerie Higgins*
Hill Towns of Tuscany · *Valerie Higgins*
Rome: from Paganism to Papacy · *Valerie Higgins*
Sorrento at Christmas · *Valerie Higgins*
The Marches · *Valerie Higgins*
Oman · *Vivienne Sharpe*

1996

Charles Rennie Macintosh · *Aileen Smart*
Velazquez & Mackintosh · *Aileen Smart*
Hadrian's Wall & the Borders · *Andrew Wilson*
Road to Damascus · *Andrew Wilson*
Ancient Lycia · *Andrew Wilson*
Prague Music Festival · *Barrie Singleton*
Medieval Bavaria · *Barrie Singleton*
Giotto & the Trecento · *Barrie Singleton*
Ravenna, Venice & Cividale · *Barrie Singleton*
Haydn at Eisenstadt · *Brian Richardson*
Music in Leipzig · *Brian Richardson*
Budapest Spring Festival · *Brian Richardson*
William Morris & Cambridge · *Carola Hicks*
Land of the Cathars · *Catherine Barnes*
Dagali & the Hardanger Vidda · *Catherine Barnes*
Norway · *Catherine Barnes*
Walking in Mallorca · *Catherine Barnes*
Georgian Yorkshire · *Charles Hind*
Medieval Burgundy · *Christie Arno*
Sicily at Easter · *Christie Arno*
Southern Italy · *Christie Arno*
Catalonia · *Christie Arno*
Road to Compostela · *Christie Arno*
Arizona · *Christie Arno*
Arizona - Cactus, Canyons, Indians & Frank Lloyd Wright · *Christie Arno*
Lady Anne Clifford · *David Bostwick*
The Green Man · *David Bostwick*
The Smythsons & Elizabethan England · *David Bostwick*
Archaeology of Malta · *David Trump*
Christmas in Salzburg · *Denis Moriarty*

Schubert in Feldkirch · *Denis Moriarty*
A Shropshire Lad · *Denis Moriarty*
An East Anglian Rhapsody · *Denis Moriarty*
Surrey House · *Denis Moriarty*
William Morris & The Arts & Crafts Movement · *Denis Moriarty*
Worcester - the Three Choirs Festival · *Denis Moriarty*
Northern India & Nepal · *Denis Moriarty*
New England · *Denis Moriarty*
Virginia · *Denis Moriarty*
Indo-China - Cambodia, Vietnam, Laos · *Denise Heywood*
Cornwall - from Fogon to Fine Art · *Douglas Ferguson*
English Imagination · *Douglas Ferguson*
Classical Rome · *Edward Herring*
Pompeii & Paestum · *Edward Herring*
Private Wealth, Public Riches · *Elizabeth Newell*
Italian Lakes, Villas & Gardens · *Francis Cheetham*
Tuscan Villas & Gardens · *Francis Cheetham*
Portugal · *Francis Cheetham*
Moorish Spain · *Francis Cheetham*
Toledo & Madrid · *Francis Cheetham*
East Anglian Houses & Gardens · *Gerald Randall*
Fenland Abbeys · *Gerald Randall*
Follies & Grottoes · *Gerald Randall*
Vermilion Bird · *Gregor Benton*
Thailand - Ancient Civilisations · *Gregor Benton*
Thailand - Ancient Civilisations · *Gregor Benton*
Christmas in Vienna · *Ian Lowson*
Bordeaux & the Wine Country · *Ian Lowson*
Guatemala · *Ian Lowson*
Mexico · *Ian Lowson*
Spring in Portugal · *Ian Lowson*
Castile & Extremadura · *Ian Lowson*
New York, New York · *Ian Lowson*
Hill Towns of Tuscany · *Joanna Saurin*
Villas of the Veneto · *Joanna Saurin*
Irish Gardens · *John Akeroyd*
Steppe, Marsh & Mountain · *John Akeroyd*
High Aragon · *John and Vivian Boucher*
Spanish Pyrenees · *John and Vivian Boucher*
Jane Austen · *Keith Connelly*
Northern Wildlife · *Kevin Hand*
Wildlife in Norfolk · *Kevin Hand*
Bison, Elk & Beaver · *Kevin Hand*
Tenerife - Whales, Flowers & Birds · *Kevin Hand*
Great Art Collections in Belgium · *Louise Leates*
Great Art Collections in Belgium · *Louise Leates*
Cezanne · *Louise Leates*
Barbizon · *Louise Leates*
Paris - 17th & 18th Centuries · *Louise Leates*
Italian Renaissance · *Malcolm Oxley*
Lord Leighton · *Malcolm Oxley*
Rome & the Campagna · *Malcolm Oxley*
Venice · *Malcolm Oxley*
Secession - Viennese Art Nouveau · *Mark Powell*
Secession - Viennese Art Nouveau · *Mark Powell*
Viennese Art Nouveau · *Mark Powell*
Architecture in Bohemia · *Mark Powell*
Splendours of Prague · *Mark Powell*
Estonia · *Mark Powell*
Cote d'Azur · *Mark Powell*
Provence · *Mark Powell*
Rhine & Moselle · *Mark Powell*
Saxony & Thuringia · *Mark Powell*
Teutonic Knights & Hansa Merchants · *Mark Powell*
Tyrol & South Austria · *Mark Powell*
Ruthenians & Ruritania · *Mark Powell*
Romania · *Mark Powell*
Persia · *Patricia Baker*
Jordan · *Patricia Baker*
Syria with Baalbek · *Patricia Baker*
Anatolia · *Patricia Baker*
Ottoman Turkey · *Patricia Baker*
London Theatre · *Paul Ranger*
Shakespeare at Stratford · *Paul Ranger*

York Mystery Plays · *Paul Ranger*
Abbeys & Cathedrals of the North · *Peter Poyntz-Wright*
Somerset - Saints, Saxons & Cider · *Peter Poyntz-Wright*
Castles of North Wales · *Peter Poyntz-Wright*
Copenhagen · *Philip B Barnes*
Annual Reunion (Jesus College) · *Philip B Barnes*
Sir Robert Walpole & Norfolk · *Philip B Barnes*
William Morris Day Course · *Philip B Barnes*
Vermeer & the 17th Century Holland · *Philip B Barnes*
Ethiopia · *Richard Snailham*
Georgian Ireland · *Roger White*
Renaissance Gardens & Villas · *Roger White*
Isles of Scilly · *Roland Randall*
Madeira: Wildflowers, Gardens & Landscapes · *Roland Randall*
Madeira · *Roland Randall*
Wildlife of Algarve · *Roland Randall*
Wildlife of Algarve · *Roland Randall*
Inner Hebrides · *Roland Randall*
Dingle Peninsula · *Sara Champion*
Russian Churches & Palaces · *Simon Franklin*
Piero della Francesca · *Simon Pierse*
Christmas in Sorrento · *Stephen Barnett*
Orkney · *Val Turner*

1997

Glasgow's Treasures · *Aileen Smart*
Scottish Exhibitions · *Aileen Smart*
Berwick & the Borders · *Andrew Wilson*
Ancient Lycia · *Andrew Wilson*
Ephesus & the Aegean Shore · *Andrew Wilson*
Medieval Germany · *Barrie Singleton*
Ravenna, Venice & Cividale · *Barrie Singleton*
Spring in Piedmont · *Barrie Singleton*
Haydn at Eisenstadt · *Brian Richardson*
Music in Leipzig · *Brian Richardson*
Music in St Petersburg · *Brian Richardson*
Walks in the Apennines · *Catherine Barnes*
Tuscany & the Apennines · *Catherine Barnes*
Dagali & the Hardanger Vidda · *Catherine Barnes*
Walks in the Hardanger Vidda · *Catherine Barnes*
Walking in Mallorca · *Catherine Barnes*
Sweden · *Catherine Barnes*
Palladio · *Charles Hind*
Forest of Dean · *Christie Arno*
Medieval Burgundy · *Christie Arno*
Sicily at Easter · *Christie Arno*
Southern Italy · *Christie Arno*
Catalonia · *Christie Arno*
Road to Compostela · *Christie Arno*
Arizona & New Mexico · *Christie Arno*
Rapallo at Christmas · *Christopher Wellington*
Umbria: Power, Piety an Patronage · *Christopher Wellington*
Verdi & the Spirit of Italy · *Christopher Wellington*
The Green Man · *David Bostwick*
The Smythsons & Elizabethan England · *David Bostwick*
Welsh Marches · *David Bostwick*
Roman Tunisia · *David Winter*
Schubert in Vienna · *Denis Moriarty*
Schubert in Feldkirch · *Denis Moriarty*
An East Anglian Rhapsody · *Denis Moriarty*
From Rosetti to Watts Winter Lecture · *Denis Moriarty*
Surrey House · *Denis Moriarty*
William Morris & The Arts & Crafts Movement · *Denis Moriarty*
Forgotten Empires: Goa & the Deccan · *Denis Moriarty*
Southern India · *Denis Moriarty*
Dublin Discovered · *Denis Moriarty*
Northern Portugal · *Denis Moriarty*
Sri Lanka · *Denis Moriarty*
Sri Lanka II · *Denis Moriarty*
Jefferson's Virginia · *Denis Moriarty*
King's Lynn Festival · *Denis Moriarty/Marina Vaizey*
Indo-China - Cambodia, Vietnam, Laos · *Denise Heywood*
Khmer Art in Paris · *Denise Heywood*
California · *Denise Heywood*

Northern Greece · *Dimitra Papagianna*
Highland Scotland · *Don Omand*
Cambridge - Art, Music & Theatre · *Douglas Ferguson*
Scottish Tower Houses · *Douglas Ferguson*
Pompeii & Paestum · *Edward Herring*
Private Wealth, Public Riches · *Elizabeth Newell*
English Alabasters · *Francis Cheetham*
Making Music in Norwich · *Francis Cheetham*
Rhodes - Island of the Knights · *Francis Cheetham*
Italian Lakes, Villas & Gardens · *Francis Cheetham*
Tuscan Villas & Gardens · *Francis Cheetham*
Historic Malta · *Francis Cheetham*
Madrid at Christmas · *Francis Cheetham*
Moorish Spain · *Francis Cheetham*
Toledo & Madrid · *Francis Cheetham*
Fenland Abbeys · *Gerald Randall*
Northamptonshire Houses & Gardens · *Gerald Randall*
Guatemala · *Ian Lowson*
Mexico · *Ian Lowson*
Peru · *Ian Lowson*
Castile & Extremadura · *Ian Lowson*
New York, New York · *Ian Lowson*
Southwest Ireland · *John Akeroyd*
Poland's Green Lung · *John Akeroyd*
Steppe, Marsh & Mountain · *John Akeroyd*
High Aragon · *John and Vivian Boucher*
High Aragon with the Ordesa National Park · *John and Vivian Boucher*
Spanish Pyrenees · *John and Vivian Boucher*
Romanesque Quercy · *Juliet Heslewood*
Stained Glass in Oxford · *June Osborne*
Jane Austen · Keith Connelly
Northern Wildlife · *Kevin Hand*
Wildlife in Norfolk · *Kevin Hand*
Crete - Flowers, Birds & Minoans · *Kevin Hand*
Madagascar · *Kevin Hand*
Tenerife - Whales, Flowers & Birds · *Kevin Hand*
Arts of 18th Century France Winter Lecture · *Louise Leates*
Eighteenth Century Gothick · *Louise Leates*
Aix-en-Provence · *Louise Leates*
Aix-en-Provence (2) · *Louise Leates*
Barbizon · *Louise Leates*
Paris & the Visual Arts · *Louise Leates*
Hogarth Day Course · *Malcolm Oxley*
Holbein Winter Lecture · *Malcolm Oxley*
Italian Renaissance Winter Lecture · *Malcolm Oxley*
Van Dyck & Genoa · *Malcolm Oxley*
Venetian Paintings · *Malcolm Oxley*
Legacy of Charlemagne · *Malcolm Oxley*
Renaissance Florence · *Malcolm Oxley*
Venice · *Malcolm Oxley*
The Grand Tour · *Malcolm Oxley*
Picasso & the Mediterranean · *Marina Vaizey*
Mondrian Winter Lecture · *Marina Vaizey*
Picasso, Portraits & Paris · *Marina Vaizey*
California · *Marina Vaizey*
New Zealand · *Mark Hanger*
New Zealand (2) · *Mark Hanger*
New Zealand's Primeval Paradise · *Mark Hanger*
Bulgarian Monasteries · *Mark Powell*
Splendours of Prague · *Mark Powell*
Estonia · *Mark Powell*
Aix-en-Provence at Christmas · *Mark Powell*
Alsace & Lorraine · *Mark Powell*
Alsace & Lorraine (2) · *Mark Powell*
Cote d'Azur · *Mark Powell*
Cote d'Azur (2) · *Mark Powell*
Provence · *Mark Powell*
Berlin & Brandenburg · *Mark Powell*
Munich · *Mark Powell*
The Hansa · *Mark Powell*
Hungary · *Mark Powell*
Hungary (2) · *Mark Powell*
Lithuania · *Mark Powell*

Lithuania (2) · *Mark Powell*
Ruthenians & Ruritania · *Mark Powell*
Towns & Palaces of Poland · *Mark Powell*
Syria with Baalbek · *Patricia Baker*
Lost Kingdoms of Eastern Turkey · *Patricia Baker*
Ottoman Turkey · *Patricia Baker*
Uzbekistan · *Patricia Baker*
Pitlochry Festival Theatre · *Paul Ranger*
Flemish Cities · *Peter Poyntz-Wright*
Flemish Miniatures · *Peter Poyntz-Wright*
Somerset - Saints, Saxons & Cider · *Peter Poyntz-Wright*
Castles of North Wales · *Peter Poyntz-Wright*
Annual Reunion · *Philip B Barnes*
Annual Reunion (Old Palace Hatfield) · *Philip B Barnes*
Carl Larsson Winter Lecture · *Philip B Barnes*
Basque Pyrenees · Richard Hall
Ethiopia · *Richard Snailham*
Ethiopia (2) · *Richard Snailham*
Brittany · *Richard Snailham*
Music in Bamberg · *Roger Rayner*
Georgian Ireland · *Roger White*
Renaissance Gardens & Villas · *Roger White*
Slovenia · *Roger White*
Isles of Scilly · *Roland Randall*
Lanzarote: Geology, Botany & Cesar Manrique · *Roland Randall*
Madeira: Wildflowers, Gardens & Landscapes · *Roland Randall*
Prehistoric Wessex · *Sara Champion*
Boyne Valley · *Sara Champion*
Zimbabwe - Animals, Art & Archaeology · *Sara Champion*
Russian Churches & Palaces · *Simon Franklin*
Ladakh · *Simon Pierse*
Piero della Francesca · *Simon Pierse*
Venice · *Simon Pierse*
Christmas in Sorrento · *Stephen Barnett*
Hill Towns of Tuscany · *Stephen Barnett*
Renaissance Florence · *Stephen Barnett*
Sicily · *Stephen Barnett*
Shetland Islands · *Val Turner*
Oman · *Vivienne Sharpe*

1998

Edinburgh's Treasures · *Aileen Smart*
Glasgow's Treasures · *Aileen Smart*
Berwick & the Borders · *Andrew Wilson*
Picts & the Kingdom of Fife · *Andrew Wilson*
Ephesus & the Aegean Shore · *Andrew Wilson*
In & around Spoleto · *Barrie Singleton*
Ravenna, Venice & Cividale · *Barrie Singleton*
Spring in Piedmont · *Barrie Singleton*
Beethoven at Bromsgrove · *Brian Richardson*
Tuscany & the Apennines · *Catherine Barnes*
Stockholm - History, Art & Design · *Catherine Barnes*
Palaces of St Petersburg · *Charles Hind*
In the Steps of St Cuthbert · *Christie Arno*
Medieval Burgundy · *Christie Arno*
Apulia · *Christie Arno*
Sicily · *Christie Arno*
Spring in Sicily · *Christie Arno*
Catalonia · *Christie Arno*
Road to Compostela · *Christie Arno*
Arizona · *Christie Arno*
Hill Towns of Umbria · *Christopher Wellington*
Italian Riviera · *Christopher Wellington*
Renaissance England · *David Bostwick*
The Green Man · *David Bostwick*
Timber-Framed Halls of Lancaster & Cheshire · *David Bostwick*
Ancient Cities of the Turquoise Coast · *David Price Williams*
Renaissance Theatre & Art · *Dawn Lewcock*
Schubert in Feldkirch · *Denis Moriarty*
Prague Music Festival · *Denis Moriarty*
An East Anglian Rhapsody · *Denis Moriarty*
Burne-Jones & Birmingham · *Denis Moriarty*
Gloucester - the Three Choirs Festival · *Denis Moriarty*
John Betjeman · *Denis Moriarty*

Copenhagen & the Danish Isles · *Philip B Barnes*
Annual Reunion (Trinity House) · *Philip B Barnes*
Ethiopia · *Richard Snailham*
Dresden Music Festival · *Roger Rayner*
Leipzig Bach Festival · *Roger Rayner*
Georgian Ireland · *Roger White*
Irish Country Houses & Gardens · *Roger White*
Sicilian Baroque · *Roger White*
Slovenia · *Roger White*
Isles of Scilly · *Roland Randall*
Mallorca - Flowers & Birds · *Roland Randall & Kevin Hand*
Haydn at Eisenstadt · *Rupert Scott*
Mozart in Salzburg · *Rupert Scott*
Vienna at Christmas · *Rupert Scott*
Kuhmo Music Festival · *Rupert Scott*
Leipzig in December · *Rupert Scott*
Music in Leipzig · *Rupert Scott*
Prehistory of the South Downs · *Sara Champion*
Archaeology of the Ring of Kerry · *Sara Champion*
Marvels of Rome · *Simon Ditchfield*
Piero della Francesca · *Simon Pierse*
Sikkim & Darjeeling · *Simon Pierse*
Hill Towns of Tuscany · *Stephen Barnett*
Shetland Islands · *Val Turner*
Oman · *Vivienne Sharpe*

2000
Glasgow's Treasures · *Aileen Smart*
Renaissance in the Alps · *Alex Koller*
Vasari - Father of Art History · *Alex Koller*
Belgian Gardens · *Andrew Sclater*
Italian Lakes, Villas & Gardens · *Andrew Sclater*
Tuscan Villas & Gardens · *Andrew Sclater*
Gardens of South Wales · *Andrew Sclater*
Northern Picts · *Andrew Wilson*
Cologne · *Barrie Singleton*
Ravenna, Venice & Cividale · *Barrie Singleton*
Spoleto & the Legacy of Rome · *Barrie Singleton*
Cheltenham Festival of Music · *Brian Richardson*
Bruges & the Flanders Early Music Festival · *Bruce Jamson*
Coleridge in the West Country · *Bruce Jamson*
D H Lawrence · *Bruce Jamson*
Palladio · *Charles Hind*
Medieval Burgundy · *Christie Arno*
Apulia · *Christie Arno*
Sicily · *Christie Arno*
Sicily at Easter · *Christie Arno*
Catalonia · *Christie Arno*
Hill Towns of Umbria · *Christopher Wellington*
Hill Towns of Umbria 2) · *Christopher Wellington*
La Via Francigena - The Road to Rome · *Christopher Wellington*
Art Treasures of Lille & Valenciennes · *Colin Bailey*
Berlin - Art & Architecture · *Colin Bailey*
The Golden Age of Dutch Art · *Colin Bailey*
Spain's Golden Age · *Colin Bailey*
American Galleries in the Fall · *Colin Bailey*
The Green Man · *David Bostwick*
Timber-Framed Halls of Lancaster & Cheshire · *David Bostwick*
Classical Art & the God Dionysus · *Dawn Lewcock*
Schubert in Feldkirch · *Denis Moriarty*
Schubert in Schwarzenberg · *Denis Moriarty*
An East Anglian Rhapsody · *Denis Moriarty*
Bloomsbury in Sussex · *Denis Moriarty*
Hereford - The Three Choirs Festival · *Denis Moriarty*
John Betjeman · *Denis Moriarty*
William Morris & The Arts & Crafts Movement · *Denis Moriarty*
Southern India · *Denis Moriarty*
Northern India & Nepal · *Denis Moriarty*
Amalfi & Naples · *Denis Moriarty*
Portuguese Art & Architecture · *Denis Moriarty*
Charleston & the Carolinas · *Denis Moriarty*
New England · *Denis Moriarty*
Caithness & Sutherland · *Don Omand*
Flowers of the Cape · *Elizabeth Ashton*

Manchester · *Elizabeth Newell*
Private Wealth, Public Riches · *Elizabeth Newell*
Norfolk & Norwich Festival · *Francis Cheetham*
Historic Malta · *Francis Cheetham*
Moorish Spain · *Francis Cheetham*
East Anglian Churches · *Gerald Randall*
Lincolnshire Houses & Gardens · *Gerald Randall*
Yorkshire Houses & Gardens · *Gerald Randall*
Blazing the Maya Trail · *Ian Lowson*
Maya World · *Ian Lowson*
Mexico · *Ian Lowson*
High Aragon · *John and Vivian Boucher*
Spanish Pyrenees · *John and Vivian Boucher*
Japan · *Julian Harvey*
Dordogne · *Juliet Heslewood*
Languedoc · *Juliet Heslewood*
Provence · *Juliet Heslewood*
Romanesque Quercy · *Juliet Heslewood*
Wildlife in Norfolk · *Kevin Hand*
Wildlife in Suffolk · *Kevin Hand*
Crete - Flowers, Birds & Minoans · *Kevin Hand & Roland Randall*
Chardin · *Louise Leates*
Arts of 18th Century France · *Louise Leates*
Aix-en-Provence · *Louise Leates*
Paris - 17th & 18th Centuries · *Louise Leates*
Art in Yorkshire · *Malcolm Oxley*
Eton College & Langley Marish Day Course · *Malcolm Oxley*
Italian Renaissance · *Malcolm Oxley*
Lombardy - Under the Visconti & the Sforzas · *Malcolm Oxley*
Popes & Princes: Umbria & the Marches · *Malcolm Oxley*
Venice · *Malcolm Oxley*
Road to Compostela · *Malcolm Oxley*
Bilbao & Barcelona · *Marina Vaizey*
Bilbao & Barcelona (2) · *Marina Vaizey*
Texas · *Marina Vaizey*
New Zealand · *Mark Hanger*
New Zealand's Primeval Paradise · *Mark Hanger*
Moravia & Southern Bohemia · *Mark Powell*
Splendours of Prague · *Mark Powell*
Splendours of Prague II · *Mark Powell*
Baltic States · *Mark Powell*
Finnish Art & Architecture · *Mark Powell*
Roussillon · *Mark Powell*
Teutonic Knights & Hansa Merchants · *Mark Powell*
Ruthenians & Ruritania · *Mark Powell*
Dordogne · *Moira Woods*
Persia · *Patricia Baker*
Sri Lanka · *Patricia Baker*
Syria with Baalbek · *Patricia Baker*
Lost Kingdoms of Eastern Turkey · *Patricia Baker*
Ottoman Turkey · *Patricia Baker*
Shakespeare at Stratford · *Paul Ranger*
The York Mystery Plays · *Paul Ranger*
Mercury Assets Management Collection Day Course · *Philip B Barnes*
Bolivia & Peru · *Richard Snailham*
Haydn at Eisenstadt · *Roger Rayner*
Dresden Music Festival · *Roger Rayner*
Leipzig Bach Festival · *Roger Rayner*
Georgian Ireland · *Roger White*
Irish Country Houses & Gardens · *Roger White*
The American Deep South · *Roger White*
Isles of Scilly · *Roland Randall*
Madeira · *Roland Randall*
Haydn at Eisenstadt · *Rupert Scott*
Mozart in Salzburg · *Rupert Scott*
Leipzig at Easter · *Rupert Scott*
Risør Music Festival · *Rupert Scott*
Chopin in Poland · *Rupert Scott*
Prehistory of the Cotswold · *Sara Champion*
Archaeology of Galway & Connemara · *Sara Champion*
Piero della Francesca · *Simon Pierse*
Orkney · *Val Turner*
Oman · *Vivienne Sharpe*

2001
Glasgow's Treasures · *Aileen Smart*
Splendours of Prague · *Alex Koller*
Splendours of Prague II · *Alex Koller*
Cologne · *Alex Koller*
Vasari - Father of Art History · *Alex Koller*
Japan · *Alex Koller*
Japan · *Alex Koller*
Italian Lakes, Villas & Gardens · *Andrew Sclater*
Tuscan Villas & Gardens · *Andrew Sclater*
Gardens of South Wales · *Andrew Sclater*
Libya · *Andrew Wilson*
Edinburgh's Treasures · *Andrew Wilson*
Picts & the Kingdom of Fife · *Andrew Wilson*
Cheltenham International Festival of Music · *Brian Richardson*
Aix-en-Provence Festival · *Bruce Jamson*
Budapest at Christmas · *Bruce Jamson*
Historic Houses in Hungary · *Bruce Jamson*
Ravenna Festival · *Bruce Jamson*
Palladio · *Charles Hind*
Palaces of St Petersburg Alumni · *Charles Hind*
In the Steps of St Cuthbert · *Christie Arno*
Medieval Burgundy · *Christie Arno*
Apulia · *Christie Arno*
Sicily · *Christie Arno*
Spring in Sicily · *Christie Arno*
Catalonia · *Christie Arno*
Arizona · *Christie Arno*
Hill Towns of Umbria · *Christopher Wellington*
La Via Francigena - Piacenza to Rome · *Christopher Wellington*
Verdi: 100th Anniversary · *Christopher Wellington*
Art Treasures of Lille & Valenciennes · *Colin Bailey*
Berlin - Art & Architecture · *Colin Bailey*
Golden Age of Dutch Art · *Colin Bailey*
Renaissance & Baroque Rome · *Colin Bailey*
Art in St Petersburg · *Colin Bailey*
Art in Toledo & Madrid · *Colin Bailey*
American Galleries in the Fall · *Colin Bailey*
The Smythsons & Elizabethan England · *David Bostwick*
Timber-Framed Halls of Lancaster & Cheshire · *David Bostwick*
Wild Man of East Anglia · *David Bostwick*
Schubert in Schwarzenberg · *Denis Moriarty*
Azores · *Denis Moriarty*
Gloucester - the Three Choirs Festival · *Denis Moriarty*
Isle of Wight: a Victorian Retreat · *Denis Moriarty*
John Piper · *Denis Moriarty*
Northumbria & the Borders · *Denis Moriarty*
One Thousand Years of Architecture · *Denis Moriarty*
William Morris & Victorian Oxford · *Denis Moriarty*
Amalfi & Naples · *Denis Moriarty*
Northern Portugal · *Denis Moriarty*
Sri Lanka · *Denis Moriarty*
Boston · *Denis Moriarty*
Charleston & the Carolinas · *Denis Moriarty*
Jefferson's Virginia · *Denis Moriarty*
Northern Greece · *Dimitra Papagianna*
Grampian through the Ages · *Don Omand*
Pompeii & Herculaneum · *Edward Herring*
Pompeii & Herculaneum II · *Edward Herring*
Manchester · *Elizabeth Newell*
Private Wealth, Public Riches · *Elizabeth Newell*
Malta at Christmas · *Francis Cheetham*
A Medieval Panorama · *Gerald Randall*
Lincolnshire Houses & Gardens · *Gerald Randall*
Yorkshire Houses & Gardens · *Gerald Randall*
Silk Road Revisited & Karakoram Highway · *Gregor Benton*
Maya World · *Ian Lowson*
The Archaeology of Cornwall · *Jeffrey May*
Madeira: Wildflowers, Gardens & Landscapes · *John Akeroyd*
High Aragon · *John and Vivian Boucher*
Spanish Pyrenees · *John and Vivian Boucher*
Albi & the Languedoc · *Juliet Heslewood*
Art on the Cote d'Azur · *Juliet Heslewood*
Provence · *Juliet Heslewood*

2003

Splendours of Prague · *Alex Koller*
Cambridge Art & Architecture · *Alex Koller*
Amalfi & Naples · *Alex Koller*
Japan · *Alex Koller*
Palaces of St Petersburg · *Alex Koller*
Russian Churches & Palaces · *Alex Koller*
Castile · *Alex Koller*
Renaissance in the Alps · *Alex Koller*
Shakespeare at Stratford · *Andrew Jarvis*
Shakespeare at the Globe · *Andrew Jarvis*
The Taming of the Shrew · *Andrew Jarvis*
Italian Lakes, Villas & Gardens · *Andrew Sclater*
Tuscan Villas & Gardens · *Andrew Sclater*
Athens at Christmas · *Andrew Wilson*
Northern Greece · *Andrew Wilson*
Peloponnese · *Andrew Wilson*
Handel Festival at Gøttingen · *Brian Richardson*
Bruges Early Music Festival · *Bruce Jamson*
Aix-en-Provence Opera Festival · *Bruce Jamson*
Budapest at Christmas · *Bruce Jamson*
Wexford Opera Festival · *Bruce Jamson*
Palladio & the Villas of the Veneto · *Charles Hind*
Palaces of St Petersburg · *Charles Hind*
Spring in Sicily · *Christie Arno*
Hill Towns of Tuscany & Umbria · *Christopher Wellington*
Hill Towns of Umbria · *Christopher Wellington*
La Via Francigena - Piacenza to Rome · *Christopher Wellington*
Rome at Christmas · *Christopher Wellington*
Art Treasures of Munich · *Colin Bailey*
Berlin · *Colin Bailey*
Berlin with Potsdam · *Colin Bailey*
Dresden · *Colin Bailey*
Art Treasures of Vienna & Budapest · *Colin Bailey*
Bergamo, Milan & Genoa · *Colin Bailey*
Bologna, Mantua & Parma · *Colin Bailey*
Renaissance & Baroque Rome · *Colin Bailey*
Historic Malta · *Colin Bailey*
Art in St Petersburg · *Colin Bailey*
Art in Toledo & Madrid · *Colin Bailey*
Art Treasures of Cadiz, Malaga & Seville · *Colin Bailey*
Manor Houses & Cottages of West Yorkshire · *David Bostwick*
The Dukeries · *David Bostwick*
Historic Malta · *David Winter*
Christmas at Shaker Mill, New England · *David Winter*
Schubert in Schwarzenberg · *Denis Moriarty*
Azores · *Denis Moriarty*
Hereford - The Three Choirs Festival · *Denis Moriarty*
Isle of Wight: a Victorian Retreat · *Denis Moriarty*
William Morris & The Arts & Crafts Movement · *Denis Moriarty*
Southern India · *Denis Moriarty*
Sikkim & Darjeeling · *Denis Moriarty*
Spring in Portugal · *Denis Moriarty*
Charleston & the Carolinas · *Denis Moriarty*
A Portrait of Skye & the West Highlands · *Don Omand*
Buxtehude in Denmark · *Douglas Hollick*
Pompeii & Herculaneum · *Edward Herring*
Flowers of the Cape · *Elizabeth Ashton*
Liverpool: Private Wealth & Public Riches · *Elizabeth Newell*
Manchester's Treasures · *Elizabeth Newell*
Georgian Norfolk · *Gerald Randall*
Lincolnshire Houses & Gardens · *Gerald Randall*
Secret History of the Mongols · *Gregor Benton*
Maya World · *Ian Lowson*
Mexico · *Ian Lowson*
Salzburg at Christmas · *John Bryden*
Albi & the Languedoc · *Juliet Heslewood*
Art on the Cote d'Azur · *Juliet Heslewood*
Provence · *Juliet Heslewood*
Romanesque Saintonge · *Juliet Heslewood*
Dordogne · *Juliet Heslewood & Moira Woods*
Flemish Painting · *Lindsey Shaw-Miller*
Vincent's Choice · *Lindsey Shaw-Miller*
City Churches after the Fire · *Malcolm Oxley*
Early Renaissance at the National Gallery · *Malcolm Oxley*

Northumbria & the Borders · *Malcolm Oxley*
Titian at the National Gallery · *Malcolm Oxley*
Alsace & its Neighbours · *Malcolm Oxley*
Normandy · *Malcolm Oxley*
Benozzo Gozzoli, Painter of Florence · *Malcolm Oxley*
Popes & Princes: Bologna & the Marches · *Malcolm Oxley*
Christmas in Madrid · *Malcolm Oxley*
Road to Compostela · *Malcolm Oxley*
New Museums across the World · *Marina Vaizey*
Bilbao & Barcelona · *Marina Vaizey*
Western Australia · *Mark Hanger*
New Zealand · *Mark Hanger*
New Zealand's Primeval Paradise · *Mark Hanger*
Bulgarian Monasteries · *Mark Powell*
Croatia · *Mark Powell*
Prague with Kutna Hora · *Mark Powell*
Baltic States · *Mark Powell*
Roussillon · *Mark Powell*
Spring in Corsica · *Mark Powell*
Saxony - Leipzig, Weimar & Dresden · *Mark Powell*
Polish Cities · *Mark Powell*
Romania & Moldavia · *Mark Powell*
Slovakia · *Mark Powell*
Ukraine & the Crimea · *Mark Powell*
La Mortella & William Walton · *Michael Aston*
Newcastle · *Michael Bellamy*
Glasgow's Treasures · *Michael Bellamy*
Andalucia & Morocco · *Michael Jacobs*
Andalucia & Morocco Day Course · *Michael Jacobs*
Moorish Spain II · *Michael Jacobs*
Morocco · *Michael Jacobs*
Moorish Spain · *Michael Jacobs*
Mexico · *Moira Woods*
Persia · *Patricia Baker*
Syria with Baalbek · *Patricia Baker*
Ottoman Turkey · *Patricia Baker*
Uzbekistan · *Patricia Baker*
Spring in Syria · *Peter Clark*
Southern Anatolia to the Euphrates · *Peter Clark*
Dorset Wildlife · *Peter Exley*
Turner & Venice · *Peter Higginson*
Barbizon · *Peter Higginson*
Renaissance Florence · *Peter Higginson*
Venice · *Peter Higginson*
Argentina · *Peter Shabbenderian*
Caucasus - Georgia & Armenia · *Peter Shabbenderian*
From Rembrandt to Rococo · *Peter Wood*
Iceland · *Richard Crabtree*
Ethiopia · *Richard Snailham*
Ludlow & the Welsh Marches · *Roger White*
Baroque & Rococo in Franconia · *Roger White*
Georgian Ireland · *Roger White*
Irish Country Houses & Gardens · *Roger White*
Great Houses of Scotland · *Roger White*
Isles of Scilly · *Roland Randall*
Crete - Flowers, Birds & Minoans · *Roland Randall & Kevin Hand*
County Donegal & Tory Island · *Roland Randall & Kevin Hand*
Sicily - Natural History · *Roland Randall & Kevin Hand*
Madeira · *Roland Randall & Kevin Hand*
Haydn · *Rupert Scott*
Mozart Festival in Salzburg · *Rupert Scott*
Kuhmo Music Festival · *Rupert Scott*
Sibelius in Finland · *Rupert Scott*
White Nights Opera Festival · *Rupert Scott*
Leipzig at Easter · *Rupert Scott*
Melk Baroque Music Festival · *Rupert Scott*
The Ring at Dresden · *Rupert Scott*
St Petersburg Music Festival · *Rupert Scott*
New England - Art, Music & Literature · *Rupert Scott*
Tanglewood Music Festival · *Rupert Scott*
Piero della Francesca · *Simon Pierse*
Anglo-Saxon Legacy · *Sue Mathews*
Sutton Hoo - Warrior King's Burial · *Sue Mathews*
Sketchbooking in Montecenero · *Tessa Henderson*
Shetlands Islands · *Val Turner*
High Aragon · *Vivian Boucher*

2004

Styria & Carinthia · *Alex Koller*
Bulgarian Monasteries · *Alex Koller*
Splendours of Prague · *Alex Koller*
Baltic States · *Alex Koller*
Vasari - Father of Art History · *Alex Koller*
Cracow · *Alex Koller*
Russian Churches & Palaces · *Alex Koller*
Slovenia & Istria · *Alex Koller*
Shakespeare at Stratford · *Andrew Jarvis*
Shakespeare at the Globe: Romeo & Juliet · *Andrew Jarvis*
Belgian Houses & Gardens · *Andrew Sclater*
Italian Lakes, Villas & Gardens · *Andrew Sclater*
Albi & the Languedoc · *Andrew Wilson*
Athens at Christmas · *Andrew Wilson*
Northern Greece · *Andrew Wilson*
Undiscovered Libya · *Andrew Wilson*
Lycian Cruise · *Andrew Wilson*
Sicily & the Reggio di Calabria · *Christie Arno*
Gerald of Wales · *Christie Arno*
Apulia · *Christopher Wellington*
Hill Towns of Tuscany & Umbria · *Christopher Wellington*
Hill Towns of Umbria · *Christopher Wellington*
Lombardy - Under the Visconti & the Sforzas · *Christopher Wellington*
Rome at Christmas · *Christopher Wellington*
Umbria & the Marches · *Christopher Wellington*
Art Treasures of Vienna & Budapest · *Colin Bailey*
Paris · *Colin Bailey*
Paris: Impressionism & its Origin · *Colin Bailey*
Berlin with Potsdam · *Colin Bailey*
Berlin, Potsdam & Dresden · *Colin Bailey*
Renaissance & Baroque Rome · *Colin Bailey*
Oslo · *Colin Bailey*
Art in New England · *Colin Bailey*
Yorkshire Mansions & Manor Houses · *David Bostwick*
Christmas at Shaker Mill, New England · *David Winter*
Haydn at Eisenstadt · *Denis Moriarty*
Cornwall · *Denis Moriarty*
Gloucester The Three Choirs Festival · *Denis Moriarty*
Schubert in Schwarzenberg · *Denis Moriarty*
Southern India · *Denis Moriarty*
Dublin Discovered · *Denis Moriarty*
Historic Malta · *Denis Moriarty*
Portugal · *Denis Moriarty*
Palaces of St Petersburg · *Denis Moriarty*
Sri Lanka · *Denis Moriarty*
Jefferson's Virginia · *Denis Moriarty*
Perth, Fife & Angus · *Don Omand*
New Year in New York · *Edmund Lowson*
Pompeii & Herculaneum · *Edward Herring*
Cape & Karoo · *Elizabeth Ashton*
Flowers of the Cape · *Elizabeth Ashton*
Liverpool: Private Wealth & Public Riches · *Elizabeth Newell*
Manchester's Treasures · *Elizabeth Newell*
King's Lynn & the Wash · *Gerald Randall*
Monastic East Anglia · *Gerald Randall*
Secret History of the Mongols · *Gregor Benton*
Glasgow's Treasures · *Hilary Macartney*
Road to Compostela · *Hilary Macartney*
Maya World · *Ian Lowson*
Salzburg at Christmas · *John Bryden*
Music from St Petersburg · *John Bryden*
New year in Vienna · *John Bryden*
Provence · *Juliet Heslewood*
Romanesque Quercy · *Juliet Heslewood*
Romanesque Saintonge · *Juliet Heslewood*
Wildlife of the Borders · *Kevin Hand*
Western Crete - Birds, Flowers & History · *Kevin Hand & Roland Randall*
Flemish Paintings · *Lindsey Shaw-Miller*
Rubens · *Lindsey Shaw-Miller*
In the Age of Rembrandt & Vermeer · *Lindsey Shaw-Miller*
Spring in Portugal · *Lindsey Shaw-Miller*
City Churches After the Fire · *Malcolm Oxley*

Clifford Country: Art & Architecture in Craven & Cumbria ·
  Malcolm Oxley
Hogarth · *Malcolm Oxley*
Northumbria & the Borders · *Malcolm Oxley*
Medieval Burgundy · *Malcolm Oxley*
Normandy · *Malcolm Oxley*
Bologna, Mantua & Parma · *Malcolm Oxley*
Christmas in Madrid · *Malcolm Oxley*
A Day at Somerset House · *Malcolm Oxley & Timothy Schroder*
Henry Moore · *Marina Vaizey*
St Petersburg at Christmas · *Marina Vaizey*
Bilbao & Barcelona · *Marina Vaizey*
California · *Marina Vaizey*
Western Australia · *Mark Hanger*
New Zealand · *Mark Hanger*
New Zealand (2) · *Mark Hanger*
Croatia · *Mark Powell*
Dubrovnik · *Mark Powell*
Baltic States · *Mark Powell*
Saxony-Leipzig, Weimar & Dresden · *Mark Powell*
Towns & Palaces in Poland · *Mark Powell*
Architecture & History of Romania · *Mark Powell*
Ukraine & the Cossacks · *Mark Powell*
La Mortella & William Walton · *Michael Aston*
Morocco · *Michael Jacobs*
Moorish Spain · *Michael Jacobs*
Moorish Spain · *Michael Jacobs*
Laos & Cambodia · *Moira Tait*
Mexico · *Nicholas James*
Syria with Baalbek · *Patricia Baker*
Lost Kingdoms of Eastern Turkey · *Patricia Baker*
Uzbekistan · *Patricia Baker*
Denmark: Architecture & Design · *Paul Brooke Barnes*
Christmas in Damascus · *Peter Clark*
Ottoman Turkey · *Peter Clark*
Dorset Wildlife · *Peter Exley*
Barbizon & Art of Landscape · *Peter Higginson*
Venice · *Peter Higginson*
Iceland · *Richard Crabtree*
Ethiopia · *Richard Snailham*
Ethiopia Extension · *Richard Snailham*
Georgian Gothick in the Cotswolds · *Roger White*
Herefordshire Country Houses & Churches · *Roger White*
Architecture of Berlin · *Roger White*
Georgian Ireland · *Roger White*
Irish Country Houses & Gardens · *Roger White*
Great Houses of Scotland · *Roger White*
Isles of Scilly · *Roland Randall*
Faroe Islands · *Roland Randall*
Wildlife in High Aragon · *Roland Randall & Kevin Hand*
Melk Baroque Music Festival · *Rupert Scott*
Mozart Festival in Salzburg · *Rupert Scott*
Kuhmo Music Festival · *Rupert Scott*
The Ring & Sibelius in Finland · *Rupert Scott*
Handel Festival at Gottingen · *Rupert Scott*
Risør Musical Festival · *Rupert Scott*
Moscow · *Rupert Scott*
New Year in St Petersburg · *Rupert Scott*
St Petersburg: Music at the Russian Court · *Rupert Scott*
Tanglewood Music Festival · *Rupert Scott*
Alfred the Great-England's Hero King · *Sue Mathews*
Northumbria – the first Anglo-Saxon Kingdom · *Sue Mathews*
Sutton Hoo: the Coming of the English I · *Sue Mathews*
Sutton Hoo: the Coming of the English II · *Sue Mathews*
Mermaids of the South West · *Terri Pearson*
Art of the Veneto · *Thomas Tuohy*
High Aragon · *Vivian Boucher*

2005

Bulgarian Monasteries · *Alex Koller*
Burma · *Alex Koller*
Baltic States · *Alex Koller*
Aix to Arles · *Alex Koller*
Naples with Pompeii & Herculaneum · *Alex Koller*
Japan · *Alex Koller*
Japan at Cherry Blossom Time · *Alex Koller*
Towns & Palaces in Poland · *Alex Koller*
Karelia & Archangel · *Alex Koller*
Palaces of St Petersburg · *Alex Koller*
Russian Churches & Palaces · *Alex Koller*
Slovenia & Istria · *Alex Koller*
South Korea · *Alex Koller*
Italian Lakes, Villas & Gardens · *Andrew Sclater*
Peloponnese with Athens & Delphi · *Andrew Wilson*
Damascus at Christmas · *Andrew Wilson*
Carian Cruise · *Andrew Wilson*
Ottoman Turkey · *Andrew Wilson*
Palladio & The Villas of the Veneto · *Charles Hind*
Palaces of St Petersburg · *Charles Hind*
Northern Cyprus · *Charles Hind*
Spring in Sicily · *Christie Arno*
Hill Towns of Tuscany & Umbria · *Christopher Wellington*
Hill Towns of Umbria · *Christopher Wellington*
La Via Francigena – Piacenza to Rome · *Christopher Wellington*
Rome at Christmas · *Christopher Wellington*
Wildlife of New England · *Clellie Lynch & Peter Exley*
Art Treasures of Vienna & Budapest · *Colin Bailey*
Edvard Munch at The Royal Academy · *Colin Bailey*
Art Treasures of Munich · *Colin Bailey*
Berlin with Potsdam · *Colin Bailey*
Dresden, Potsdam & Berlin · *Colin Bailey*
Art Connoisseur's Dublin · *Colin Bailey*
Renaissance & Baroque Rome · *Colin Bailey*
Art in St Petersburg · *Colin Bailey*
Art Connoisseurs' Edinburgh · *Colin Bailey*
Art in Madrid & Toledo · *Colin Bailey*
Art in New England · *Colin Bailey*
Derbyshire Halls & Houses · *David Bostwick*
Green Man · *David Bostwick*
Finland with Alvar Aalto · *David Brady*
New Year in Malta · *David Winter & Teresa Zammit*
Schubertiade: Schubert in Schwarzenberg · *Denis Moriarty*
From Montreal to Boston · *Denis Moriarty*
Cornwall · *Denis Moriarty*
Eric Gill: Sculptor & Master Craftsman · *Denis Moriarty*
John Piper · *Denis Moriarty*
William Morris & the Arts & Crafts Movement · *Denis Moriarty*
Worcester Three Choirs Festival · *Denis Moriarty*
Christmas at Dresden · *Denis Moriarty*
Cave Temples & Moghul Palaces · *Denis Moriarty*
Forgotten Empires: Goa & the Deccan · *Denis Moriarty*
Historic Malta · *Denis Moriarty*
Oporto, Coimbra & the Douro Valley · *Denis Moriarty*
New Year in New York · *Edmund Lowson*
Pompeii & Herculaneum · *Edward Herring*
Cape & Karoo · *Elizabeth Ashton*
Flowers of the Cape · *Elizabeth Ashton*
Liverpool: Private Wealth & Public Riches · *Elizabeth Newell*
Manchester's Treasures · *Elizabeth Newell*
Fenland Abbeys · *Gerald Randall*
Georgian Norfolk · *Gerald Randall*
Lincolnshire Houses & Gardens · *Gerald Randall*
Glasgow's Treasures · *Hilary Macartney*
Road to Compostela · *Hilary Macartney*
Vienna Music Festival with Humphrey Burton · *Humphrey Burton*
Los Angeles With Humphrey Burton · *Humphrey Burton*
Haydn at Eisenstadt · *John Bryden*
Salzburg at Christmas · *John Bryden*
Dresden Music Festival · *John Bryden*
Handel Festival at Gottingen · *John Bryden*
Music Celebrations in Dresden · *John Bryden*
New Year in St Petersburg · *John Bryden*

Albi & the Languedoc · *Juliet Heslewood*
Art on the Cote d'Azur · *Juliet Heslewood*
Provence · *Juliet Heslewood*
Romanesque Quercy · *Juliet Heslewood*
Brittany · *Juliet Heslewood & Moira Tait*
Wildlife in Norfolk · *Kevin Hand*
Crete - Birds, Flowers & Minoans · *Kevin Hand & Roland Randall*
Pembrokeshire · *Lindsay Evans*
Art Nouveau in Belgium · *Lindsey Shaw-Miller*
Dutch Paintings of the Golden Age, Buckingham Palace · *Lindsey Shaw-*
From Castles to Capability Brown · *Lindsey Shaw-Miller*
Newcastle: Tyneside Revived · *Lindsey Shaw-Miller*
Surrey House · *Lindsey Shaw-Miller*
Wellington Museum, Apsley House · *Lindsey Shaw-Miller*
Holland & Van Gogh · *Lindsey Shaw-Miller*
Art & Architecture of Oxford · *Malcolm Oxley*
City Churches After the Fire · *Malcolm Oxley*
Clifford Country: Art & Architecture in Craven & Cumbria · *Malcolm Ox*
Rubens: International Painter in England · *Malcolm Oxley*
Venetian Paintings at the National Gallery · *Malcolm Oxley*
Yorkshire Minsters & Monasteries · *Malcolm Oxley*
French Gothic Art & Architecture · *Malcolm Oxley*
Medieval Burgundy · *Malcolm Oxley*
Princely Courts of Northern Italy · *Malcolm Oxley*
Medieval Catalonia · *Malcolm Oxley*
Christmas at St Petersburg · *Marina Vaizey*
Bilbao & Barcelona · *Marina Vaizey*
Swiss Art Treasures · *Marina Vaizey*
Christo in New York · *Marina Vaizey*
New Zealand · *Mark Hanger*
New Zealand · *Mark Hanger*
New Zealand's Primeval Paradise · *Mark Hanger*
Bulgaria's Danube & The Black Sea Coast · *Mark Powell*
Dubrovnik · *Mark Powell*
Splendours of Prague · *Mark Powell*
Roussillon · *Mark Powell*
Spring in Corsica · *Mark Powell*
Saxony-Leipzig, Weimar & Dresden · *Mark Powell*
Weimar at Christmas · *Mark Powell*
Silesia & Western Poland · *Mark Powell*
Architecture & History of Romania · *Mark Powell*
Moldavia · *Mark Powell*
Ukraine · *Mark Powell*
La Mortella & William Walton · *Michael Aston*
Bolivia · *Michael Jacobs*
Morocco · *Michael Jacobs*
Gastronomic Spain · *Michael Jacobs*
Moorish Spain · *Michael Jacobs*
Trafalgar · *Michael Jacobs*
West of Ireland · *Niamh Whitfield*
Heart of Mexico · *Nicholas James*
Persia · *Patricia Baker*
Syria with Baalbek · *Patricia Baker*
Uzbekistan · *Patricia Baker*
Barbizon & Paris · *Peter Higginson*
Venice · *Peter Higginson*
Venice · *Peter Higginson*
Ancient Libya · *Philip Kenrick*
Iceland · *Richard Crabtree*
Ethiopia · *Richard Snailham*
Ethiopia Extension · *Richard Snailham*
Dorset Manor Houses & Gardens · *Roger White*
English Baroque · *Roger White*
St Bartholomew's Hospital & Charterhouse · *Roger White*
Painted Rooms · *Roger White*
Baroque & Rococo in Franconia · *Roger White*
Irish Country Houses & Gardens · *Roger White*
Sicilian Baroque · *Roger White*
Great Houses of Scotland · *Roger White*
Isles of Scilly · *Roland Randall*
Shetland Islands · *Roland Randall*
County Donegal & Tory Island · *Roland Randall & Kevin Hand*
La Gomera, Whales, Dolphins, Plants & Birds · *Roland Randall & Kevin*
Haydn at Eisenstadt · *Rupert Scott*

Cyclades · *Andrew Wilson*
Northern Greece · *Andrew Wilson*
Pompeii & Herculaneum · *Andrew Wilson*
Jordan · *Andrew Wilson*
Ancient Libya · *Andrew Wilson*
Morocco · *Andrew Wilson*
Outer Hebrides · *Andrew Wilson*
Roman Scotland · *Andrew Wilson*
Roman Tunisia · *Andrew Wilson*
Lycian Cruise · *Andrew Wilson*
Ottoman Turkey · *Andrew Wilson*
Palladio & the Villas of the Veneto · *Charles Hind*
Palaces of St Petersburg · *Charles Hind*
Apulia · *Christopher Wellington*
Christmas in Milan · *Christopher Wellington*
Hill Towns of Tuscany & Umbria · *Christopher Wellington*
Via Emilia · *Christopher Wellington*
Velazquez at the National Gallery · *Colin Bailey*
Sargent & Sorolla in Paris · *Colin Bailey*
Berlin with Potsdam · *Colin Bailey*
Germany's Hidden Art Treasures · *Colin Bailey*
Picture & Palaces of Saxony · *Colin Bailey*
Bologna, Mantua & Parma · *Colin Bailey*
New Year in Florence · *Colin Bailey*
Piero della Francesco · *Colin Bailey*
Renaissance & Baroque Rome · *Colin Bailey*
Renaissance Florence with Siena · *Colin Bailey*
Art in St Petersburg · *Colin Bailey*
Unexplored St Petersburg · *Colin Bailey*
Art in Toledo & Madrid · *Colin Bailey*
American Galleries in the Fall · *Colin Bailey*
Derbyshire Halls & Houses · *David Bostwick*
Chinese Civilisation · *David McMullen*
Schubertiade: Schubert in Schwarzenberg · *Denis Moriarty*
A Weekend of English Song · *Denis Moriarty*
Elgar's 150th anniversary & The three Choirs Festival ·
   Denis Moriarty
Isle of Wight · *Denis Moriarty*
Thaxted Festival · *Denis Moriarty*
William Morris & the Arts & Crafts Movement · *Denis Moriarty*
Budapest at Christmas · *Denis Moriarty*
Cave Temples & Moghul Palaces · *Denis Moriarty*
Forgotten Empires: Goa & the Deccan · *Denis Moriarty*
Historic Malta · *Denis Moriarty*
From Jamestown to Washington 1607–2007 · *Denis Moriarty*
Pompeii & Herculaneum · *Edward Herring*
Flowers of the Cape · *Elizabeth Ashton*
Liverpool: 800 Years of History · *Elizabeth Newell*
Manchester's Treasures · *Elizabeth Newell*
Suffolk Houses & Gardens · *Gerald Randall*
Mongolia · *Gregor Benton*
Kingdom of the Asturias · *Hilary Macartney*
Road to Compostela · *Hilary Macartney*
Hidden Treasures of Central India · *Hilary Smith*
Vienna Music Festival · *Humphrey Burton*
St Petersburg: City of Music · *Humphrey Burton*
Wagner's Ring Cycle in New York · *Humphrey Burton*
Chinese Civilisation · *James Lin*
Salzburg at Christmas · *John Bryden*
Bach Festival in Leipzig · *John Bryden*
Handel Festival at Gottingen · *John Bryden*
Munich Opera Festival · *John Bryden*
Beethoven Festival in Warsaw · *John Bryden*
Mendelssohn in Scotland · *John Bryden*
Castile · *Julia Boadle*
Art on the Cote d'Azur · *Juliet Heslewood*
Provence · *Juliet Heslewood*
Dordogne · *Juliet Heslewood & Moira Tait*
Hidden Coast & Woods of Lincolnshire · *Kevin Hand*
Wildlife in Norfolk · *Kevin Hand*
Wildlife of Ethiopia · *Kevin Hand & Roland Randall*
Crete - Birds, Flowers & Minoans · *Kevin Hand & Roland Randall*
Sardinia: Birds, Flowers & Nuraghi · *Kevin Hand & Roland Randall*

New Year in The Azores · *Kevin Hand & Roland Randall*
Wildlife of Andalucia & the Strait of Gibraltar · *Kevin Hand & Roland Randall*
Canaletto at The Dulwich Gallery · *Malcolm Oxley*
Carr & Adam in Yorkshire · *Malcolm Oxley*
City Churches after the Fire · *Malcolm Oxley*
Italian Renaissance at the National Gallery · *Malcolm Oxley*
Renaissance Siena: Art for a City · *Malcolm Oxley*
William Hogarth & the Foundling Hospital · *Malcolm Oxley*
Medieval Burgundy · *Malcolm Oxley*
Hanover & Hesse · *Malcolm Oxley*
Art Treasures of Bologna · *Malcolm Oxley*
Princely Courts of Northern Italy · *Malcolm Oxley*
Treasures of Turin & Piedmont · *Malcolm Oxley*
New in St Petersburg · *Marina Vaizey*
Bilbao & Barcelona · *Marina Vaizey*
Art Treasures of Switzerland · *Marina Vaizey & Alex Koller*
Copenhagen · *Marina Vaizey & Paul Brooke Barnes*
Tasmania with Melbourne · *Mark Hanger*
New Zealand · *Mark Hanger*
From Sofia to the Black Sea · *Mark Powell*
Dubrovnik · *Mark Powell*
Moravia & Southern Bohemia · *Mark Powell*
Splendours of Prague · *Mark Powell*
Roussillon · *Mark Powell*
Saxony - Leipzig, Weimar & Dresden · *Mark Powell*
Montenegro & the Adriatic Coast · *Mark Powell*
Romania & Transylvania · *Mark Powell*
Gastronomic Spain · *Michael Jacobs*
Moorish Spain · *Michael Jacobs*
County Mayo · *Niamh Whitfield*
Mexico · *Nicholas James*
Dukes of Normandy · *Pamela Marshall*
Plantagenets · *Pamela Marshall*
Persia · *Patricia Baker*
Lost Kingdoms of Anatolia · *Patricia Baker*
Uzbekistan · *Patricia Baker*
Belle Epoque Alexandria · *Peter Clark*
Damascus at Christmas · *Peter Clark*
Venice · *Peter Higginson*
Venice · *Peter Higginson*
Spring in Sicily · *Philip Kenrick*
Ancient Libya · *Philip Kenrick*
Iceland · *Richard Crabtree*
Kenya: Rift Valley Safari · *Richard Crabtree*
Ethiopia · *Richard Snailham*
Dorset Manor Houses & Gardens · *Roger White*
English Baroque · *Roger White*
Greenwich · *Roger White*
Irish Country Houses & Gardens · *Roger White*
Bergamo: Villas, Gardens & Palaces · *Roger White*
Italian Marches · *Roger White*
Castles & Mansions of Grampian · *Roger White*
Swedish Houses & Palaces · *Roger White*
Shetland Isles · *Roland Randall*
Extremadura · *Roland Randall & Kevin Hand*
Haydn at Eisenstadt · *Rupert Scott*
Melk Baroque Music Festival · *Rupert Scott*
Mozart Festival at Salzburg · *Rupert Scott*
Glyndebourne Autumn Festival · *Rupert Scott*
Sibelius Anniversary Festival in Finland · *Rupert Scott*
Christmas at Dresden · *Rupert Scott*
Leipzig at Easter · *Rupert Scott*
Schwetzingen Music Festival · *Rupert Scott*
Riga Opera Festival · *Rupert Scott*
Moscow · *Rupert Scott*
Orkney - St Magnus Festival · *Rupert Scott*
Opera in New York · *Rupert Scott*
Sketchbooking in Monteconero · *Tessa Henderson*
Sketchbooking in Monteconero · *Tessa Henderson*
Impressionists by the Sea · *Thomas Cocke*
New Year in Oman · *Tony Walsh*
Shakespeare at Stratford · *Vivien Heilbron*

2008 (–May)
Burma · *Alex Koller*
Vasari – Father of Art History · *Alex Koller*
Japan at Cherry Blossom Time · *Alex Koller*
Italian Lakes, Villa & Gardens · *Andrew Sclater*
Nile Cruise · *Andrew Wilson*
Cyclades · *Andrew Wilson*
Ravenna · *Andrew Wilson*
Jordan · *Andrew Wilson*
Apulia · *Christopher Wellington*
Art on the Cote d'Azur · *Colin Bailey*
Paris: in the footsteps of the Impressionists · *Colin Bailey*
Bologna, Mantua & Parma · *Colin Bailey*
The Grand Tour – Part One: Turin to Milan · *Colin Bailey*
Art in St Petersburg · *Colin Bailey*
Art in Toledo & Madrid · *Colin Bailey*
Historic Malta · *Denis Moriarty*
Sri Lanka · *Denis Moriarty*
From Jamestown to Washington 1607-2007 · *Denis Moriarty*
Pompeii with Herculaneum · *Edward Herring*
Chinese Civilisation · *Hans van de Ven*
Vienna Music Festival · *Humphrey Burton*
St Petersburg Shrove Music Festival · *Humphrey Burton*
Beethoven Festival in Warsaw · *John Bryden*
The Hidden Coast & Woods of Lincolnshire · *Kevin Hand*
Wildlife in Norfolk · *Kevin Hand*
Crete - Birds, Flowers & Minoans · *Kevin Hand & Roland Randall*
Sardinia: Birds, Flowers & Nuraghi · *Kevin Hand & Roland Randall*
Coptic Egypt · *Lukas Amadeus Schachner*
Early Italian Renaissance at the National Gallery · *Malcolm Oxley*
Pompeo Batoni at the National Gallery · *Malcolm Oxley*
William Hogarth & The Foundling Hospital · *Malcolm Oxley*
New Zealand · *Mark Hanger*
Dubrovnik · *Mark Powell*
Montpellier · *Mark Powell*
Roussillon · *Mark Powell*
Romania & Transylvania · *Mark Powell*
Gastronomic Spain · *Michael Jacobs*
Moorish Spain · *Michael Jacobs*
Syria with Baalbek · *Patricia Baker*
Castles of Cilicia · *Peter Clark*
The Somerset Levels · *Peter Exley*
Venice · *Peter Higginson*
Ancient Sicily · *Philip Kenrick*
Ancient Libya · *Philip Kenrick*
Kenya: Rift Valley Safari · *Richard Crabtree*
English Baroque · *Roger White*
Sicilian Baroque & Rococo · *Roger White*
Wildlife on Holy Island & The Northumbrian Coast ·
   Roland Randall & Kevin Hand
Mozart Festival at Salzburg · *Rupert Scott*
Leipzig at Easter · *Rupert Scott*
Wagner's Ring in Berlin · *Rupert Scott*
Opera in New York · *Rupert Scott*
Painting in Andalucia · *Stephen McGuinness*
Shakespeare in Stratford · *Vivien Heilbron*

From our customers . . .

"A most enjoyable tour"
YVONNE RAY,
Irish Country Houses and Gardens

"The tour was, in every respect,
a fulfilling and enjoyable experience"
Mrs M J FAIRBURN,
Wagner's Ring in New York

"Meticulous advance planning
by Roger White meant that
everything went so smoothly"
EVELYN HARRIS,
English Baroque

"I have easily gone on over
500 tours in my lifetime and
this has to be in the top 1%"
BARBARA NORVELL,
Baltic States

"The hotel was ideally
situated and very
comfortable. The service
was first class"
A CATHERINE GUNN,
Roman Scotland

"Altogether a most enjoyable
and instructive visit"
Dr D WAKEFIELD,
Pictures and Palaces of Saxony

"A very good leader – everything
ran smoothly, and in a relaxed,
friendly way"
JANET MARTIN,
Iceland

"One of the prettiest hotels
I have ever stayed in"
MARGARET RAYNER,
Mediaeval Burgundy

"Colin Bailey is a remarkably
fine lecturer – well-informed and
maintains interest at all times"
Mr G A BAKER,
Piero Della Francesca

"Absolutely spot-on. As always,
Denis Moriarty pitched his talks
so very well with his customary
good-humour and expertise"
LOIS HELLER,
Elgar's 150th Anniversary
and Three Choirs Festival

"Everything ran like
clockwork and we
didn't need to worry
about anything"
JENNY GARLAND,
Road to Compostela

"A very interesting
and varied programme.
I would have loved to
spend longer there"
Mrs R A BEYNON,
Shetland Islands

"An absolutely first-rate tour in every way"
RICHARD THORPE,
Sibelius Festival in Finland

"I found it all absolutely fascinating"
Mrs R A SKINNER,
Vienna Music Festival

"This tour was excellent value for money"
AMANDA MARTIN,
Swedish Houses and Palaces

"It is important to have a sympathetic leader, and in Denis Moriarty we had the master – excellent at all times"
Mrs M HIGGINS,
Schubertiade: Schubert in Schwarzenberg

"This was my first ACE tour and it was wonderful. The tour manager was warm and caring, the lecturer very learned"
Ms S N COOMBES,
Rome at Christmas

"I honestly cannot fault this week"
Mrs ELIZABETH MELLY,
Roussillon

"The two lecturers were so knowledgeable and their enthusiasm was infectious"
Prof R KNECHT,
Crete, Birds, Flowers and Minoans

"The choice and variation from day to day was excellent"
ROSEMARY MORRIS,
Mozart in Salzburg

"As a first time ACE-traveller, I really enjoyed every aspect of the trip. The programme was stimulating and very informative and varied"
LYNDA M DAY,
Berlin with Potsdam

"A most enjoyable combination of wonderful music and interesting visits, all underpinned by the enthusiasm and knowledge of our leader, Denis Moriarty"
Mr & Mrs COFFIN,
Christmas in Dresden

"I cannot speak highly enough about Hilary. An excellent guide who went way beyond what one would expect"
Mrs J HERBERT,
Road to Compostela

"The course director was the best I have ever encountered on such a trip, both on the academic side and the smooth management"
Mr B REID,
Schwetzingen Music Festival